The Complete Junk Food Book

BY MICHAEL S. LASKY

McGraw-Hill Book Company

New York   St. Louis   San Francisco   Düsseldorf   Mexico   Toronto

234567890 DODO 783210987

Library of Congress Cataloging in Publication Data

Lasky, Michael S
  The complete junk food book.

  1. Food, Junk. 2. Nutrition. I. Title.
II. Title: Junk food book.
TX370.L37   641'.01'3   77-9367
ISBN 0-07-036501-6
ISBN 0-07-036502-4 pbk.

The Complete Junk food Book

To my sisters, Patricia and Laurel

Acknowledgments

During a year's worth of junk food, there were many people whose help went beyond the call of duty. By now many of these slightly heavier friends and colleagues are, I am sure, either vegetarians or, at best, closet noshers. I would like to express my sincerest appreciation and gratitude for their patience, support, and sound advice.

To Kathryn Marx, without whose invaluable, dogged, and resilient research much of this book would not exist.

To Kristin Anundsen, who read over the manuscript and then, mirabile dictu, retyped it. To Carolyn Franklin and Margaret Phillips of the Society for Nutrition Education, who offered valuable help by letting me into the Society's small but resourceful library. To Michael Jacobson at the Center for Science in the Public Interest for his tireless efforts to bring truthful nutrition information into the open and to point the way to unfamiliar material.

To Roslyn Kramer, Christopher Eskeli, Rose Boche, DuMont Howard, Dennis Martin, and John Tuttle, who volunteered as trusting guinea pigs on my relentless junk journeys, for their continued support and tolerance.

To the many companies and trade associations that supplied me with copious information about pop food, with special thanks to Tootsie Roll Industries.

And, of course, to my agent, Rhoda Weyr, for her faith and belief in me and my work. . . .

To all of you three cheers, one Milky Way, and a couple of Tums.

"The Americans are the grossest feeders of any civilized nation known. As a nation their food is heavy, coarse, and indigestible. . . . The predominance of grease in the American kitchen, coupled with the habits of hearty eating, and of constant expectoration, are the causes of the diseases of the stomach which are so common in America."

James Fenimore Cooper—Early 1800s

"Topps Chewing Gum, Inc. has introduced a unique child-pleasing candy product called "GARBAGE CAN-dy" featuring a plastic can filled with pressed candy in the shape of shoes, cans, fish bones, and bottles. Each garbage-type can holds an assortment of these unusual candy shapes in lemon, orange, cherry and tutti-frutti flavors."

News Release—June 1975

CONTENTS

INTRODUCTION   XV

Part One: "The Joys of Junk Food?"

  1. THE PSYCHOLOGY OF JUNK FOOD: WHY WE EAT IT /
     AND THE EXCUSES WE MAKE FOR IT   3
  2. TAKING THE BAD WITH THE GOOD: JUNK FOOD AND
     YOUR HEALTH   22

Part Two: A Junk Food Almanac

  3. CONFECTIONERY FOIBLES   45
  4. THE BIG CHEW   52
  5. FIZZLE   58
  6. IF I KNEW YOU WERE COMING I'D HAVE BAKED A . . .   66
  7. DOUGHNUTS: THE HOLE TRUTH   69
  8. IT'S AS EASY AS . . .   76
  9. THERE'S A COOKIE MONSTER IN ALL OF US   78
 10. WHAT WE ALL SCREAM FOR   83

CONTENTS

11. SNACKS FACTS   88
12. BREAKFAST CEREALS: THE *REAL* SUGAR BOWL   95
13. BUCKETS AND BURGERS: FAST FOOD   99
14. FAST FOOD CHAINS: A TRAVELER'S GUIDE TO EATING
    ACROSS AMERICA   108

Part Three: **Now That You Know Why You Eat Junk Food and How Much,**
            Choose Carefully From the Ratings in this Selective Compendium

CANDY   138
CAKES, PIES, PUDDINGS AND ICE CREAM   193
COOKIES, CRACKERS, AND CHIPS   220
CHEWING GUMS AND MINTS   266
SODA POP AND SOFT DRINKS   277

(The Ballad of the) Junk Food Junkie

Well, you know I love that organic cookin'
I always ask for more.
And they call me Mister Natural
On down to the healthfood store.
I only eat good sea salt—
White sugar don't touch my lips
And my friends is always beggin' me
To take 'em on macrobiotic trips.
But at night I take out my strong box
That I keep under lock and key,
And I take it off to my closet
Where nobody else can see.
I open that door so slowly
Take a peek up North and South,
Then I pull out a Hostess Twinkie
And I pop it in my mouth.

CHORUS
In the daytime I'm Mister Natural
Just as healthy as I can be.
But at night I'm a JUNK FOOD JUNKIE,
Good Lord, have pity on me.

Well, at lunch time you can always find me
At the Whole Earth vitamin bar,
Just suckin' on my plain white yogurt
From a hand thrown pottery jar.
And sippin' a little hand pressed cider

With a carrot stick for dessert
And wipin' my face in the natural way
On the sleeves of my peasant shirt.
But when that clock strikes midnight
And I'm all by myself,
I work that combination
On my secret hide-a-way shelf.
And pull out some Fritos corn chips,
Doctor Pepper and an old Moon Pie,
And sit back in glorious expectation
Of a genuine junk food high.

CHORUS
In the daytime I'm Mister Natural
Just as healthy as I can be.
But at night I'm a JUNK FOOD JUNKIE,
Good Lord, have pity on me.

My friends down at the commune
They think I'm pretty neat,

I don't know nothing 'bout arts and crafts
But I give 'em all something to eat.
I'm a friend to old Euell Gibbons,
And I only eat home grown spice,
I got a John Keats autograph Grecian urn
Filled up with my brown rice.
Oh, but lately I have been spotted
With a Big Mac on my breath
Stumblin' into a Colonel Sanders
With a face as white as death.
I'm afraid some day they'll find me
Just stretched out on my bed,
With a handful of Pringle's potato chips
And a Ding-Dong by my head.

CHORUS
In the daytime I'm Mister Natural
Just as healthy as I can be.
But at night I'm a JUNK FOOD JUNKIE,
Good Lord, have pity on me.

INTRODUCTION

Each year, from the time I was six years old until I was fourteen, my parents would send me off to summer camp to get me out of their hair. I used to dread going off to that godforsaken pine-tree wilderness, ostensibly to play with other children who had also been forced to attend the June-to-September refuge. One of the reasons I disliked camp so much was the strict control the counselors had over what we ate.

Junk food was *verboten*. Sure, sure once a day we were allowed to select a puny nickel candy bar from a skimpy assortment, but otherwise we got what was put on our plates at the three scheduled meals and nothing more.

By midsummer there was invariably a crisis as over ten dozen kids who had become hooked on candy bars and potato chips during the other months of the year grew berserk with lust for even the smell of cellophane or foil wrappings. Fistfights became common, and sneak thieves would steal packages of goodies that Mom or Dad had mailed to Junior as a CARE package.

At one camp, a cat burglar systematically robbed my bunk of all the CARE-package Milky Ways, Fritos, Hersheys, and Snickers that we had stowed away like squirrels before a hard winter.

Each of us hysterically accused the other of being the Snickers Snatcher, until one day, alone in the bunkhouse retrieving a pair of Keds from under my bed, I saw a counselor tiptoe in and case the cubbyholes for Oreos. I kept quiet, hardly breathing, until he left. Then I ran gleefully to report him to the owner of the camp.

The pimply eighteen-year-old made a tearful confession. He was fired, as the owner put it, for "the worst kind of thievery there is—taking candy from the mouths of babes."

Looking back, I can understand how that counselor must have felt. All that sunshine and fresh air, three square meals, and no between-meal snacks. In a word, torture. And just as a junkie commits heinous deeds to get drug money, so our counselor, desperate to quiet a nagging sweet tooth, had embarked on his career of crime.

So ends the Candy Caper and so begins my confession . . . this ode to the unwholesome.

I love trash. Any kind: a tawdry novel, a TV game show, lurid gossip—or junk food. Yes, I admit it, I love junk food. If it has sugar in it or oil on it, I'll eat it. And yes, I feel guilty about it, but not long enough to stop eating frozen Milky Ways or Sara Lee Cheesecake tomorrow.

Besides, I have the comfort of knowing that I am one in a large crowd; junk food is at the root of the most powerful addiction in the United States today.

In this book, after revealing exactly how and why we addicts became hooked on junk food, I offer an A-to-Z compendium of all the major popular junk foods available in the United States. Hopefully you will be able to differentiate not only between those that taste good and bad but between those that are nutritious or barren.

Naturally the word "junk" has pejorative connotations. This is unfortunate, because some of what is classified as "junk" is surprisingly nutritious.

Some of it.

Separating the gold from the glop can be as simple, sometimes, as reading the ingredients label. Other times you need a Ph.D. in chemistry to figure out the value of the food. When strange-sounding additives are included, I will explain what each of them is and its function in the food—and your body.

No matter what the manufacturer dumps into it, there is always a certain amount of guilt you must accept when eating junk food. You know it's bad for you. You know that in one way or another the junk food nemesis will return to haunt you. Either you will break out in a rainbow of zits or you will miraculously gain weight overnight. The accumulation of sugar and oil you are stuffing into your mouth will eventually find its way to some unwanted place in your body.

Yet the lure of chocolate bars and fried foods is like the temptation of the apple in the Garden of Eden, the sirens in Homer's *Odyssey*, or a life-and-death blood transfusion.

So you indulge anyway. Each time you make excuses, each one more elaborate than the last, and with your conscience partially cleared, your brain says to your mouth, "Open Sesame!" The only control you have is in deciding *which* junk food you will eat.

We eat junk food for the pleasure of it, for the pleasurable association it beckons from our memories, for its uncomplicated taste. Perhaps we even eat it because we know that it's bad for us. After all, "anything worth doing is probably illegal, immoral, or fattening." Eating junk food may be an act of anti-Puritanical defiance, a stroke for independence of thought.

If it is indeed true that "you are what you eat," then we all might as well tie ourselves up inside a Hefty bag and throw ourselves away. More than half the food an average American consumes each year is junk.

This is no idle accusation. Last year, according to government calculations, each American consumed 100 pounds of refined sugar; 55 pounds of fats and oils; 300 cans or bottles of soda; more than 200 sticks of chewing gum; over 20 gallons of ice cream; 18 pounds of candy; five pounds of potato chips; a couple more of popcorn, pretzels, corn chips, and other snack products; 63 dozen doughnuts; and a conservatively estimated 50 pounds of cookies and cakes.

And, I presume, we loved every empty calorie of it, making us the first nation to have malnutrition extending to all income levels—from rich to poor.

There are many reasons why we *enjoy* our addiction to junk food and make no great effort to break the habit. Perhaps the most alarming fact is that even if we wanted to change our ways tomorrow we would find it difficult. Each year there are more and more of the foods which contribute to our junk food habits.

In the past decade close to 9,700 new items have been introduced into supermarkets, the majority of them convenience foods, distinguished by a remarkable lack of nutrients as the result of overprocessing. Further, we eat one out of every three meals (one out of two by 1980) outside the home, and most restaurants rely on the same factory-prepared, ready-frozen overwrapped schlock.

Junk food. Pop food. Trash. Fun food. Call it what you will, we'll still eat it. We are virtually assaulted with it by manufacturers, and its sheer superabundance hampers our ability to escape. Wherever we travel, wherever we shop, it's there, staring at us, teasing us.

And if it all disappeared from the face of the earth tomorrow, you know what would happen? Riots in the streets. Panic in the pantries. Black market Twinkies! Bathtub Pepsi! Tootsie Rolls at caviar prices! Catastrophe!

Sugar is virtually synonymous with junk food. So are fats. Therefore, this book assumes that *any food that relies on sugar and/or fat as its primary ingredients is a junk food*. As you will see, there are many guises that sugar and fat can take. It doesn't have to say "sugar" to be sugar or "fat" to be fat. For example, sugar comes as corn syrup (glucose) and as dextrose. Fat comes as butter, vegetable shortening, margarine, or peanut oil.

But refined sugar is the chief source of junk food and our cravings for it. Sugar is eight times as concentrated as refined flour; when sugar is refined, 90 percent of the cane or beet is removed, while only 30 percent of the wheat disappears in making flour. It is because sugar has most of its natural qualities removed that it becomes addictive. It fools our taste buds and appetites.

You most likely wouldn't want to consume—or even consider consuming—2½ pounds of sugar beets a day, but that's exactly the amount needed to produce a mere five ounces of sugar.

If we are going to eat junk food, we should at least avoid the trashier varieties. There is some good junk and there is much bad junk. I want you to be aware of exactly what you are eating, why you are eating it, and how its manufacture has come to be the largest portion of the mammoth food processing industry. The compendium at the end of this book lists each class of junk food and the major brands—with some facts and anecdotes about each. As should be clear by now, I even love talking about junk food. But I must take time out now for a Hostess Ding-Dong.

PART ONE
"THE JOYS OF JUNK FOOD?"

2.
THE PSYCHOLOGY OF JUNK FOOD WHY WE EAT IT/AND THE EXCUSES WE MAKE FOR IT

"People do not eat foods because they are good for them—rather because they appeal to their appetite, to their emotions, to their soul."

Dr. Robert S. Harris,
Professor of Nutritional Biochemistry,
Massachusetts Institute of Technology

We really have no control over our fondness for sweets. From the time we are born—and even before that—we accept food that tastes sweet over any other. The first food to pass through our mouths is milk, and whether it's mother's or processed it contains lactose, one of the basic natural sugars.

"The primary function of taste sensitivity (is to) determine which parts of the environment contain substances suitable as food and which do not. Of the four basic taste sensations—sweet, salty, sour, bitter—the first two [are associated] with the possible presence of food and the last two indicate to us possible harmful substances," explains Dr. R. J. Watson of the Department of Nutrition at the University of London.

Behavioral psychologists tell us that flavor is probably the most important characteristic in satisfying our appetites—the instinctive craving. Which flavors are acceptable to us and which are not is determined by experience. The flavors we like best are not necessarily found in those foods that form part of a well-balanced, nutritious diet. We seem to be born junk food junkies. Well, not quite. But we are ideal candidates for the blitz of external brainwashing stimuli that will convince us that the sweetened, the oily, and the salted provide the greatest pleasure.

While the advertising of the multibillion-dollar food industry is the most persistent influence on what we decide to eat, we have to look no further than home to find the true instigators of our junk food habits.

Mom and Dad are more adept at making us junk food fanatics than all the millions of dollars spent on advertising.

Food, psychological studies show, is the single most powerful emotional stimulus in our lives. From the first day of life it is associated with intimacy. "It carries not only the feeling of security, protection, love, and developing strength but also the sense of pain, rejection, deprivation, and the potential terror of starvation," notes Dr. Charlotte Young, professor of medical nutrition at Cornell University.

From our earliest childhood we are taught to regard sweet foods as rewards. We come to feel that desserts and between-meal snacks are something special, bonuses to strive for. From the moment we are able to sit down at the dinner table, we have one fact drummed into us: "You won't get dessert if you don't finish eating your dinner."

Dinner is interpreted as a chore—a means to getting something even better. We carry this misconception with us through our adult life. We want to please Mommy and Daddy so they will bestow the fruits of love upon us—the sugar-laden dessert. Thus, we are made to believe that the junk at the end of the meal is somehow better than the meal itself.

The preponderance of sugar hidden in the other foods we eat maintains and physiologically reinforces our sweet tooth. Presweetened breakfast cereals with up to 68 percent sugar are the most successful and deceitful pusher catering to our junk food habit.

As *Sugar Blues* author William Dufty states: "Refined sugar is an incomplete food. All nutrients have been processed out. Incomplete foods are addicting. If a body is nourished it has a cut-off point for foods it has obtained enough of, a natural reaction. But with incomplete foods such as refined sugar, the body is fooled and continually demands more and more. It can't get its fill."

Expressions and phrases about sweets handed down through the ages all compound our acceptance of the idea that *anything sweet is good*. Shakespeare says in *Hamlet:* "Sweets to the sweet, farewell!" Sweets as a gift, as something valuable, are a symbol of bonds and friendship.

The Bible proclaims: "Out of the eater came forth meat, and out of the strong came forth sweetness." Strength is an admired quality and sweetness is its equal.

My mother was forever saying to me when I was a child: "Be nice to your sisters—you'll get more with honey than with vinegar."

The message is always the same. Western culture is overflowing with it.

This continual overt and subliminal bombardment of impressionable, growing children sinks deep as they form their food and eating habits.

KIDDIE LITTER

Welcome to the world of *kiddie litter*—junk food made and sold expressly for children. The makers of cereals, sodas, and candy flood schools with free literature packed with misleading information and downright lies, say nutritionists.

One booklet distributed to some 60,000 students and teachers by the National Confectioners' Association includes such claims as:

• Candy is vital for weight watchers. "To reduce, eat candy before and/or after each meal. We can promise you it works!"

• Candy plays a decisive role as a fever fighter and actually prevents vomiting, diarrhea, and convulsions.

• Cavities in your teeth are caused by "the lack of use of the teeth in hard chewing." Candy is passed off as only a minor source of dental decay.

Dr. Jean Mayer, head of the Nutrition Department at Tufts University, maintains that these are "outrageous, misleading, and contrary-to-fact" statements.

The National Soft Drink Association promotes sugary soda pop to children in literature that claims soda is a good source of water.

"In that case, it would be better to drink water," says Dr. Michael Jacobson, co-director of the Center for Science in the Public Interest.

General Foods, makers of Post cereals, recently launched a relatively inexpensive program (boxtops for fun and fitness) where they offered to give gym equipment to school systems that collected specified numbers of Post Cereal boxtops. They sent letters to every school principal across the country with a well-scripted spiel about how the money crunch meant that much-needed physical education equipment couldn't be obtained by cost-cutting schools. Here was a great free way to get it.

The effect of this would have been to place school systems in a position of endorsing the sugar-coated cereals children would have to eat to get the box-tops. Many school principals enthusiastically responded to GF's offer.

The major avenue of approach to children, however, is still television.

The tantalizing invitations to partake in sugary sweet foods parade in front of the young TV viewer about twenty times an hour on most kiddie programs. This compares to seven to nine commercials an hour on prime-time adult pro-gramming, according to the *Broadcast Advertisers Report* (BAR). Each com-mercial is designed with the impressionable child in mind. The ideas evoked in the ads harp on concepts the child has most likely picked up in the home. And if he hasn't, the power of the TV picture is the new instructor. As kiddie-litter critic Robert B. Choate told the Senate Subcommittee on the Consumer which was investigating TV advertising to children:

"When you take a child who sits and watches television from the age of two to ten or eleven and sits in front of the Saturday morning TV box and listens to sugar, sugar, sugar, sweetness, sweetness, sweetness, chocolate, chocolate, that child picks up a habit which is going to continue through life."

A group of outraged and concerned parents and teachers who had seen first-hand what the continual barrage of junk food commercials preach to children formed the Action for Children's Television in the early 1970s and formally complained to the Federal Communications Commission and the Federal Trade Commission. In one petition to the FTC, Action for Children's Tele-vision (ACT) documented the misinformation and false picture of true ideals that kiddie-litter commercials provided for American kids.

One of ACT's chief complaints was that parents who limit the amount of sweets their children eat are pitted against "television ads that come fast and furious." Cereal, one of the hallowed "basics"—a food children are taught to eat as part of a balanced diet—is advertised only on the merits of being "supersweet." Children are taught to equate eating the "goodies" with basic human values.

BROTHERHOOD: "Learn brotherhood," croons Post's Sugar Bear, "and we *all* love Super Sugar Crisp. Share it with your friends."

FRIENDSHIP: Joe Namath introduces a young boy to his "old pals"—various football stars—and finally to his *old pal* Ovaltine.

POWER: "Have breakfast with the King." King Vitaman Cereal.

COMMON SENSE: "If you put Sweet Pebble in your mouth, you'll never have rocks in your head."

HAPPINESS: "There's nothing like the face of a kid eating a Hershey bar, there's nothing like it you'll ever see, a face as happy as it can be."

FUN: "You get a big delight in every bite." Hostess Cupcakes.

ECOLOGY: "Help, Blob is polluting the ocean." But Sugar Bear in his best Bing Crosby voice comes to the rescue bearing Super Sugar Crisp and triumphing over evil.

Studies of child television viewing conducted by the Surgeon General's Scientific Advisory Committee on TV and Social Behavior found that the junk food products advertised on TV are more frequently requested by the child than other products.

The repetitive ads seen by children on TV are not the only force of persuasion to which they are exposed. The Cereal Institute, a public-relations arm of the cereal-processing industry, estimated that a fantastic one billion package "backsides" are shown to Americans each year—that's like half a million billboards by space. Most of these package backs carry hoopla for toy premiums or free items that can be gotten by sending in boxtops.

And surprise surprise: four of the major cereal manufacturers now own toy companies.

The names of products are often designed to be emotive or pixyish enough to lure children like the Pied Piper. Cheerios, Alpha Bits, Sugar Sparkled Corn Flakes, Captain Crunch, Captain Crunch Crunberry, Kaboom, Cocoa Puffs, Frankenberry, Count Chocula, Orange Quangaroos, Quisp, Boo Berry, Baron von Redberry, Vanilly Crunch, Froot Loops, Pink Panther, Lucky Charms, Sugar Smacks, Super Orange Crisp, Trix, and so on . . . can, by name alone, be attractive friends to children.

Look at the names of these popular candies and gums—names that are created purposely with the "Pepsi Generation" in mind: Abba Zaba, Baffle Bar, Biggest Sucker in Town, Bubble Gum Smokes, Chee Wees, Chocolate Cartoon Funnies, Cinnamon Teddy Bears, Crazy Mixed Up Kids, Double Bubble, Fizzies, Fudgies, Funny Faces, Good & Plenty, Graperoo, Groovy Grape Stix, Happy Face, Laughs, Lotsa Loot, Nice Mice, Peek-a-Vue, Santa Prize Package, String-a-Zings, Super Skrunch, Yoyos, Zooper-Dooper, and Willy Wonka Oompas.

When the Quaker Oats Company, one of the top three cereal manufacturers in America, noticed that the candy industry was four times as large as the cereal business and growing rapidly, it entered the confection business itself. In the late 1960s they purchased the movie and TV rights to a cute book by Roald Dahl, *Charlie and the Chocolate Factory*. After massive rewriting to push the name Willie Wonka, they hired David Wolper to produce the kiddie flick, *Willy Wonka and the Chocolate Factory*. When the movie was released in 1971, the "coincidental" benefits to the company became clear. The movie debuted at the same time Willy Wonka chocolate bars were introduced: Super Skrunch, Peanut Butter Oompas, and lest we forget, Scrumdidilyumptious!

The movie, starring Gene Wilder, came and went but the candies, more successful than ever, are profitable items for Quaker's candy subsidiary, Concorde Confections.

Usually they rely on tried and proven methods but no matter how they do it, junk food manufacturers manage to mesmerize the small-fry audience to clamor for their products.

It just isn't fair! We are all proselytized at an innocent age into consuming puppets of the junk food barons. We have no choice about it. They gang up on us like bullies. Our parents inadvertently abet them, being recipients of the same kind of persistent persuasion themselves. We grow, unaware of the junk food habit we have come to possess, and by the time we are capable of decision we are hooked from years and years of indulging in what we were conditioned to think is *good* junk.

When you stop to think about it, the dietary patterns nurtured and developed by parent and advertiser are really obvious. But because they are so ingrained, these patterns or habits are familiar and taken for granted.

The California Raisin Advisory Board recognized this when it set out to illustrate the junk food ways most children have picked up. In a simple, yet pointed, 30-second commercial for raisins as an alternative to the kiddie-litter habit, the raisin pushers dramatize that most children don't know any foods other than junk. They have a kiddie-litter mentality because that is all they have ever been exposed to by parents and media.

Here's how the raisin ad goes:

Little Girl: Can I have a Mr. Chunko?
Mother: Not now, dear.
Girl: Then can I have some Giggle Chips?
Mother (patiently): No, Darling.
Girl: Can I have a Butter Dream?
Mother (trying to restrain herself): No.
Girl: Then what can I have? (obviously confused)
Mother: How about some raisins?
Girl (face lighting up): OK!
Announcer: Ever think there'd be a snack you'd want your children to get their hands on? There is. Raisins from California. (voice and picture) Nature's candy. (voice and picture)

Alas, even the California Raisin Advisory Board falls into the trap with its description of wholesome raisins as "nature's *candy*."

Does it have to be called candy before children will eat it? In a nation of junk food junkies of all ages, the answer seems to be: Yes.

Even without the reinforcement of this parental and cultural learning process, we would still eventually get hooked on junk food for two other reasons: the overwhelming, ubiquitous availability of junk food and the massive psychological advertising we are exposed to as children and adults. This advertising appears most blatantly on television, less so in radio and print, and is insidiously inconspicuous in the food packaging itself and the manipulative displays in the supermarket.

THE NAME IS THE GAME

One purpose of repeated advertising for any product is to entice us not only to buy a particular type of item but to accept a certain *brand name* as the almighty. Because we are surrounded by a constant buzz and blurr of brand names, they become part of our world. They are familiar to us and we feel comfortable and safe with them.

No wonder. The largest advertisers on TV are marketers of supermarket products. Together they spend, according to *Progressive Grocer* magazine, "an astounding $2.58 *billion* on network, spot, and local TV time each year. That's about half of all TV advertising dollars. Add the millions spent on radio and magazine and newspaper advertising and the total figure is $3.87 *billion*.

"This comes to about $60 for every household in the U.S. [All of this advertising] is not so much to sell as to presell, to precondition the consumer so that when the moment of purchase comes she will choose that brand."

We have been brainwashed into accepting brand names as tantamount to dependability and goodness. Brand names are the most potent advertising tools food companies have, because when the actual screaming TV ad doesn't convince you to buy a product, your subliminal familiarity with a brand takes over. The name is "good" even if the food isn't.

That's where packaging helps determine what you buy and eat. "The average supermarket carries more than 10,000 products—all in competition for your choice," explains psychologist and package design veteran Dr. Edmund W. J. Faison, who is chairman of the Department of Marketing at the University of Hawaii.

The manufacturer will spend between $5 and $10 million a year just to design packages that carry a strong "buy me" message.

"For example," Dr. Faison points out, "the most popular brands of cooking oil (Crisco, Wesson, etc.) are sold in bottles that have an hourglass shape. This helps to overcome the resistance of weight-conscious women who know that oil is fattening. The bottle is 'thin in the waist,' presenting a slender silhouette, thus subtly implying the product is not so fattening after all.

"White bread is now put in soft polyethylene wrappers instead of the older type of cellophane wrap. The new package is softer to the touch and softer means fresher to the consumer, so the bread sells better.

"A maker of frozen pies increased sales 25 percent just by changing the picture on the package. The old box showed the pot pie in its throwaway foil container. When the picture was switched to a pie served in a china casserole, sales zoomed! The tin foil picture made shoppers feel guilty—it implied the product was 'tinny' and that the consumer wasn't going to much trouble to serve the pie. The same pie in a china dish made the consumer feel he or she was serving a food that looks choice and took trouble to prepare."

The paradox of convenience foods is that while we will pay extra for a convenient, get-out-of-the-kitchen-quickly product, we don't want to be reminded about the convenience. That fact in itself implies that convenience food is somehow inferior in quality and nutrition compared to its homemade counterpart.

To illustrate how subtly a food package design can affect our decision-making process, Dr. Faison tells how one cake mix manufacturer upped sales just by moving the flavor designation from the top to the bottom of the box.

"The shopper had to scan the entire box to find the flavor. In so doing, she saw the luscious cake pictured on the box and was more tempted to buy the product."

The package can be considered the best sales seducer a manufacturer can have. No wonder packages are called "the world's greatest mobile billboards."

According to Louis Cheskin, a marketing design consultant, "While we don't realize it, we practice 'sensation transference.' This means we unconsciously transfer our perception of a package and other elements of the design to the product itself."

Our overall psychological perception of a product is based on the product, name and logo (which may communicate the product's character by color and typeface alone) and the total package design—its size, shape, and packaging material.

Marketers know that Americans are forever in a hurry. They like to get their food shopping over with quickly. Experts calculate that it takes just four seconds for us to scan the shelves of a supermarket where a particular product may be found. We see 317 items per minute and one in one-fifth of a second.

A package, then, has just a glimmer of a moment to grab our attention and convince us it should be bought. Elaborate and costly test marketing is performed with various package designs before a product is finally released on consumers. The effectiveness of a package in a display is tested meticulously, for it can mean millions in sales.

Tests to determine how well the package can be seen, how readable the brand name is on the store shelf, and how the eye moves across a package (which determines how easily a message is read and what material on the package actually *is* read) are all part of the marketing effort. As a result, the package design of a junk food you wouldn't ordinarily want very often appeals to you for some subconscious reason.

More than 50 percent of the purchases made in a supermarket occur on a whim. It's called impulse buying and it's the way the majority of the junk food we consume is purchased. Even if you had no intention of buying the Sara Lee brownies, the Hires root beer, the Pringles, the Baby Ruths, or the Oreos when you went into the store, chances are better than the house odds in Las Vegas that you will spend money on some junk food before leaving the supermarket.

In her penetrating analysis of *The Supermarket Trap*, author Jennifer Cross points out that "once inside the store the shopper today is exposed to a floor layout which is a scientifically designed compromise between our need to find things easily and the store's need to induce us to spend more than we intended. . . . Studies of supermarket traffic patterns show that 75 percent of shoppers normally walk around the store perimeter."

So supermarkets are arranged to lead shoppers to the staple items such as milk and bread by taking them willy-nilly through aisles loaded with impulse items. While you shop—or rather, hunt—for the items you really need, you are forced to pass through rows of temptation foods. It's all done in a rather low-key way to make your shopping pleasant. Gently the supermarket design eases you from products you need to ones you really don't. There is such an array of the latter that one or more is bound to end up in your cart.

Marketing studies demonstrate that 70 to 90 percent of the time the purchase of such junkie favorites as candy, cookies, snacks, and frozen desserts is the result of an in-store decision. As it happens, they are all products with high profit margins. That's no casual coincidence; obviously the stores are going to push items that give them the biggest return, and junk food happens to be one of the easiest of those enticements because we are predisposed to it anyway.

"Merely exposing shoppers to [all these] products, however, is not enough. In the mass of 10,000 items screaming for attention almost anything can get lost unless it is given star billing," says Jennifer Cross.

This is exactly why we tend to buy at least one item from a special display. These displays are usually featured at the end of a shopping aisle where they most readily catch your eye. Retailers consider these end spots best for especially high-margin impulse items.

Even a person with a cast-iron will (who, remember, has probably been weaned on sweets and exposed to junk food commercials since birth) cannot avoid the subliminal psychological effects employed in supermarket sales methods.

Our senses are so heavily blitzed by the flood of items in a supermarket that they tend to become one massive blur. As this happens, we tune out logic and common sense as well.

When psychologist Monroe O. Friedman challenged 33 young college-educated married women to select the best deals on 20 popular items in a supermarket, they made the most uneconomic choices 43 percent of the time. They were even given an hour to shop, or about three times as long as is usually required to gather 20 items. If a well-educated young woman with lots of time can fare so poorly, think how it is for the rest of us—who shop not under test conditions, in a rush, and with other matters on our minds.

Even grocers who are savvy to the ways of their aisles buy on impulse, so sophisticated and potent are the strategies they themselves create.

Here are some of the other crafty devices we and our weak-willed, junk-food-prone natures are up against:

"Tumble" or "Jumble" Displays: When a display is neat and symmetrical, like boxes of animal crackers arranged in a pyramid, people feel guilty about removing a package and ruining the design. Tumble and jumble displays are purposely piled in disarray to overcome that feeling. Also, messy bins suggest that what's in them is a bargain.

Product Spotters: Makeshift signs, often hand written, catch our eye and focus our attention on a product by simply giving its name or an appealing, emotive word such as *New!*, *Special!* or *Featured*. The amateurish design suggests that you are getting a today-only bargain—but that's all it is: a suggestion.

Tie-Ins: Because we think in terms of whole meals when shopping—the old "what-should-I-get-for-dinner" syndrome—supermarkets will place an impulse junk food next to a staple. For example, the store will "tie in" potato chips with cheese or put those all-sugar, non-maple, maple syrups next to the pancake mix.

Last Chance Displays: High-profit impulse items such as candy, cookies, and other junk food favorites are always found at the checkout counter near the cash register. Here, mommies can silence their children's "buy me something, buy me something" fits with a 20-cent candy bar, or with a package of chocolate chip cookies. Or Mommy herself will indulge in a Hershey bar as a reward for doing the shopping or to reduce the stress of her day.

Pricing Techniques: Give the shopper the illusion of a bargain—that's the market maxim. As a result of psychological pricing, nearly every price ends in a "9" because, for example, "39" sounds so much cheaper than "40." Multiple pricing is another technique which induces us to stockpile or buy more than we originally planned to (if, indeed, we intended to buy the product at all). Studies have shown that we will buy a food that is marked "3 for 99" more often than the same item offered for 33 cents each. Presumably, people do not or cannot figure out that the most they *might* save is a penny by buying more. "Some shoppers even think that that's the only way the store will sell the item," boasts Robert Muller, former editor of *Progressive Grocer*, a supermarket trade magazine.

Eye-Level Displays: "There is a definite resistance every time a store requires physical exertion by a customer," notes Jennifer Cross. Stores prey on our laziness and accustomed acceptance of convenience in America. The end of the Golden Rainbow for supermarkets is the shelf at eye level. Tests of customer behavior conclude that the same items sold 66 percent more during a two-week period when raised from waist to eye level and a whopping 400 to 500 percent more when raised from floor to eye level.

Of course, with kiddie litter (junk food for kids), the lower the level the better. If the child can reach the Snap, Crackle, and Pop and manage to sneak it into the shopping cart, chances are Mommy will be more apt to buy it—especially if she does not discover it until she reaches the cash register.

BUYING NAMES, NOT PRODUCTS

The names of junk foods—and the adjectives that accompany the basic brand name—can make or break them. For example, why anyone would want to buy, let alone eat, imitation margarine (a substitute for a substitute) is beyond imagination. Yet Diet Mazola is a brisk seller. Its success only goes to prove that if the name is right—in this case the word "diet" is the grabber—we can often be persuaded we want the product.

These days, if a product is labeled "natural" or "made from natural ingredients" or "country fresh" it is a shoo-in for our bucks. Foods that used to come wrapped in jazzy-colored plastic are suddenly appearing in earth-brown boxes with the inscription "Made from All Natural Ingredients." The packages suggest that their contents are healthier, safer, and more nutritious to eat. It's the same junk, essentially, but the way we view it is different. Manufacturers, perceiving the trend toward the "natural," have stumbled over themselves in a mad dash to change their package designs and take advantage of our self-inflicted misconception: that the "natural" way is the best, if not the only, way to go.

And why does the word "natural" have such a high emotional value for us?

Simply because we've discovered too late that much of our food isn't *all* food but a mess of test-tube chemicals. While many of them are harmless, they sound—and their printed names look—scary.

We had been ingesting chemicals in our foods for years—mainly since the end of World War II—without ever paying much attention to them. We took their safety and purity for granted. But then suddenly came those ominous FDA reports that some of them may cause cancer and other illnesses.

Let's face it: the idea of pulling Polysorbate 60 from the cupboard to add to Mother's recipe for coffee cake is repulsive even if the sterile-sounding chemical is safe to consume. And we're not going to be overly eager to have it in the food we purchase either. The chemicals only remind us that we are buying overprocessed, factory-made junk. We are on a heavy enough guilt trip about buying and eating junk foods; the presence of chemicals actually makes us afraid of food.

Not that Americans don't have a phobia about food anyway—one that dates back to Puritan times, when food was looked upon as basically unclean, a tainter of the body, according to historian Daniel Boorstin. Despite all the subsequent processing to clean up our food—pasteurizing, sanitizing, hulling, coring, bleaching, refining, enriching—we still have a deep-seated unconscious paranoia about germs in what we eat.

Packagers are well aware of this paranoia and are ingeniously inventive in their ways to capitalize on it. For example, they are trying to make everything instant.

HOW WE EAT: NOW YOU SEE IT, NOW YOU DON'T!

Linked to our subliminal fear of food is our passion for consuming it quickly. If you can gulp it down quickly, the food will not bother you. And besides, eating takes too much time—the American "on the go" has other things to do. We

consider meals to be joyless obligations or routine chores and we wolf our way through them as perfunctorily as possible.

Or we nibble between meals. Nibbling, noshing, munching require little thought or attention. Meals are something to eat between snacks.

How many times have you gone to a quality restaurant and nibbled on bread or noshed on cheese and crackers while waiting for the main course, so that when it came, you barely wanted to bother with it? This passion for pecking is directly related to our adoration of junk food and our craving for speed in everything we do. Junk food is fast food.

There's that old cliche "Let's get a bite to eat!" the national anthem of the American muncher. Having a bite is like a reflex, an act performed without consideration.

And whatever food we eat quickly must be pure, or at least look as though it is. Hence only virgin white sugar, refined of its dirty-colored nutrients into instant winter wonderland purity, is acceptable to us. Flour bleached to a hospital white and containing lower levels of most of its original components goes into our cakes, cookies, and breads. Because eating is from birth an emotionally related act, the colors, texture, and flavor of food—which are also cues to past experiences—contribute significantly to our decision to eat it.

Colors are put into food primarily to provide it with an appetizing appearance, as they are inextricably linked with the perception of flavor. Just try to imagine a white cherry sourball candy or brown-colored vanilla ice cream. Everyone knows that green is for mint or lime, yellow for lemon, orange for orange, red for cherry or raspberry, and pink for strawberry. Then there is golden brown for wheat and earth brown to indicate natural earthborn qualities. (Ironically, most of these natural colors do not remain stable under cooking and processing and their artificial or imitation counterparts hold up better under the rigors of food manufacturing.)

The texture or "feel" of food in our mouths can also cue past associations from our childhoods when our food habits were formed. Hence, the value we associated with crispy, crunchy, snap-crackle-pop or sugar-laden cereals makes us want cereal and snack foods to have a grainy texture and a corresponding sound.

In the final analysis, though, it is the taste of foods that determines our acceptance or rejection of them. And in America, blandness reigns supreme. Fondness for the undistinguished (in foods) is a national trait. Mass manufacturing, geared to feed millions of people, dictates that most food be made as neutral as possible. If you are in the business of feeding the masses, food must be standardized so as not to offend anyone's individual tastes. Let them add their own seasonings.

Evidence from extensive studies of food preferences of men in the Army— whose likes and dislikes correspond to those of the general civilian population— indicates that Americans, in general, opt for bland, simple foods. When asked what foods they preferred, the Army men rated milk first and then hot rolls and biscuits with butter, ice cream, strawberry shortcake, fried chicken, french fries, turkey, and hamburgers.

Among these foods, the most prevalent ingredients are sugar and oil, which are not only bland but tend to smother other flavors. We accept foods relying on these ingredients; manufacturers give us more and more of them; and they become so familiar that any detour from the bland convenience-food taste is suspect. Blanketed in oil and sugar, junk food soothes our primal association of sweet-and-smooth with safe-and-good. Naturally, everything we eat is judged against the criterion these daily dependables have established.

Other results from the Army surveys pointed out that the "fillingness" of a food is also a substantial factor in its consumption. We like our food not only bland but bulky.

This provides a clue as to why fast food franchises are so successful. Their limited menus of carbohydrate bulk are monotonously unpretentious, and the food is prepared in the same familiar assembly-line style of the food-in-plastic-pouches we are accustomed to at home. We patronize fast food emporiums not only because they are fast but also because we are sure of what we are going to get.

Even the burgeoning Mexican fast food chains, which could offer the traditionally hot and spicy South-of-the-Border dishes, provide us instead with Americanized versions devoid of their original gutsy fire, so they will appeal to an unadventurous public.

ADVERTISING: THE RULER OF THE PALATE

Television and magazine advertising uses catch words to make junk food sound mouth-watering. Crispy, crunchy, smooth-and-creamy, ice-cold, chewy, and so on. Or it relies on sounds with strong associations: ice clinking in a glass and effervescent bubbles sparkling and singing; potato chips crackling.

On television the most effective commercials use evocative scenes for their food ads. Happy families picnicking together, people laughing in an amusement park. Recreational settings. Funny cartoons that charm and beguile us at the same time they pique our salivary glands.

Then, using popular misconceptions and generally accepted beliefs, neglecting some disparaging facts and playing up trivial ones, they sell us food we might suspect or even know to be junk, but that we want to believe isn't.

Some commercials make junk food products sound positively healthful. ITT-Continental Baking's campaign for Hostess cakes, for instance, declares that their Twinkies, Creme Filled Cupcakes, and Fruit Pies are "so good and wholesome"—merely because they are enriched with a few vitamins.

The fact is, of course, that Twinkies and the like are just oozing with empty caloried sugar, which in itself classifies them as junk food. Adding vitamins to junk food does not make a food wholesome. But we are led to believe it does, especially in the case of breakfast cereals, by far the most insidious class of junk food we eat.

Cereal manufacturers prey on parents' meager reservoir of nutrition knowledge and easily convince them that "fortified" flakes, puffs, and shreds are just the thing they and their children need to stay fit. One reason we are willing to believe this is that breakfast cereals fit into our lifestyle. We roll out of bed as late as we possibly can and gulp down breakfast cereal. What an easy way to get the vitamins and minerals we need each day! We sacrifice wholesome meals because they are invariably time-consuming—a tedious exercise in any event.

EXCUSES, EXCUSES, EXCUSES!

It is easier to accept what we hear on TV or read in a newspaper ad than to heed the advice of an expert who may tell us our food is junk. So, if we are the least bit aware that what we are about to consume is junk, we rationalize. We find comfort in the advertisers' message that quick and easy food has the added value of the vitamins that we need to stay healthy.

Most of the time our guilt over eating junk food is only fleeting. But when it threatens to be traumatic—"rich" junk like ice cream sundaes, candy, and cake provoke the strongest guilt—we overcome it by telling ourselves that the pleasure derived from it is greater than any harm it may do.

To assuage our guilt, we invent "benefits" that result from eating junk food. If we are with friends we eat junk because they are eating it. If we are alone, we tell ourselves that we have "earned the goodie" or that we've eaten enough "good" food to balance out any subsequent junk. Or we excuse ourselves by pretending that "since I don't eat it too often, this one time won't hurt."

Although we really don't have to make up excuses to eat what we want, we relieve a certain amount of anxiety by doing so.

And now, I don't care what *anyone* says: it's time for my Pepsi Light and Fritos!

2.
TAKING THE BAD WITH THE GOOD: JUNK FOOD AND YOUR HEALTH

If the body is the temple of the soul, then anybody who consumes junk food is an atheist. And I, confessing love for it, have been shouting blasphemy.

Junk food is the single largest class of the pollutants that we inflict on our bodies. Medical and dental evidence from decades of extensive research has repeatedly demonstrated its harmful effects.

The good news is that we don't have to stop eating junk food *entirely*. But that's it for the good news. The bad news fills the rest of this chapter. To sum it up: we must learn to restrain ourselves. For the excessive consumption of junk food is, if not killing us slowly, gradually making us malnourished and unhealthy.

The food processors make it sound as though we have nothing to worry about. They are proud of their Ding-Dongs, Yoo-Hoos, Yum-Yums, and It's-Its. They strut and crow about the sterling qualities of their junk food. They claim that it is "high-energy" food, supplying us with necessary carbohydrates, and that the term "empty calorie" applied to their products by nutritionists is a meaningless epithet.

For example, Hershey Foods Corporation tells us in its slick "Nutrition

Information" booklet, "*Calories are important, and foods which supply only calories can, if used correctly, contribute to good nutrition.*"

Believe that and you'll most likely believe anything. If a food's only quality is calories, then it is not a quality food, it's junk.

Almost all junk food is empty calories and should be consumed only for the fun and enjoyment of it. If there happen to be some nutrients in the particular food, that's wonderful, but to say, as the processors do, that junk food is a necessary part of our diet is like saying that cigarette smoking saves lives.

A startling and controversial report issued in January 1977 by the U.S. Senate Select Committee on Nutrition and Human Needs paints a bleak picture of the effect of processed foods on our health. After lengthy hearings of expert medical, dental, and nutritional testimony, the committee reported that over the last seventy years the "composition of the average diet in the United States has changed radically. Complex carbohydrates—fruit, vegetables, and grain products—which were the mainstay of the diet, now play a minority role. At the same time, fat and sugar consumption—the so-called "empty calories," according to the Committee, has risen to where it now comprises at least 60 percent of total caloric intake. In the view of doctors and nutritionists these and other changes in the diet amount to a wave of malnutrition of both under- and over-consumption. The over-consumption [is] related to six of the ten leading causes of death in the United States.

"At the same time current dietary trends may also be leading to malnutrition through under-nourishment. For fats and sugar are relatively low in vitamins and minerals."

The food industry defended itself at the hearings by suggesting that the decline in nutrients in various food items isn't all that important because the nutrients needed for optimal health could be readily found in great abundance in other foods in the marketplace.

But are we finding them?

Studies by the U.S. Agriculture Department show that "more than 50 percent of the United States diet undergoes some form of processing before it enters the home." And how are we to know about the other, nutrient-rich foods when so much of the information we get about nutrition comes from commercial TV? Since World War II, the largest expenditure for public dietary information in the United States has been made by the food industry—for food advertising.

Testimony prepared by Northwestern University Medical School revealed that the most frequent advertisers on TV were "non-nutritive beverages, sweets, oils, fats, and margarines, baked foods, snacks, and relishes—nearly 70 percent of all time devoted to food advertising. That's on weekdays—junk food advertising shot up to 85 percent on weekends."

Robert Choate, a veteran opponent of the breakfast cereal companies, explained to the Senate committee that "the repeated hammering on a single theme—sweetness and sparkle—makes the sugar campaign of cereal ads resemble the now-outlawed cigarette campaign. It was not the individual cigarette ad that threatened the nation's health; it was their combined impact."

It's not that we don't know junk food can be bad for our health. Various authorities have informed us many times that, for starters, it contributes to tooth rot and causes diabetes, heart ailments, and cancer. But these reports never explain whether one type of food is more dangerous than another, or how much is too much. We know that sugar promotes cavities in our teeth, but we are never told which foods with sugar are worse than others.

This chapter contains an overview of what the experts now know about the effects of junk food ingredients on our health.

For a clearer picture of how each ingredient in junk food affects you I will deal individually with the three significant groups: sugar, fats and oils, and chemical additives.

SUGAR AND YOUR MOUTH

Dental research has pinpointed refined sugar and sucrose as a leading contributor to tooth decay—the most widespread disease related to nutrition.

In our American sweet-tooth culture it is estimated that 98 percent of the children have some tooth decay and that by the age of fifty-five about half of us have no teeth.

Dr. Abraham Nizel of Tufts University School of Dental Medicine supplies a shocking statistic to illustrate the state of our dental health: For every 100 Army inductees there are 106 teeth to be pulled and 600 cavities to be filled. That's an average of one tooth and six cavities per man.

Okay, we know that the massive amount of sugar in the junk food we eat isn't doing our teeth any good. Do dentists have any information about how the cavities are caused and which junk foods are the worst offenders?

Sure. A pioneering study revealed that it's not so much the *amount* of sugar we consume that triggers tooth decay, but the form and frequency of sugar ingestion.

The classic study, which has been corroborated by subsequent independent work, was performed on more than 400 subjects during a five-year period in Sweden. From that study and others, this is what you should know about sugar and tooth decay:

•   The form of the food you eat is critical in cavity formation. The less sticky and more fluid a food, the less chance it has of being cariogenic (decay caus-

ing). So, for instance, soda pop isn't as culpable as caramels.

• Foods with sugar eaten frequently between meals are more apt to cause cavities than foods with sugar eaten at meals only. In the Swedish study, when foods such as sugar-laden bread which tend to stay on the teeth were consumed at meals alone, the chance of cavities forming was low, but when sugary foods of this kind were eaten frequently between meals, the chance of increasing decay was greatest.

• The amount of time a sugar is retained in the mouth is a major determinant in tooth decay. Similar amounts of glucose sugar were given to subjects in cake, gum, liquid, and wafer forms. It was found that the people who sucked on the wafers retained sugar in their mouths three times longer than the others and were most susceptible to tooth decay. The experiment proved that it was the actual form of the food the sugar is in, rather than the amount of sugar eaten, that determines the probability of cavities.

• Any carbohydrate (not just sugar) can be an enemy of your teeth. According to Dr. Nizel, even bread, the starchy staff of life, can stick to your teeth. It does not, per se, cause cavities, but it creates a foundation on teeth which lets sugar foods adhere to the dental plaque.

Tooth decay and cavities are caused when bacterial enzymes, ever-present in your saliva and food, start to ferment sugar on your teeth. The acids they release decalcify the protective outer tooth enamel when they are allowed to react with carbohydrates (sugars and starches) retained in your mouth.

Ever since Aristotle named figs as a cause of dental decay, man has been aware of a connection between sweets and tooth rot. But it is only recently that dental technology has been able to grade specific foods in the order of their cariogenic potential.

Foods high in acid were found to have a low cariogenicity. This means that fruits, juices, and—surprisingly, considering the amount of sugar in them—carbonated beverages are somewhat less harmful. But sticky foods like dried fruits, toffee, caramels, and chocolates are easily retained on the teeth for the time it takes the enamel-decaying acids to form in the mouth.

Other sweets which stick to either your teeth or your gums after ingestion include (in alphabetical order):

Cakes and cake frostings	Pastries and sweet rolls
Cookies	Pies
Doughnuts	Puddings and toppings
Ice cream	Sugar-coated cereals
Jams and jellies	Sugar-coated chewing gum
Marshmallows	Vegetables cooked or glazed with sugar.

All candies are basic tooth rotters, but some wreak more havoc than others. Caramel and chocolate are most often cited as causing decay, but hard candy, because it is retained for long periods in the mouth, is equally bad. This includes Life Savers and all the other candies we suck on, such as cough drops, sour balls, and lollipops.

Uncarbonated sugar-based soft drinks (Kool Aid, Welchade, Hi-C), while they produce less decay than candy and cake, are by no means friendly to teeth. Studies have shown that when sugary liquids hit the plaque on our teeth, the cariogenic acids are produced in a quick 20 seconds and can linger for up to 30 minutes before our saliva neutralizes them. In that half hour there is enough time for the bacteria to start the decay process on its potholing way.

(As noted earlier, pure fruit juices and carbonated soft drinks are less of a threat than hard foods and other liquids.)

Depending on the type of flour used and the amount of sugar included, certain kinds of cookies are more apt to cause decay than others. High on the list of chopper-boppers are shortbread-style cookies, chocolate chip cookies, oatmeal cookies, and coconut cookies. The more shortening a cookie or cake or bread contains, the better it adheres to teeth.

Corn meal snacks also tend to stay on or between teeth, so items like corn chips, tortilla chips, and others promote tooth decay.

Sugar-coated or presweetened cereals are particularly risky because they are sticky on the outside and the starchy consistency of the grain lingers on teeth. Since most people don't brush after breakfast they carry the sugar particles from these cereals in their mouths for hours.

The best rule to prevent tooth decay is to remember that it's not the amount of sugar you consume that causes cavities, but the frequency with which you eat junk food. Cutting down the number of times you snack and nosh can mean a reduction in the amount of eventual decay. Of course, this assumes that you take good care of your teeth and gums each day.

"SUGAR-FREE" FOODS

So-called sugar-free foods, such as sugarless gum, can also cause decay. Sugarless gums contain sorbitol and mannitol, which are sugar alcohols. According to Dr. Ben Hammond, head of the microbiology department at the University of Pennsylvania Dental School, "These chemicals have a similar effect to sucrose (table sugar). The claims that the gums are noncariogenic are false. Both sorbitol and mannitol can be broken down in combination with food bacteria in the mouth to produce the acid which eats away at the teeth to cause cavities."

(In addition, the gums are made of a gum base which is less elastic and tends to pull more at pre-existing fillings.)

SUGAR AND THE REST OF YOUR BODY

Of the 100 or more pounds of refined sugar we dump into our systems annually, more than two-thirds, says the Department of Agriculture, comes in food products and beverages.

"Moreover, beverages now comprise the largest single-industry use of refined sugar, accounting for over one-fifth of the total refined sugar in an American's diet," reports the USDA.

Most of the increase in sugar use over this century is directly traceable to profit-motivated food manufacturers who use it to create new junk foods that will give them a competitive advantage.

For example, the addition of sugar to cereals in 1948 led to the recovery of a slumping cereal market. Since then the number of sweetened cereals has increased ten times over.

Although our bodies need carbohydrates for energy, they are better for us if they come from foods containing *complex carbohydrates*, which are also high in micro-nutrients. Sugar is an empty energy source, with any other nutritional value refined away.

In our diet, sugar-based foods have actually displaced nutrient-rich natural carbohydrate-containing foods like fruit and grains. Nutritionist Dr. Jean Mayer suggests that refined sugar calories are even more insidious: they can actually rob the body of vitamins it has attained from other sources.

For example, sugar calories eat up vitamin B-1 (thiamin), which is used by the body to metabolize carbohydrates. This means that other parts of our diet must make up for this vital loss, to compensate for the emptiness of the sugar calories.

In addition, sugar has been linked to heart disease and diabetes, and, needless to say, obesity.

The United States has not kept records comparing levels of sugar consumption and the occurrence of diabetes, but the connection between the two has long been recognized.

Statistics show that the incidence of diabetes dropped sharply during World War I, when sugar was rationed. But reports of diabetes among soldiers increased drastically during wartime, for the troops were supplied with the very sugar that civilians had been forced to cut down on.

Diabetes results from excess sugar in the blood which the body can't metabolize because of an insulin deficiency. (Insulin is a hormone secreted by the pancreas which regulates carbohydrates by controlling blood sugar levels.)

The sugar disease is most often connected with the obese and people over forty but any age group can get it, and the earlier the malfunction occurs the more abrupt is its onset, doctors say. It has been considered mainly a hereditary ailment but that does not mean that people susceptible who overconsume sugar may not induce it in their systems.

Back in 1929 the discoverer of insulin, Dr. Frederick Banting, noted that his discovery was not a complete cure for diabetes but that a reduction of sugar consumption was a sound preventative. "The incidence of diabetes," he said, "has increased proportionately in the United States with the per capita consumption of sugar." He advised that something in the refining process of sugar cane altered the plant into a "dangerous foodstuff."

Since that time a number of correlations between sugar and diabetes have been documented by scientists, but the American Medical Association still does not fully acknowledge the evidence connecting the two.

Nor does the AMA acknowledge what author William Dufty calls "Sugar Blues": hypoglycemia. This is a disease of low blood sugar (as opposed to high in diabetes) whose symptoms can include sweating, the shakes, rapid heartbeat, headaches, intermittent feelings of weakness, a drugged appearance, and even seizures and comas.

The controversial nutritionist Dr. Carlton Fredericks has co-authored a remarkably lucid bestselling account of hypoglycemia entitled *Low Blood Sugar and You*, which is widely available in paperback. Dr. Fredericks offers persuasive evidence of the epidemic proportions of low blood sugar in America— commonly unrecognized by doctors and victims alike.

After the illness had attracted widespread media attention in the early 1970s, the AMA declared in 1973 that "the majority of people in America do not have hypoglycemia." This statistic disturbed Marilyn Hamilton Light, a director of the Hypoglycemia Foundation. She had found that most of the people who contacted the group complained that they had visited an average of twenty doctors and four psychiatrists before their conditions were correctly diagnosed. She wrote to the Department of Health, Education and Welfare asking if they had any statistics about the prevalence of the disease. They replied that they had in their possession unpublished records which reported that "Out of 134,000 people interviewed [over time] 66,000 cases of hypoglycemia were reported. This represents 49.2 percent of those interviewed."

So the AMA was correct in stating that a majority of Americans don't have low blood sugar. But they were only nine-tenths of one percent away from a lie.

Because this information is inexplicably still unpublished a decade later, the medical powers-that-be can continue to play down the mammoth problem, claiming that there is no published medical evidence to prove it.

Meanwhile, if you eat junk food, you should find out if your body has a tolerance for it all. Ask your doctor for a glucose tolerance test to determine how well your body produces sugar.

Hypoglycemia is a prediabetic condition, according to the American Diabetes Association. The ADA also states that compared to other people, diabetics are more often afflicted with hardening of the arteries, heart attacks, strokes, and other similar ailments because of the excessive amounts of fatty foods in the diets doctors have prescribed for them. There are between 5 to 12 million diabetics in America.

Although diabetics might have a predilection to heart-related illness because of their prescribed diets, heart disease is still the number one killer in America. Junk food diets based on too much sugar and fat contribute heavily to heart disease.

FAT IN YOUR FOOD
CAN BE FAT ON YOUR BODY

Americans like to chew the fat.

The USDA says about 42 percent of the calories in our diet is now composed of fat; 26 percent "unsaturated," and 16 percent saturated.

A certain amount of fat in your diet is essential to health. It is a basic nutrient, as are vitamins, minerals, proteins, and carbohydrates. Fats provide our bodies with energy.

The problem is that one gram of fat provides double the energy of a gram of protein or carbohydrate; with more than double the calories (nine vs. four).

On the positive side, though, body dietary fat provides necessary cushioning around vital organs, helps to retain body heat, and supplies steady inner warmth in cold temperatures.

Fat is the vehicle that transports vitamins A, D, E, and K through the body. These vitamins are therefore called fat soluble; they require fat if they are to be assimilated by the body.

Besides being used as an intestinal lubricant, body fats cushion nerves by forming the myelin sheath which insulates them; they also provide us with fatty acids which aid in the growth of body cells and tissues.

The last benefit provided by fat is the easiest to recognize: fats make food taste good. In many cases they are the only thing that makes some foods worth tasting at all.

Despite these benefits, all the scare reports and idle talk about cholesterol have given fat a lousy reputation. Although not totally unwarranted, it's a reputation based on misleading generalities.

There are three types of fats: the Good, the Bad, and the Ugly.

The good fats are *polyunsaturated* fats. These are the liquid cooking oils that come from plants. Common ones include corn oil, safflower oil, sunflower oil, soybean oil, and margarines. They actually help to lower blood cholesterol. *Monounsaturated* fats, found in fowl and nutmeats such as peanuts, pecans, and almonds, don't reduce cholesterol like polyunsaturated fats, but they don't contribute to building it either.

The bad fats are *saturated* fats. Lard. Grease. Found in dairy products and red meats—whole milk, cream cheese, butter, ice cream, shortening, chocolate, coconut, beef, pork, and lamb—saturated fats are inescapable in most American diets.

This type of fat is said to raise the level of blood cholesterol which is then thought to be deposited within the artery wall. When enough of an accumulation develops, heart ailments may ensue.

The difference between the cholesterol-producing saturated fats and oils and the unsaturated ones is their atomic structure. All fat is composed of carbon, hydrogen, and oxygen atoms, all in a chain pattern. Saturated fats are comprised of many more hydrogen atoms than unsaturated fats. Hydrogen is the chemical that solidifies fats at room temperature and makes the fats saturated, so, basically, the less hydrogen contained in the fats we consume, the better for our health.

The manufacturers of confectionery products have found, however, that low-hydrogen fats or oils turn rancid quickly. To prevent this, they hydrogenate the fat, pumping hydrogen into it to keep it fresher tasting for longer periods in the factory and the home. As a result almost all candy which requires oil (and the majority do) relies on hydrogenation to convert the oil into saturated fat. If the candy is chocolate-coated then you have double trouble: the cocoa butter used in the preparation of chocolate is a natural saturated fat, also.

Most fried food is cooked in vegetable oil because it imparts less of its taste to food than animal fats. But an oily taste does not necessarily mean that a saturated fat is being used. Poor quality control in frying can make food absorb more oil and taste greasy.

Would you believe that the same report that called attention to the connection between cancer and cigarettes also shows that the more fried food you eat, the longer you live?

Yale Professor Harold Morowitz, an expert in molecular biophysics and biochemistry, studied the sweeping Hammond report of 1963 which surveyed more than 422,000 men over three years. He found that the statistics showed the death rate for men who ate no fried food was 72 percent higher than the death rate for those who ate fried foods more than fifteen times a week: Men who ate fried foods once or twice a week had a death rate 16 percent lower than men who ate none at all. Those who ate them five to nine times a week had a 35 percent lower death rate than the abstainers. And those who ate them ten to fourteen times a week had a 40 percent lower death rate.

Says Dr. Morowitz: "We cannot ignore these results any more than we can ignore the Surgeon General's warning that 'cigarette smoking is dangerous to your health.' Both are derived from the same report."

You figure it out. One thing is certain: foods fried in polyunsaturated fats are somewhat safer, but if they are cooked in animal fats, you have more to worry about.

Other than the cholesterol problem—which is easily controlled by diet watching—fats also create one not so simply avoided.

The ugly fat is the *fat on your body*.

Fats are contagious. Those who eat fat beget fat of their own. As one of the characters in the television comedy series "Rhoda" says when indulging in a piece of Sara Lee cheesecake: "I don't know why I even bother to eat this—I might as well apply it directly to my hips!"

Obesity. Overweight. Flab. Junk food loaded with sugars and fats is turning us into a nation of fatsos. As junk food has become a national pastime, weight watching has become a national preoccupation.

Obesity is no laughing matter. It is a risk factor directly related to a hospitalful of diseases. As one doctor put it to the Senate Committee on Nutrition:

"Obesity aggravates cardiovascular disease and increases the liability to hypertension, atherosclerosis, hernias, and gall-bladder disease. It can facilitate the emergence of latent diabetes in predisposed individuals and it adds hazards to surgery. The mortality from cirrhosis of the liver in obese males is 249 percent that of the non-obese. Now statistics make it quite clear that the obese do not live as long as the lean."

A reduction in fat in our diet is the best means of reducing weight and lowering health risks. But the ever-present temptation of high-calorie junk food seems to be more potent than our will to lose weight.

We have seen that unsaturated fats are the best for our diet. Unfortunately, hardly any junk food label lists the type of oil used in the ingredients. We have no way of knowing if our potato chips are cooked in corn oil or our Kentucky Fried Chicken dipped in peanut oil. Until packaging laws are changed we won't know. You pay your money and you take your chance.

But before you put that Cool Whip on your dessert, remember one thing: fake toppings may contain as much saturated fat as real whipped cream—and sometimes more. And with substitutes you get a sea of chemicals as well.

WHAT CHEMICAL ADDITIVES ADD UP TO

When the perturbed mother brought her eight-year-old son to the doctor she was ready to lock the kid in a filing cabinet. He wouldn't stop fidgeting and running around or keep his mouth shut for a second. She knew that children have unlimited energy, but this was ridiculous!

The pediatrician had seen this often. He knew of the theory proposed by San Franciscan Dr. Ben Feingold that children who eat foods with chemical additives—for coloring, flavoring, and other purposes—become hyperactive. (Feingold's theory appears in his bestselling book *Why Your Child Is Hyperactive*, Random House, 1975.)

The mother told the doctor that yes, she let the child have sweets, "just to quiet him down."

"What type of sweets?"

"Oh, the regular thing—cookies, candy bars, soda, that sort of thing."

The eight-year-old was diagnosed as a *colaholic*. He had been guzzling Cokes and Pepsis and was ingesting more caffeine than his body could handle. The result was hyperactivity. Between the cola (30 mg. for every eight ounces) and the chocolate bars (25 mg.), the boy was loading up more than 60 mg. of caffeine daily.

Physicians have reported to Senate Committee hearings that "caffeinism" among youngsters is resulting in a flood of cases of irritable, nervous, and head-achey kids.

After coffee, soda pop is the most popular beverage in America (also the most advertised food). And over 60 percent of all soda sold in the United States is cola. More cola is consumed in this country than milk!

Acres of sugar and tons of caffeine go into soda pop; so do concentrated amounts of colors, flavors, and preservatives.

There are now around 2,000 chemicals available as ingredients for food. Junk foods in particular rely on these substances to stabilize, texturize, emulsify, solidify, bleach, and moisturize them.

True, without some of these additives many varieties of foods would not be available for sale; they would rot on the shelves within days instead of lasting for months as they do now.

But are all the thousands of additives necessary?

Not really.

In fact, it's surprising that we have put up with them at all. In a recent survey of 2,000 consumers, 75 percent said they were concerned over the use of chemical additives in the foods they buy and eat, and nearly half those asked said they would be willing to pay more for "natural" foods so they could avoid potentially harmful additives.

Food additives have been with us since the middle of the nineteenth century but it has only been in the past decade that we have become conscious of them in our food supply. It's the old story of too little awareness, too late. Because we are now dependent on the very foods that rely on chemicals the most.

The food additive business got under way in 1859 when Sir William Henry Perkins synthesized the color mauve from coal-tar oil. It was found that foods could be dyed with it to give them a more appealing appearance. People were unaware that the very same dyes were coloring the clothes they wore.

In less than fifty years coal-tar oil had become the basis of some eighty dyes for food. A perceptive chemist at the Department of Agriculture, Dr. Henry Washington Wiley, examined some of these chemicals and, horrified at what he saw, said: "The American people are being steadily poisoned by the dangerous chemicals that are being added to food with reckless abandon."

Teddy Roosevelt, probably the best consumer advocacy President we ever had, signed the resulting Food and Drug Act in 1906. It banned all but seven of the eighty-plus coal-tar dyes. Of those seven, only two remain today. A third one, Red Dye No. 2, was only recently removed from the Food and Drug Administration's GRAS list (Generally Recognized As Safe) after tests found that the dye caused cancer in animals. The remaining pair are Food, Drug, and Cosmetic (FD&C) Red No. 3 and Blue No. 2. There are over thirty food dyes from sources other than coal tar, some of which are only provisionally approved and can be withdrawn at any time.

Still, dozens of replacement additives are formulated annually. Since food processors are eager to jazz up what we eat with something new, junk foods have become the chemists' playground.

Pretesting of these chemicals is generally extensive, but its effectiveness in determining their overall long-term safety is questionable.

As Betty Furness said on the NBC-TV documentary "What Is This Thing Called Food?":

"The fact of the matter is that the best scientific minds today are not able to tell us which food chemicals, if any, will cause us bodily harm, when they will strike and how many of us will be hurt. We do know that we are taking into our bodies large numbers of man-made chemicals. We know that some chemicals by themselves or acting with others can cause harm. We know there is strong evidence that some of the damage may not show up for years."

Among the profusion of chemicals put into foods today are ones that are unquestionably safe. Their names just sound scary. Others sound scary and are of unproven safety.

Here is a list of popular food additives with short descriptions. Perfectly safe chemicals are followed by the word "GO" and those whose safety has yet to be fully established are followed by the word "STOP."

Information for this list was obtained by consulting, among other references, a worthwhile book called *Eater's Digest: The Consumer's Factbook of Food Additives* by Dr. Michael Jacobson, co-director of the Center for Science in the Public Interest (Doubleday, 1972).

Agar (go):   A seaweed extract, this is a gel-like substance used mainly to prevent cake frosting from drying out.

Brominated Vegetable Oil—BVO (stop): See rating of Fresca, page 280.

BHA/BHT—butylated hydroxyanisole, butylated hydroxytoluene (stop): Although on the GRAS list, these preservatives improve shelf life only for short periods of time and test results of them have been mixed. Scientists have shown that they accumulate to some extent in our body fat. Whether they cause cancer or not has never been established.

Calcium and Sodium Propionate (go): These are expedient preservers that stop mold and some germs from growing in baked goods.

Carrageenan (go):   A gel derived from seaweed, it helps disperse cocoa in chocolate milk and desserts. There is evidence, however, that suggests it should not be fed to infants.

Citric Acid (go):   Found naturally in citrus fruits and berries, it is used as a flavoring in candy, gum, and soda and as a preservative in many foods.

Corn Syrup (go):   This is a sugar-based solution made from cornstarch and enzymes. It is used to retard the crystallization of regular sugar cane in candies, frostings, and fillings and reduces moisture loss in baked and whipped foods.

Dextrin (go):   Another substance to stop sugar from crystallizing when heated, this modified natural starch chemical is also used to encapsulate flavoring oils used in powdered mixes.

Dextrose (go):   This is a natural sugar sweetener to help baked goods get that brown-colored look, especially on crusts, and to provide soft drinks with "body." about 25% less sweet than sugar.

Dioctyl Sodium Sulfosuccinate—DDS (go):   This sounds bad but isn't; it's used in powdered beverages (Kool Aid, etc.) to help the powder dissolve in water.

Gum Arabic (go): The sappy gum from the acacia tree is used in candy, drinks, ice creams, and puddings. Some 30 million pounds of this vegetable gum was imported last year from the Sudan, where the tree grows best.

Guar Gum (go): Naturally found in plants, this is a thickener of ice creams, puddings, and beverages.

Invert Sugar (go): This is a mixture of glucose sugar and fructose sugar used in candy and other foods where a sweeter-than-regular sugar is needed. Liquid encases sugar crystals to produce a smooth, pleasing feel as candy is eaten.

Invertase (go): This is the yeast enzyme capable of inverting sucrose. A doctoring agent.

Lactose (go): One-sixth as sweet as refined sugar, this natural sugar is found in milk and is used in whipped topping mixes along with other foods where a less sweet sugar is required.

Lecithin, Soya Lecithin (go): A soybean derivative, this healthful additive is used as an emulsifier in chocolate, ice cream, baked goods, and margarine. Added to chocolate, lecithin reduces the expensive cocoa butter content from 36 percent to 32 percent.

Mannitol (go): Ever notice the "dust" on a stick of chewing gum? It could be sugar, but more likely it is this sweetener—also a major substitute for sugar in "sugarless" gums. Because it isn't absorbed into our bodies easily, doctors have been known to use it sometimes as a laxative. It is also used by drug pushers to cut heroin.

Mono- and Diglycerides (go): These make cakes fluffier, prevent overstickiness in caramel, stop breads from getting stale quickly. They are derived from natural sources.

Polysorbate 60 (go):   This helps oil to stay dispersed in water. As an emulsifier, it is often found in baked goods, fake whipped cream, and snacks. Polysorbates have been found safe repeatedly and are even used as an aid for people who have illnesses that prevent easy absorption of fat into the bloodstream.

Propyl Gallate (stop):   This synthetic preservative has never been tested fully even though it is now on the GRAS list. The tests that were performed two decades ago do not meet the more stringent test protocols required today. Used in snack foods, chewing gum, candy, and other junk, it keeps fats from oxidizing and turning rancid.

Propylene Glycol (go):   This is found in candy, baked goods, frostings, coconut shreds, and soft drinks. It keeps food moist and maintains the proper texture.

Saccharin (stop & go):   The most oft-used sugar substitute, this man-made sweetener is at least 300 times sweeter than sugar. Found in diet junk foods among others, its safety is now in question. Some tests performed in Canada indicate that in large quantities it could eventually cause cancer. If continuous testing shows that it does in fact cause cancer in test animals, it will be totally banned. Until then. . . . ? (Also listed as SODIUM SACCHARIN.)

Salt (stop & go): We overeat salt not only when we shake it on the top of our food but also when processors put it in at the factory. It has been found to produce in some individuals an increase in blood pressure and hypertension, which may lead to heart disease and migraine headaches. However, because of its versatility as a flavoring agent it is one of the largest additives in our food supply. It can increase the sweetness of sugared foods, yet in the right amount it also reduces extremely sharp sugar tastes. One of the dietary goals of the U.S.

Senate Nutrition Committee is to get Americans to reduce their salt consumption by 50 to 85 percent. Start by not putting any directly on your food.

Sodium Benzoate or Benzoate of Soda (go): For nearly this entire century, this preservative has been found in soda, fruit juices, and other foods (such as Maraschino cherries). Remarkably concentrated, it is used in proportions of less than one-tenth of one percent to keep foods fresh.

Sorbic Acid (go): Found in soft drinks, canned frostings, syrups, and baked goods, this preservative and inhibitor of mold and fungus is used by the body as if it were a real fat.

Sorbitan Monostearate (go): This emulsifier is often found in chocolate candy as well as cakes and frostings, frozen puddings, and other foods. It also prevents the discoloration that occurs due to fats moving to the surface and hardening when chocolate is warmed and later cooled.

Sorbitol (go): This synthetic sweetener is used in sugarless gums, but turns into a sugar once in the body. It is also used to take away the unpleasant taste of super-strong saccharin in sodas and to maintain firmness in chewable sweets. It does act as a laxative in larger amounts (one ounce for kids and double that for adults).

Tartaric Acid (go): This comes from grapes and is used in grape-flavored junk food.

Textured Vegetable Protein (go): This soy derivative is used as a filler in hamburgers and as a meat substitute when other additives are mixed with it. It is also found in candy.

Tragacanth Gum (go): A thickening agent, it is used mostly in acidic foods.

Vanillin (go): This is a man-made substitute for vanilla, which isn't grown in large enough quantities as a natural product to meet the demands of food processors. The chemical tastes close to real vanilla and is cheaper but does not match real vanilla's quality and versatility.

Whey, Whey Solids (go):   Whey has half the solids of the milk from which it comes. It is the waste product in cheese production and is found in candy, cake, and ice cream. In cake particularly, it provides good texture.

Why so many chemical additives? One chemical manufacturer, Arthur Schramm, president of Food Materials Corporation, explained it best:

"We really eat with our eyes. So, foods that are unattractive to us will not develop beneficial digestive juices. You know—like the mouth-watering concept in advance of consuming the food. Flavor, color, and texture are imparted to the processed foods to make them attractive."

"Somehow," says Betty Furness, "we are made to feel that we *asked* for it: for the convenience meals, brighter colors, zingier flavors, the whole processing miracle that uses thousands of chemicals to restructure what we eat.

"I don't remember any such request. It all sneaked up on us until we were enveloped by it. And though we are told we are the beneficiaries, there is an ever-growing feeling that we may be the victims."

We did ask for it, though, indirectly. Manufacturers only produce what we buy. They make products we like or are made to think we like. TV dinners, frozen pot pies, and other adulterated glop got us out of the kitchen faster. We liked that idea.

We have reached the point where fast food franchise emporiums and factory-prepared meals in the home are the rule, not the exception; we have obtained a food supply dominated by additives, imitations, and substitutes; we have allowed junk to be our basic diet.

Would you excuse me for a moment? My Kellogg's Pop-Tart is burning . . .

PART TWO
A JUNK FOOD ALMANAC

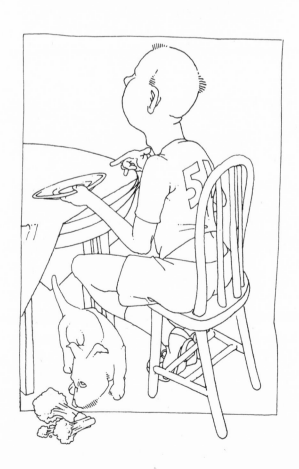

3.
CONFECTIONERY FOIBLES

Ogden Nash was right. Candy *is* dandy. It can make you high or bring you down. It can erase boredom. As a gift it can open doors. It can be shared, or be a luxurious self-indulgence. It can break the ice and get people talking. And it's a godsend for shutting up kids.

Although the bulk of all candy is sugar, it can be concocted in an endless variety of wonderful tastes, colors, shapes, sizes, textures, and forms.

There are eight basic candy types, according to the National Confectioners Association. Each is a result of the versatile way in which sugar can be processed. The finer the grain of the sugar crystal—that is, the less moisture it retains—the harder the candy will be. As moisture decreases, so does chewiness.

Hard Candy: Sour balls, peppermint (candy canes), and lollipops have 98 percent or more of their moisture removed by heating and vacuum processing. This reduces the grain of the sugar until it is very fine. Hard candies are prepared to a basic recipe of three parts sugar, three parts corn syrup, and one part water. Flavoring comes mainly from citric acid (the more acid, the sourer the taste), but mint oils and others are also used in minute amounts. All candy requires some corn syrup because it not only reduces sweetness but keeps down

the size of the sugar crystals. Water is also a vital ingredient, especially in hard candy, because it breaks down sugar crystals before it evaporates itself; H_2O also allows the boiling of the sugar to be regulated.

Creams and Cream Fillings (Fondants):   Candy corn and chocolate fillings have a coarser grain than other candies. If candy is manufactured with poor quality control you will notice it most easily in this variety. It will actually feel "sugary" or gritty from over-crystalization.

Caramel, Toffee, Fudges: One of the most popular candy varieties, made of refined and brown sugar, corn syrup, cream and butter (or fat-based substitute), and flavorings. Moisture content is high, resulting in the characteristic chewiness. The caramel coloring is produced by letting the sugar cook until it's browned. Fudge is a hybrid of caramel and fondant, and when made properly includes a cooked mixture of milk, cream, and butter added to a sugar and corn syrup base. The whole brew is then agitated until it arrives at a palatable degree of crystalization. As with fondants, it's the cooking temperature that determines the size of the crystals; the cooler it is, the creamier the resulting texture.

Marshmallows and Nougats: Marshmallows were originally a medicine from the marshmallow root. But it was found that when sugars and gelatins were added to albumen (egg or vegetable) and the mixture whipped with air, the result was fluffy candy versions of marshmallows. Nougat is simply marshmallows that have been cooked at a higher temperature.

Jellies: These include gum drops, fruit slices, fruit pectins, and jelly beans.

Vegetable gums, pectins, and flavorings are added to the sugar and corn syrup base, with a dash of concentrated day-glo colorings. The resulting candy can range from hard and gummy to soft and chewy.

Taffy: A sugar wallop—80 percent or more—combined with aerated albumen and flavorings yields the chewy, pliable taffy.

Panned candies: Jordan almonds, sugar-coated licorice, and chocolate-covered "bridge" mixes (nuts, raisins, etc.) make up this class. They are actually made in revolving pans not unlike the cement mixers you see on construction sites. A fine mist of chocolate or some other coating is sprayed around the revolving candy centers while cold air to solidify the coating is shot in simultaneously.

Chocolate-Covered Bars and Pieces: Seven hundred bars are made per minute in massive football-field-size machines. As they glide by on conveyor belts they are sprayed with melted chocolate above and below. Fancy boxed chocolate miniatures are made in the same way or dipped into pots of chocolate.

Our adoration of candy is reflected by the awesome size of the confectionery business in America. According to the U.S. Department of Commerce we ate more than 3.4 billion pounds of candy in 1975. For this pleasure, we shelled out close to 3 billion dollars. That's a nationwide average of 16.3 pounds per person.

You'd think that $3 billion would smother the candy companies in profits. It did, but they still complained that the pots of gold were realized on an 8 percent drop in poundage from the previous year. Profits were up, but the amount of candy sold was actually less.

Rising prices for the mountains of ingredients dumped into our candy were passed on to the candy customers. We purchased less but paid more—one reason why we purchased less. Sugar supplies rose and fell dramatically, so manufacturers took advantage of the "sugar crisis" of spring 1975 to raise the price of candy. When sugar prices dropped again, though, they kept the higher candy prices where they were, for clear profits.

More than 1.25 billion pounds of sugar found its way into candy in 1975, down from a peak of 1.5 billion in 1973. Also, 380 million pounds of chocolate coatings and flavorings, 142 million pounds of shelled peanuts, 51 million pounds of fats and oils, 14 million pounds of almonds, and 23 million pounds of coconut meats were consumed in candy form by Americans.

Our favorite type of candy, as reflected in sales figures, is chocolate-covered anything. We gobbled 1.7 billion pounds of chocolate candy in 1975, both individual 15-cent bars and "family size" supermarket packs. (Despite this, the Swiss still eat more chocolate on a per capita basis than we do.)

Non-chocolate candy—hard, caramel, marshmallow, nougat, etc.—reached 1.3 billion in sales, with a little more than a third of it in hard candy form.

The most popular price range is between 15 and 24 cents, with 50 to 99 cents following.

It takes about 900 companies and 1,000 factories to produce our candy supply, but you need only one hand to count the companies that dominate production and profits. The ten top-selling candy bars in the nation are made by the three largest companies: Mars, Hershey, and Peter Paul.

The consistent Number One bestselling candy of them all is Reese's Peanut Butter Cup, made by Hershey. The famous chocolate company bought out Harry B. Reese's company, one he had formed after leaving the Hershey Company. Reese worked on a Hershey dairy farm, but quit in 1923. "I figure if Hershey can make a million dollars selling his candy, I can at least make a living selling mine," he declared when he started turning out his chocolate-covered peanut butter confections.

Next in line comes Mars' Snickers. Frank and Ethel Mars made their world-famous candy bars by hand when they started their business in a Minneapolis loft in 1920. The bars proved so popular that by 1939, when the company had relocated in Chicago, it was grossing $30 million. Mars thought he had reached the absolute peak in sales, but was talked into an unprecedented candy advertising campaign anyway. He sponsored a radio show called "Dr. I.Q." and watched in amazement as his sales tripled.

The company behind the Number Three bar, Hershey's Milk Chocolate, was started in 1901 after Milton Hershey sold his successful Lancaster, Pennsylvania, caramel business for a million dollars. Within a decade, the Hershey Company reported earnings of $5 million in chocolate products. Today, sales of Hershey Food products are well over the $500 million mark and still climbing.

The other most popular candy bars in America (in order of preference) are Mars' Three Musketeers, Milky Way, Hershey's Almond, Peter Paul's Mounds, Mars' M&Ms Plain, Peter Paul's Almond Joy, and Mars' M&Ms Peanut.

Peter Paul, the third large candy manufacturer, also had humble beginnings. Peter Paul Halajian ran two candy and ice cream shops in Connecticut. When he noticed that his Konabar—a blend of coconut, fruits, nuts, and chocolate—was always selling out, he formed the Peter Paul Candy Manufacturing Company in 1919 to increase production. With enlarged facilities he developed the Mounds coconut bar which became such a hit that he had to expand to a three-story factory in Naugatuck, Connecticut, where the company operates today.

CHALK-OLATE OR CHOCOLATE: TAKE YOUR PICK!

Not all chocolate bars are really made with chocolate.

Only a certain mixture of ingredients qualifies by Food and Drug Administration standards as chocolate. Candy bars must contain chocolate liquor, sugar, lecithin or other emulsifier, and cocoa butter in order to have the word "chocolate" on their label. Milk chocolate must also contain milk or cream.

The majority of chocolate-covered candy bars today are actually spread with what confectioners euphemistically call "compound chocolate," in which cocoa butter and chocolate liquor—the two expensive ingredients—are replaced with cocoa powder and vegetable fats. FDA requirements about chocolate apply only to candy, so junk food companies can legally call cookies, puddings, and other ersatz chocolate-flavored items "chocolate."

Curtis candy bars, including Baby Ruth and Butterfingers, were the pioneers with the cheaper chocolate compound and have been using it since the Second World War. Apparently we never noticed, because their sales have increased steadily ever since.

As the average price of the cocoa bean, which is produced mainly in Ghana, has shot to almost $2.00 a pound, most other candy companies have switched from real chocolate to the hybrid compound. How much this matters to you is a question of individual taste. Chocolate connoisseurs may bicker but otherwise there seem to be few audible complaints.

The following chart shows the composition of the various types of chocolate coatings used in candy, cookies, and ice cream. The more butter fat and chocolate liquor derived from the cocoa bean they contain, the more expensive the final product will be.

CHOCOLATE COATINGS
Types and uses

Type and content	Use
Chocolate Liquor (bitter) Fat: 50–58%	Coating for very sweet centers for balancing effect

Bittersweet
    Liquor: 44–49%
    Sugar: 32–42%
    Fat: 36–38%
	Cordials, fudge, peppermints, and marshmallow centers

Dark Sweet
    Liquor: 39–43%
    Sugar: 32–42%
    Fat: 36–38%
	Enrobing nougats, cordials, creams, and fudges

CHOCOLATE COATINGS
Types and uses

Type and content	Use

Medium Dark Sweet
    Liquor: 34–38%
    Sugar: 41–46%
    Fat: 36–39%
	Molding chocolate bars and solid chocolate; enrobing caramels, nuts, and soft centers

Milk Chocolate
    Liquor: Not less than 10%
    Milk solids: Not less than 12%
    Sugar: 43–55%
    Fat: 28–40%
	Coating for mild centers low in sweetness, such as bars

Ice Cream Coating*
    Fat: 50–60% for thin running chocolate.
    May be dark sweet, medium dark, or milk*
	Enrobing ice cream pops

* Lecithin is added to combat thickening due to moisture absorption from melting ice cream. A full, rich chocolate flavor is required because of diminished flavor from low temperatures.

Although the sugar in chocolate qualifies it as a junk food, would you believe that chocolate can actually have beneficial side effects? Like all cocoa-based products, chocolate contains "theobromine," a natural chemical which stimulates the brain and mental processes. This might explain why chocolate bars have always been included in emergency kits during wartime and why they were part of the moon mission astronauts' lunchpail.

We associate chocolate with sweetness, but its name is from the Aztec "chocolatl," which means "bitter water." Cocoa beans, grown only on trees found in the tropics, come in pods, each with twenty to forty beans. The beans themselves have no flavor until they are fermented and blended.

Fine chocolate should smell like chocolate, and melt like smooth butter once it is in the mouth. When you break a piece from a bar it should come apart firmly with clean edges. Without preservatives, quality chocolate should last up to a year if wrapped well. Milk chocolate lasts half as long. In ice cream, vanilla is America's favorite flavor. In all other types of confections chocolate is king.

4.
THE BIG CHEW

"Does Your Chewing Gum Lose Its Flavor on the Bedpost Overnight?" was a popular song in the early sixties. The answer to that popular song title question is generously provided by the largest chewing gum manufacturer in the world: William Wrigley, Jr., Company.

Attempting to defend chewing gum from the accusation of being a leading cause of tooth decay, Wrigley points out in its fact-sheet that "about 90 percent of the sugar in a stick of gum is chewed out in two or three minutes and less than one percent remains after ten minutes."

Sugar carries the flavor in gum. When the sugar goes, so does the flavor. In three minutes! (In your mouth, not on the bedpost.)

Wrigley adds that, "furthermore, the excess saliva that gum-chewing stimulates tends to neutralize mouth acidity, which is harmful to teeth."

Any dentist will tell you flat out that this is a crock of spit.

No matter what gum does to our teeth, it will remain popular. It has been with us since the days of Ancient Greece when the people chewed on mastiche, a resin from the Mediterranean mastic tree.

In America we've been chewing ever since the *Mayflower* parked at Plymouth

Rock. The gum from the spruce tree was chewed to sweeten breath and relax nerves. Like the food served during the first Thanksgiving dinner, gum chewing was a custom given to us by the American Indians. Gradually paraffin wax gum replaced spruce until 1869, when a Mexican general named Antonio Lopez de Santa Ana, searching for a rubber substitute, happened across chicle in South America. The general went with his discovery to American inventor Thomas Adams, who tested it but found it a poor replacement for rubber.

Adams did, however, see value in chicle as a chewing gum base. He persuaded a local druggist to carry it. The rest, as they say, is history.

It was discovered that chicle carried flavors better than spruce or paraffin and was more springy and elastic. It is still the base of many gums available today, but other latexes from natural and man-made sources are also used. Chicle comes from the Sapodilla tree found in South American rain forests. The 100-foot-tall trees cannot be tapped for their latex until they are at least a quarter century old, and then a tap produces only 2½ pounds of gum. The tree can't be tapped again for another three to four years. In other words, you could say that once tapped, it has shot its wad.

A decisive change in the gum business occurred at the turn of the century, when William Wrigley, Jr. noticed that the gum he used as a premium incentive for the purchase of his baking soda was more popular than the soda itself.

Barely out of his twenties, he ventured into an already competitive field, but his unique and perceptive use of advertising to gain public faith in a brand name paid off. By 1910 Wrigley's Spearmint was America's best-selling chewing gum. Juicy Fruit, introduced before the new century began, also grew in appeal. In 1914 Wrigley released the peppermint-flavored Doublemint gum. At first sales were slow. Today it is the best-selling gum in the nation, with Juicy Fruit and Spearmint in a close race for second.

What is it about chewing gum that Americans enjoy so much—to the tune of $800 million in sales last year? Wadded together, all the gum chewed by us last year would make a 200-million-pound ball.

Psychologists suggest that the rhythmic action of chewing has an effect similar to that of hypnosis. It somehow eases tension in nerves and muscles. On the job, particularly exacting work or repetitive chores make us bored or tense. We become fidgety. Chewing gum—a fine substitute for erasers, rubber bands, or toothpicks—breaks up the routine and helps to ease it along. Tension expended in chewing facilitates concentration, and prevents you from clenching and grinding your teeth, an alternative way in which the mouth is used for the release of tension energy.

Gum comes in four basic shapes: the stick, the pellet, the ball, and the wad.

Pellet gum like Chiclets and gumballs with "candy coatings" are actually coated with nothing more than pure liquid sugar, which is then whirled in pans with beeswax or some other wax to provide it with its characteristic sheen. Manufacturers are continually making "improvements." One found that a way to boost sales (and prices) is to give sticks and pellets of gum a color that psychologically matches their particular flavor. A number of gum makers have had to resort to the most glaring psychedelic colors to catch the eye of youngsters jaded by the constant blur of color from the TV screen. Shiny Kelly greens, iridescent turquoise blues, flaming oranges, and blinding lipstick reds leap at us from the gum wrappers. Soon we may need sunglasses just to avoid the glare.

THE ETIQUETTE OF CHEWING GUM

Gum chewing is still considered a bit gauche in some civilized circles—but what do they know?

True, there are certain places or occasions where it *is* universally impolite to chew gum, such as church, lectures, and theatrical performances.

Children, of course are still taught never to chew gum in school. My junior-high-school history teacher caught one of us with a wad of gum during a lesson on the Erie Canal. He harangued the humiliated student about the "evils of the chicle," and then forced him to write on the blackboard 500 times: "I will never masticate upon the chicle again in history class." We giggled about it for days afterward.

Emily Post has a few choice rules on gum-chewing manners, which I feel would enhance the credibility of gum-chewers around the world if they were followed:

- First of all, gum should be chewed quietly. Don't pop or crack it.

- And please, folks, remember to close your mouths when you chew.

- When you are finished with gum, get rid of it carefully. Many of us stick it firmly under the table in whatever restaurant we happen to be in. Wrong! Put it in the wrapper it came in and dump it into a wastebasket.

- Considering the universal popularity of gum, it is impolite to take out a piece for yourself without first offering some to the people around you. If you only have one piece, offer to share it with the person you are with. If you are with more than one person, don't chew at all. Dividing a stick of gum into more than two pieces is as complex as trying to split the atom.

PUTTING THE BUBBLE IN BUBBLE GUM

Bubble gum has a thicker consistency than regular gum, plus more flexibility and cohesiveness. Blowing bubbles with it is an acquired skill, like riding a bike.

Bubble gum should first be chewed until its flavor is lost—about three to five minutes. Then stretch or knead the pliable wad over your tongue as if it were dough being fitted into the bottom of a pie shell. Then place your tongue behind the gum, push it forward so that an air pocket is formed, and blow air into the pocket so that it expands in all directions, forming a round shape. The larger the bubble the thinner its skin. Finally, pop!

THE GUM BUSINESS: "DOG *CHEW* DOG"

Wrigley's has been the leading gum company during this century, but two pharmaceutical houses, eager to extend their profit centers, are now muscling in on Wrigley's realm.

Warner Lambert, which owns American Chicle, now controls an estimated 40 percent of the market, and Squibb's Life Saver Division has chalked up about 20 percent.

In an effort to regain its almost monopolistic control of the gum market Wrigley, which hadn't produced a new variety for decades, has released two new products in the last two years and is test marketing a couple more.

AFTER WRIGLEY'S:

American Chicle		Life Savers		Reed Candy Co.
Adams	assorted flavors	Fruit Stripe	assorted flavors	Clark Teaberry
Dentyne	"	Beech-Nut	"	Cinnamint
Beemans		Beechies (pellets)	"	Fruit Bunch
Chiclets	"	Care*Free	"	Spearmint
Trident	"	Life Savers	"	Peppermint
Clorets		Breath Savers	"	Superstick

Wrigley's Big Red, with its uninspired copies of Marlboro cowboy commercials, is a cinnamon-flavored gum that is aiming for the Dentyne market. Its Freedent gum contains a gum base especially formulated so as not to stick to most acrylic resin dentures. So far, it's proved to be a big hit with those whose teeth are not their own.

The reason the other gum firms have been able to take away Wrigley's business is their development of sugarless gums. Today one out of every four sticks of gum sold is sugarless. Trident brand is the pioneer—but because the sticks look so meager, Live Savers' Care*Free has climbed in sales with an ad pitch that it has more on the stick by weight.

Life Savers has also jumped into the small but lucrative bubble gum area with Bubble Yum, a softer gum that adults as well as kids have turned into a best-seller. In fact, the gum proved so unexpectedly successful that Life Savers has had to operate its plant on a twenty-four-hour-day basis and increase payroll and staff by more than 50 percent just to meet the demand.

Although baseball and other sport trading cards are still a hit with each new generation of kids, since the late 60s an increasing number of children have been eating the gum and throwing the cards away! Manufacturers have started to add monsters and other video personalities to the card lineup so children will return for more and continue the save-and-trade custom.

The competition in the gum world, which is populated by only a dozen or so manufacturers, has resulted in some new gimmicks that are paying off in record profits, although the nickel pack now costs 15 cents—and you get less gum.

American Chicle's instant hit and its pride and joy is called Freshen-Up. It sports a liquid center that spurts—some say, *comes*—when you bite into it. It is packaged like a stick, but each piece is in a soft pellet form. Originally test marketed in three flavors—spearmint, peppermint, and cinnamon—its production is now limited to spearmint because demand for the gum exceeded the company's ability to produce it. All American's machines are now grinding out the one flavor full time.

The major companies remain leaders because they have the marketing savvy to second-guess what the public wants in their chews. A few smaller, less resourceful companies have offered numerous "Edsels" to Americans. Sharp advertising can fool most of us, but our taste buds remain the ultimate judge. So celery-flavored gum has come and gone. Gum with nicotine, designed to ease smokers out of their habits, flopped too. People stopped smoking but got hooked on the gum. There was even once chewing gum for dogs. Licorice-flavored gum seemed a sound idea, but it turned chewers' mouths into pitch-black coal mines which even chimney sweepers couldn't clean.

5.
FIZZLE

In the early decades of this century it was considered improper for ladies to drink the hard liquor that men were pouring down their gullets. Women and children were stuck with so-called "soft" drinks: fruit juices, tea, and a new-fangled invention, flavored carbonated beverages. Softness used to be a quality associated with femininity but the rising popularity of carbonated drinks has hooked many men as well.

The first carbonated water was made in the late 1700s when an Englishman, one Joseph Priestley, a theologian and the discoverer of oxygen, produced "fixed air" by pouring acid over chalk. He perfected a good-tasting sparkling water in 1772.

By 1807 Benjamin Stillman was operating a firm in New Haven, Connecticut, exclusively for producing and selling plain soda water. The first flavored soda was made when Eugene Roussel of Philadelphia opened a perfume shop to which he added a soda counter to draw more business. The same year, 1825, Elie Magliore Durand added cigars and soda water to his pharmacy store.

In 1849 there was more than a California Gold Rush—there was a donny-brook for soda plants. Sixty-four of them serviced the entire nation; ten years later this figure had doubled and mineral waters and flavored pop were being made. Bottling was still not perfected, and when bottles filled with the effervescent water were opened there was invariably a popping sound from the escaping gas. Later in the nineteenth century pop was known as "belch water."

It was a $25 million business by 1900, when 2,763 plants were operating. By 1930 it took more than 6,000 plants to meet the demand. The number of bottlers has since declined as more efficient methods of shipping and manufacture have been introduced. In 1960, with 2,398 plants, 30 billion bottles were produced, or 185 bottles for each American.

Think that's a lot? This year we will consume almost three times that amount.

Just as in 1860, flavors today run the gamut of fruits and herb roots (ginger, sarsaparilla, birch), but cola is still the overwhelming favorite. Lemon-lime is second; orange, ginger ale, root beer, and grape follow in that order.

In fact, of all soda pop sold in the United States, a little more than 62 percent is cola. That converts to about 2.8 billion cases (each containing 24 eight-once servings). Lemon-lime makes up about 13 percent of sales or 577 million cases. Orange and root beer combined comprise 16.5 percent of soda sales with the remaining 8.5 percent for every other type.

About 10 percent of all soda sold in the United States, or 432 million cases, is diet soda.

Soda is made with local tap water, purified of odor and taste by treatment with lime, sand filtration, and other methods. Some private-label sodas, which shall be nameless, have lower prices because their manufacturers don't bother "fixing" the water. You can taste the pennies you may save in the metallic tang that even strong flavorings and sugar can't mask.

TOP SODA COMPANIES
IN THE U.S. IN 1976

Firm	% of market
Coca-Cola	35.3
Pepsi-Cola	21.1
Seven-Up	7.6
Dr. Pepper	5.5
Royal Crown	5.4
Canada Dry	3.4
All Others	21.7

TOP BRANDS OF SODA*

Brand	Millions of cases	% of all soda sold
Coca-Cola	1170	26.2
Pepsi	778	17.4
Seven-Up	295.5	6.6
Dr. Pepper	217	4.9
Royal Crown	153	3.4
Sprite	115.3	2.6
Tab	115	2.6
Diet Pepsi	75	1.7
Mountain Dew	56	1.3
Canada Dry Ginger Ale	55.5	1.2

*This accounts for 2980.3 million cases of soda, of the 4460 million sold, or 67.9%

OTHER LARGE SELLERS INCLUDE:
Mr. PiBB, Fresca, Sugar Free Seven-Up, Sugar-Free Dr. Pepper, Diet Rite Cola, Hires Root Beer, Orange Crush, Shasta Flavors

A CONNOISSEUR'S GUIDE TO SODA POP

It takes no more than one taste test to know that the best soda comes in bottles or cans and the worst comes from soda fountains. Outside the bottling plant it is virtually impossible to prepare the exacting proportions of water and flavored syrup required to make a satisfactory beverage. Rare is the occasion when you find a soda-fountain pop that isn't too watery or sickeningly syrupy.

According to soda industry sources, fountain syrups are in most instances formulated to produce a finished product in a 1:5 ratio. That is, *one* ounce of syrup for every *five* ounces of water equals *six* ounces of good-tasting soda. Accordingly, one gallon of 1:5 syrup will turn out 128 six-ounce drinks or 768 ounces of finished product.

In soda-industry parlance the correct ratio is called "brix." This is an indication of the percentage by weight of sugar solids in solution at a given temperature. If the brix of the soda is *below* the correct level the drink doesn't have

WHAT'S IN SODA BESIDES THE BUBBLES? A GUIDE TO INGREDIENTS

Flavor	% of sugar by weight	Other ingredients*
Cream	11–13	vanillin, caramel color, citric acid
Cola	11–13	extract of cola nut, lime oil, spice oils, caffeine, caramel color, phosphoric acid
Ginger Ale	7–11	ginger root, oil of ginger, lime oil, caramel color, citric acid
Root Beer	11–13	oil of wintergreen, vanilla, nutmeg, cloves or anise, caramel color, citric acid
Orange	12–14	oil of orange, orange juice, sunset yellow color, citric acid
Grape	11–13	methyl anthranlate, oil of cognac, grape juice (optional), brilliant blue color, tartaric acid
Cherry	11–13	benzaldehyde or oil of bitter almond, red coloring (whatever is allowed these days), tartaric acid or citric acid
Lemon	11–13	oil of lemon, lemon juice, citric acid (if lemon juice isn't enough)
Tom Collins	7–9	lemon juice, coloring

* Correct carbonation is needed because of the pungent taste it provides. Mixers have most carbonation, cola next, and flavored drinks the least.

enough syrup. While the operator gets more yield per gallon, the finished drink will taste weak and unappealing. *Above* the correct level means too much syrup has been used. The icky sweet drink reflects a reduction in revenues for whoever served it. He is losing too much syrup—and, eventually, too many customers.

Soda served without ice should be at 40°F or less when dispensed. Higher temperatures seem to make soda sweeter than it should be.

You can tell you have good soda if the carbonation has that bite that tingles the nose, has no strange or metallic taste or odor, and has a flavor that carries through without being watery.

America's favorite source of soda pop is the ten-ounce nonreturnable bottle.

TALES FROM THE BUBBLE BUSINESS

The story goes that the first batch of Coca-Cola syrup was made in a three-legged cast-iron pot in the back yard of its creator, druggist Dr. John S. Pemberton. The first sale was for five cents per glass on May 8, 1886, at Jacobs' Pharmacy in downtown Atlanta.

Dr. Pemberton didn't think much of his concoction and two years later, in need of funds, he sold his interest in the new beverage for $1,700. For an additional $600 investment, Asa G. Candler, a rural Georgia man who had come to Atlanta fifteen years previously with $1.75 in his pocket, took over all rights in 1889.

Twenty years later Candler sold the company to a group of Atlanta businessmen. The sale price was $25 million. Until the 1950s when the company ventured into multi-flavored sodas, Coca-Cola was the only product it made. It came in the familiar Mae-West-shaped 6½-ounce bottle or by the glass at a fountain. It wasn't until about 1959 that the soda was offered for sale in cans.

Today, according to the Coca-Cola Company, Coke alone is called for—worldwide—more than 175 million times a day. Applying the typical eight-ounce measure that the soft-drink industry uses for comparisons, this means 1.4 billion ounces of Coke are downed daily.

Pepsi-Cola had its roots in New Bern, North Carolina, where in the summer of 1898 Caleb Bradham, a pharmacist, fiddled around with cola beans and other flavorings to find a new soft drink for his drugstore's fountain. He discovered that a blend of sugar, vanilla, spices, and cola nut extract made a pleasant-tasing drink. Within five years he was no longer in the drugstore but in the bottling business, with his new company selling the trademarked Pepsi-Cola. Unlike Coca-Cola, Pepsi's business fluctuated up and down and by the Depression only two of the more than 300 bottlers it had franchised at its peak during World War I remained. Advertising saved the day: in 1934 the now-famous jingle "Pepsi-Cola hits the spot, Twelve full ounces, That's a lot . . ." turned the company's profits into a tidal wave. Pepsi continued to adopt catchy advertising slogans, capping its efforts with "Come alive, you're in the Pepsi Generation."

Seven-Up was the creation of C. L. Grigg, a Missouri country boy who had come to the big city (St. Louis in this case) to make good. He started the Howdy Company with an associate in 1920. Howdy was an orange drink which, while a modest success, was not sufficiently smashing for Grigg. He continued to test new formulas and on the eleventh shot produced what we now know as Seven-Up. Only in 1929 it was called "Bib Label Lithiated Lemon Lime Soda."

Lemon Lime would never have been his final flavor choice if he had used any test-marketing procedures like the ones employed today. There were 600 different lemon-lime sodas available then.

The brand name wasn't particularly catchy either. Grigg soon changed it to Seven-Up. When Grigg died at the age of seventy-three in 1940, the Seven-Up Company was another national rags-to-riches success story. But his colleagues forgot to ask him, before he died, one important question: how had he arrived at the name "Seven-Up"? Nobody will ever know.

To this day it remains one of the few soft drinks not to use artificial flavors or colors. Seven-Up is the third largest soda company in America today, and with its new campaign advertising it as the "UnCola," it's doing better than ever.

You have to feel sorry for the fellow who must be the world's biggest loser: the man who invented Six-Up.

THE $450 MILLION LEMONADE STAND— NON-CARBONATED SOFT DRINKS

One of the best ways for a child growing up in America to find out if he has what it takes to be an entrepreneur is to operate his very own lemonade stand. Before 1928 kids had it rough. Lemonade and any other fruit punches had to be made from scratch. From, *mirabile dictu*, real fruit.

A year before the stock market crash General Foods changed all that by pioneering in mix-it-yourself powdered drink mixes. A packet of powdered flavoring and sugar was dumped into a quart of water and abracadabra, instant fruit drink.

Today General Foods, long the sole manufacturer of these soft drinks, has some tough competition. The $450-million-plus powdered drink market has Borden Inc.'s Wyler's Drink Mixes, R. J. Reynolds Food Division's Hawaiian

Punch, and Pillsbury's Funny Face, among other companies, joining the powder glut.

Canned fruit beverages, a $400-million industry in itself, are losing sales rapidly to the powdered varieties. Packaged liquids are getting to be too expensive, and besides they take up a lot of space. Powdered mixes, even if they are mostly sugar, appeal to us because they are compact, easy to prepare, and capable of lasting indefinitely on the shelf. Because we add the water, the mixes take less room and seem cheaper, because of the amount of drink produced from one packet.

With the exception of lemon, just about all the flavors are geared for children's undiscriminating palates. As long as it's sweet, kids will drink it.

Powders have been gaining sales at the incredible rate of 50 percent a year since 1974. One reason for this trend is the continual improvement in taste since the first powders came out in 1928. Another reason is that soda pop takes the brunt of attacks from nutritionists and dentists.

Actually, any fruit-based beverage is junk if the label doesn't say "juice." Drinks, ades, nectars, punches, and mixes are predominantly sugar or sugar-based syrups. A "juice drink" is 50 percent juice, an "ade" is only 25 percent, and a "drink" only has to contain 10 percent, by law. The remaining ingredients are sugar and water with the obligatory artificial colors, flavors, and preservatives.

America's favorite flavors are orange, lemon, and grape, particularly orange. Manufacturers spend millions each year in research and development to come up with synthetic flavors that come as close as possible to the real juice taste. With orange, it is easy enough to add dehydrated pulp for instant realism. But lemonade and other flavors still resemble what kids perennially refer to as "bug juice." That's the Day-Glo punch that doesn't taste like any fruit in particular but manages to seem "fruity" enough to deserve its euphemistic name, Tutti-Frutti.

Chocolate drink mixes also try to duplicate the real flavor but with a conspicuous lack of success. When Consumers Union tested chocolate drink mixes in 1976 they found only one in twenty-one that actually contained chocolate. All contained cocoa. Some were even called cocoa mix. But chemical flavorings are relied upon to doctor the taste.

Sugar is the primary ingredient in cocoa and chocolate-flavored mixes. Some are mixed with water to produce a weak chocolatey taste. Others, mixed with milk, come closer to real chocolate flavor.

They are all junk, though—with more calories (up to 250 for eight-ounce portions) than flavor. Every one tastes better cold than hot. The best advice is, if you want chocolate *eat* it—don't drink it.

6.
IF I KNEW YOU WERE COMING I'D HAVE BAKED A...

Maybe it's because we Americans cherish our independence so much that we dislike being told what we can't do. Maybe that's why nobody has ever understood the meaning of the old saying "You can't have your cake and eat it too."

We can so. The baking industry estimates that commercial cake production in the United States is well over 2 billion pounds annually. Furthermore, manufacturers of instant cake mixes produce close to 800 million pounds of ready-to-use ingredients yearly, yielding a whopping 1.5 billion additional pounds of finished cake.

Pillsbury, General Mills (Betty Crocker), and Procter & Gamble (Duncan Hines) are responsible for most of the cakes we make at home. Then there are the millions of cakes created by local retail bakeries and the factory-made ones found in the frozen-food display cases of supermarkets. (Sara Lee and Pepperidge Farm are responsible for most of these.)

We are still left with the 700 million or more air mattresses known as "Twinkies" that ITT-Continental Baking makes in its coast-to-coast bakeries. Children eat about 80 percent of these Twinkies—light sponge cakes filled with a white sugar filling. The other 140 million are gulped down by grown-up junk fooders.

Twinkies were the brainstorm of James Dewar, who first "creamed" them up in 1930. His bakery made the sponge cakes as a foundation for strawberry short-cake. But sales came to a halt when the short strawberry season ended. To maintain year-long consumption he got the idea of filling the plain cakes with cream. He christened the new creation after "Twinkle Toes Shoes," a name he noticed on an advertising sign in St. Louis.

Twinkies are a national commodity now although their largest sales are still in the Midwest. ITT-Continental sells about $50 million in Twinkies each year and is aiming for $70 million.

Junk food devotees tend to be a desperate bunch when it comes to Twinkies. In 1975, for example, somebody ripped off a Continental Baking delivery truck in Marysville, Michigan. The police say they found the truck but the 1,800 Twinkies on board had vanished. A house in Kennett Square, Pennsylvania, was burglarized twice in the same year and each time the culprits, overlooking valuables, raided the pantry and took the Twinkies.

ITT-Continental also manufactures Ho-Hos, and Snoballs, the chocolate creme-filled cupcakes, among other snack cakes, for the bakery shelves of grocery stores. These products have a loyal following, too, but nothing compared to the Twinkies aficionados. Even Archie Bunker goes berserk if Edith don't put a Twinkie in his lunchbox.

Twinkies, however, are *bas cuisine* compared to the stupendous lineup produced in the Kitchens of Sara Lee. If I could take only one type of food with me to a desert island, it would be *anything* Sara Lee makes.

The Kitchens of Sara Lee, now a division of Consolidated Foods, began in 1949 when Charles Lubin decided to ignore the marketing experts' belief that people wouldn't be willing to pay a little more in the supermarket for baked goods, no matter how fine the ingredients. At that time, $3 billion worth of bread and bakery products was sold in the United States but none of it was frozen. By 1953, frozen baked goods were a multimillion-dollar business, with most of the millions going to Sara Lee.

Lubin named his new company after his young daughter. Besides the original cheesecake with which the company started, and for which it became famous, dozens of new products were added, all prepared with fresh dairy ingredients.

In fact, Sara Lee is the single largest user of dairy goods today. More than

200,000 pounds of Grade AA butter is whipped into their all-butter products each week—totaling some 11 million pounds per year. The company's milk delivery amounts to 60,000 quarts a week or 3 million quarts a year. More than 1½ million pounds of sour cream, 3 million pounds of baker's cheese, and 4 million pounds of cream cheese a year all find their way into the 90,000 cheesecakes we gobble up daily.

Sara Lee even has its own egg-breaking plant in Rock Island, Illinois, where 50,000 pounds of whole eggs are cracked at the rate of 2,000 per minute.

The company is dedicated to meticulous quality control, as any tour of the Deerfield, Illinois, plant will prove. The place is immaculately clean (the floors are washed every twenty minutes) and the visitor is dumbfounded by the rows and rows of computerized machinery that whirls out cake after cake. The pastry dough that oozes forth is 108 or more layers *thin*, pressed so fine that all we notice is its lightness and flakiness.

Sara Lee has made for itself such a heaven-high reputation that demand for its products goes beyond our shores. Factories are now operating in Europe, Canada, and Australia.

Many people argue convincingly that Sara Lee desserts are *not* junk food. Perhaps not. But what are they, then? Pop food? Maybe. Ambrosia? Yes.

7.
DOUGHNUTS: THE HOLE TRUTH

There's a small clique of Wall Street analysts who amuse themselves by relating the health of the national economy to the sale of doughnuts. They point out that as the economy crumbles, for some strange reason the sales of doughnuts skyrocket. They cite as irrefutable evidence the depression of the early 1930s when doughnuts became one of the most popular foods in the country. Ultimately the U.S. Census Bureau was persuaded to go to the herculean effort of determining just how many doughnuts were purchased per year during that period. The census revealed that an incredible 216 million dozen doughnuts were consumed in 1929, the year of the crash.

This year, no doubt, we should expect sales of what in '29 was dubbed "the poor man's rich food" to be monumental. When you consider that in 1974, as the economic downturn began we bought some 15 *billion* doughnuts, it becomes unsettlingly clear that those wiseacre Wall Streeters really aren't selling us a bill of goods after all.

Just what is it about these little life-preserver-shaped cakes—these gentile bagels, as it were—that makes them adored so fanatically by Americans?

Simple.

Doughnuts are the ultimate junk food. Fortified with globs of sugar and then fried in heavenly oceans of hot grease—polyunsaturated vegetable oil, if we're lucky—doughnuts have found their niche in our stomachs.

Our love affair with doughnuts is not just a twentieth-century fling; it dates back to when America was first colonized. Fried cakes, as they were called in the 1600s, were a Dutch or English tradition, depending on which one of the assorted histories of the doughnut you want to believe. When the Dutch (and/ or English) settlers emigrated to New England they brought with them the savvy to prepare the sweet fried cakes. Since the mounds of dough were shaped like nuts and then quick-fried, the result was christened "doughnuts."

How the doughnut got its hole is quite another story. Of all the myths, however, the most ludicrous one seems to be the most authentic. This was established in the Great Doughnut Debate, held in New York in late November 1941, just before Pearl Harbor. The heated discussion took place at the Hotel Astor and was sponsored by the National Dunking Association.

The judges were Clifton Fadiman, Franklin P. Adams, and Elsa Maxwell. Speaking in favor of the traditional view was Fred E. Crockett of Camden, Maine. In opposition was one Henry A. Ellis, a Cape Code attorney who claimed that doughnut hole was invented when a Yarmouth Indian shot an arrow through a fried cake being cooked by a Pilgrim woman over an open fire.

However, Mr. Crockett's story, actually supported by affidavits and letters, is the one that goes down in the history books: In the late nineteenth century a brawny Maine sea captain, Hansen Gregory, was snacking on a fried cake during a violent storm at sea. (Why anyone would be snacking on *anything* during a violent storm is beside the point.) Somehow the ship lurched, forcing the captain to push the cake he was eating into one of the spokes of the steering wheel, creating—a hole! How convenient! Gregory talked his hometown bakery in Camden, Maine, into preparing his favorite doughnuts with holes so he could take them on all his voyages.

Our doughnut mania received a further impetus from World War I. The Salvation Army began serving doughnuts as an inexpensive novelty to boost soldier morale. Apparently they made the soldiers happier and hungrier. Doughnuts were dished out so often and in such quantities that they were considered a major war supply. The infantry was so enthusiastic about doughnuts that eventually its soldiers were nicknamed "doughboys."

Enter the 1920s and the machine age. A new-fangled doughnut machine invented by an enterprising baker was able to produce almost 1,000 of them per hour. Now the whole nation could have doughnuts. But as with anything which exists in excess, doughnuts soon became passé. It took the rise of the fast-food franchises in the 1950s to start up the doughnut craze once again.

Dunkin' Donuts, headquartered near Boston, started its operations in 1950 and now has more than 800 individual stores around the world. It brought glamor and pizazz to the doughnut by offering fifty-two different varieties. Five years later, Mister Donut, also near Boston, became Dunkin' Donuts' chief rival. Today, with more than 500 stores in the United States, Canada, Japan, and God knows where else, Mr. Donut offers "53 basic varieties and 200 variations based on our recipe formulas."

The good old plain doughnut became the subject of intense experimentation. And like some hybrid creatures from Dr. Frankenstein's laboratory a motley menagerie of new doughnuts emerged from doughnut stores around the country. Peanut butter, banana, apple strudel, pumpkin, Bavarian creme coconut, squash, bacon 'n egg—flavor upon flavor, *ad nauseam*.

Whether or not the weird flavors sold, they brought people to the doughnut shops where they would purchase the old dependable standards: cinnamon, powdered sugar, chocolate, honey dip, chocolate honey dip, jelly, plain.

Doughnuts come in three basic styles: yeast-raised, cake, and filled cake. The first is a light concoction which doesn't have air pumped into it but owes its puffy, cloudlike texture to natural yeast action. Most often glazed in sugar, this is the doughnut that is most popular in America and throughout the world.

The cake doughnut, more amenable to flavor modifications, is a heavier, not to say more leaden, variety. It comes in various shapes and sizes and is your basic doughnut for dunking. Filled cake doughnuts are holeless and rely on the same cake recipes but are pumped full of flavorings from jelly to custard, the filling replacing the hole.

Each region of the United States has its own favorite, according to the doughnut bakers. The honey dip or glazed sells almost three to one against the other varieties. It is a yeast-raised confection which is iced in an almost color-less sugar. Honey has absolutely nothing to do with it, so the name is definitely misleading.

Older people tend to prefer the less complicated plain cake doughnut. In the West, the "old fashioned"—a crusty sort of crumb bun doughnut, is popular, while the chocolate cake doughnut is preferred in the North and Southeast.

Doughnuts are considered by most devotees to be basically a breakfast food. Two doughnuts and a cup of coffee is a quick and filling repast. Accordingly, the mammoth food conglomerates have viewed doughnuts as vehicles for fresh profits.

The first of them to market doughnuts nationally was Morton Foods, a division of ITT-Continental Baking, manufacturers of frozen lemon cream pies that contain neither lemon nor cream. In 1974, after intensive test marketing, Morton began full-scale production of what it fancifully calls its "Donut Shop Donuts." Within six months the food giant was able to declare that "the donuts had attained 20 percent of the frozen breakfast baked goods area," or in simpler terms, a nice round $55 million in sales. Not to be outdone, Pillsbury has moved in and so, too, has Welch Foods, the latter known mainly for its grape products. Welch's gimmick is to stick in some of their famous brand of grape jelly natch, whereas Pillsbury is riding on its name as the All-American bakery goods leader.

When such hefty profits can be obtained so quickly it seems surprising that the companies took so long to realize the potential of America's passion for doughnuts. According to a spokesman for Morton, the reason that company hadn't cast its doughnuts upon the waters sooner was the "time-consuming effort of R & D to find the exact recipe formulation which could withstand the freezer."

Unfortunately, there is one problem. Frozen doughnuts tend to be sticky and gummy when defrosted. And no technology or test tube chemistry has yet been able to change this. Quality doughnuts depend upon split-second timing in the frying, the ingredients, and the oil temperature. So doughnuts are one of the most perishable junk foods. Let them sit around for more than four or five hours and they become mushy and limp or hard and stale.

Every doughnut receipe emphasizes that they must be fried exactly at 375°. If the fat is too hot they will brown before they are cooked enough. If the fat is too cool, the doughnuts will absorb too much oil before they brown. The industry doesn't like to talk about this kind of doughnut, but it certainly serves enough of them. They're known as *sinkers*.

A sinker is just what it sounds like. A doughnut that's so heavy in oil as to be almost indigestible. You will find them most often in coffee shops and diners serviced by factory bakeries that don't know real doughnuts from borscht. If they weren't shaped like life preservers you could mistake them for anchors.

Which brings us to one theory about why the "ugh" was taken out of the word doughnut. Apparently the "ugh" suggested to people that doughnuts were heavy. So the name "donut" was created, a much more economical word that said the same thing. In the beginning, though, it took a lot of convincing to persuade people that donut was not pronounced doo-nut."

Mass-produced doughnuts packaged for supermarkets usually contain enough stabilizers and preservatives to keep them alive on borrowed time. They come from huge assembly-line machines which do everything from preparing the dough to packaging the final product at the modest speed of 2,400 dozen an hour.

With the rising price of ingredients and labor, the price of doughnuts has shot up in some places to 30 cents each. And where they don't get you in the pocketbook, they'll still find a way to get you: notice how that hole in the middle is gradually getting larger?

Doughnuts are as rich in mystique as they are in carbohydrates. Take the curious habit of dunking. Supposedly the legendary silent movie actress Mae

Murray accidentally dunked a doughnut at her hangout, the Roseland Ballroom in New York, thereby starting the trend. Other celebrities over the years have followed suit. Funnyman Red Skelton put dunking into his pantomime act. Shipwreck Kelly, the famous flagpole sitter, reportedly dunked a baker's dozen in coffee, while standing on his head on a plank extended from the roof of a towering New York City skyscraper.

There was even a National Dunking Association for a while. Skelton served as president and so did Johnny Carson, Jack Lemmon, Joey Bishop, and others. It got to the point where Emily Post was obliged to create a new rule on dunking. She decreed that it was socially acceptable to dunk, if you first break the doughnut in half.

Incidentally, it could be said that doughnuts help to keep the country awake. Approximately 75 percent of all stores that sell doughnuts exclusively stay open

twenty-four hours a day dispensing them with fresh hot coffee. And most do a lucrative business after midnight.

One of the most unusual recipes for doughnuts is offered by a small, widely scattered chain called Spudnuts. Started in 1939 in Salt Lake City as a neighborhood shop by two brothers, Bob and Al Pelton, Spudnuts is now a national franchise with 130 outlets from Maine to California. The Peltons' success lay in finding a way to grind potatoes into a cake flour (hence, spudnut) which can be used to make an extremely fluffy, satisfying doughnut. Spudnuts don't taste anything like potatoes, but they have the smooth texture of whipped ones.

Every doughnut chain has its own particular recipe, although (except for Spudnuts) they closely resemble each other. Good doughnuts are fried only in top grade polyunsaturated vegetable shortening. Animal fat tends to leave a telltale taste, as does any oil when it is overused. Oil for doughnuts must therefore be changed constantly. Normal cake doughnuts absorb about 18 percent of the fat; yeast-raised, 15 to 25 percent. Cake has up to 15 percent sugar, though, while yeast-raised has 3 percent or less.

So popular is the doughnut that the Field Museum of Natural History in Chicago has one in its collection "identified as a glazed donut by the eminent gastro-ethnologist A. Cruller-Dunquer."

And that's the hole truth.

8.
IT'S AS EASY AS...

My grandmother was a truly great baker. The fragrant smells that would waft out of her kitchen still linger in my mind. Golden coffee cakes, delicate sugar cookies, and the richest chocolatey brownies in all creation were a small part of of her repertoire. But nobody dared ask her to bake a pie. She just couldn't do it—and that gave her a bigger inferiority complex than any shy teenager ever had about getting a Saturday night date.

A kindly old German lady up the street from my grandmother's summer cottage, however, produced a vast array of scrumptious pies. They were practically artistic achievements, worthy of a museum showcase.

Grandma Annie couldn't hide her jealousy. Whenever anybody would mention the wonderful piece of apple pie they had had at Mrs. Frieden's, she would be sure to retort icily, "You really shouldn't eat that woman's pie—she's a dirty Nazi!"

Despite the old "easy as" saying, pies are difficult to make, which explains why they constitute such a large proportion of the frozen convenience bakery items in the supermarket. Some 400 million pounds are sol this way every year. That's nearly double the combined volume of other frozen baked goods.

While pies are not an American invention, we have made them almost a national trust. Why else would we say, "It's as American as apple pie"?

A European creation, pies are by definition a baked dish consisting of a filling with either a lower or an upper crust or both. When the lower crust is missing, the result is sometimes referred to as a "deep dish" pie.

Commercial and retail bakers make over one billion pounds of pie a year. The largest firm exclusively devoted to pies is Mrs. Smith's Pies. But Sara Lee has recently joined the ranks. Lloyd Harriss is the other major pie manufacturer whose product finds its way into the frozen-food display cases in America's supermarkets.

Pies are really overgrown pastries. The crust is usually a flaky pastry type and the fillings are similar to those found in turnovers, danishes, and tarts, only in larger quantity.

America's favorite fillings are apple (natch), cherry, and blueberry. Cream pies, usually a custardy pudding on top of crushed graham crackers, are also beloved, with chocolate the most popular and banana, coconut, and custard close behind.

9.
THERE'S A COOKIE MONSTER IN ALL OF US

The "cookie monster" doesn't dwell only on Sesame Street. It lives in every household in America. We are all cookie monsters! Whether we are dunking our Oreos or overdosing on a freshly baked batch of Toll House chocolate chips, cookies remain our greatest passion. Take away our cookies and you take away our very souls.

A common misconception (love *is* blind) is that cookies are an American invention. Actually, we derive the name from a Dutch specialty, *koekjes*, which were first baked in colonial Nieuw Amsterdam (New York). The British, who still refer to cookies as "biscuits," used them as tea cakes or scones. As our nation grew, so did our sweet tooth. Americans in the New World gradually experimented, adding new and sweeeter varieties of cookies to the originally slim lineup.

The current American favorite is the chocolate chip cookie. There is even a chain of stores, Famous Amos, which sells nothing but variations of chocolate chip cookies: peanut butter, butterscotch, and raisin-filled.

If $3 a pound for Famous Amos Chocolate Chip Cookies is too steep, there is a host of other types and brands to choose from, including Chips Ahoy, Chip-aroos, Rich 'n' Chips, and Cocochips.

Nabisco, the largest manufacturer of cookies, would probably disagree that the chocolate chip cookie is the American favorite, and claim that their Oreo Creme Sandwich leads in sales. But Nabisco buttons up when you ask for figures. In fact, when I attempted to get information about their products from this mammoth cookie and cracker company, they refused on the grounds that their cookies "couldn't possibly be considered pop food."

Nabisco actually has many accomplishments about which to be proud, if not snooty. It produces more than 150 types of cookies and crackers, totaling half a billion pounds a year. Its Sugar Wafers, Animal Crackers, Lorna Doones, and Oreos are found in virtually every grocery store in this country. As a pretzel maker it produces 25 percent of our total supply and its behemoth machines can whip out 40 million in eight hours.

Nabisco executives have apparently always been prone to pomposity. When the company first began business back at the start of this century, a company spokesman declared: "In my opinion, Nabiscos are one of the major gastronomic achievements of the human race, as important as the development of ice cream."

When Nabisco was formed in 1898, by the merger of local bakeries across the country, it was known as the National Biscuit Company. Within a year some 65 million packages of crackers and cookies had been sold. The initial products were well-known standard cookies. Ginger snaps were known as "jinger wayfers" before Nabisco baked them by the millions on a national scale. Delicate, golden Biscos Sugar Wafers, the first cookie with the Nabisco name, followed in 1901 and production couldn't keep up with demand.

Social Tea Biscuits were familiar long before Nabisco existed but it took the baking giant to package and trademark it to new popularity.

Part of Nabisco's unique success came because it packaged its products in a newly developed "In-Er-Seal," a trademarked process which kept products fresh long after they left the factory. Americans, long accustomed to poorly packaged, short-lasting products, were quick to appreciate this new development.

In 1912 *Lorna Doone* was the number one bestselling romance. Nabisco capitalized on the book's vogue and changed the name of its Scottish-type shortcake from Hostess Jumbles to Lorna Doone Jumbles. It was a marketing coup that has made the cookie one of the company's perennial profit staples.

But of all the days in the company's history, April 2, 1912, stands out as the most important. That was the day the firm introduced the Oreo Biscuit to the world: two beautifully embossed chocolate-flavored wafers with a rich cream filling, all for just 30 cents per pound. In 1921 the cookie was renamed the Oreo Sandwich, and twenty-seven years after that, the Oreo Creme Sandwich.

Today the company is a $2 billion conglomerate that may have become too big for its own—or our—good.

Its Vanilla Wafers, a favorite in the South, are now a national product but no longer contain real vanilla; hence their new name, Nilla Wafers. However, Nabisco's chief competitor, Sunshine Biscuits, still produces a quality Vanilla Wafer for a reasonable price. Where Nabisco skimps to save a penny, this company still uses natural ingredients when artificial ones can be avoided—in all its products.

Sunshine Biscuits has been with us since 1902 when James Loose, his brother, and a friend, John Wiles, formed the Loose-Wiles Candy and Cracker Co. in Kansas City, Missouri. With only a handful of employees, the bakers worked under uncomfortable conditions in a cellar. But they had a dream: to get the bake shop out of the cellar into a building where the working area would be flooded with sunshine. By 1908 their fortunes had improved and they opened new bakeries around the country. The one in Boston was the first of many "Thousand Window Bakeries." Four years later, the company opened the world's largest bakery under one roof in Long Island City, New York. It wasn't until 1946 that the Loose-Wiles name was changed formally to Sunshine Biscuits, Inc.

Sunshine is now owned by American Brands (an outgrowth of the American Tobacco Company) but is still dedicated to quality ingredients in its cookies and crackers. Says a spokesman: "The difference between our products and others is that we still use pure vegetable shortening in everything."

Its leading cookies are Vienna Fingers and Chiparoos. Its snack crackers, Cheezits, are made with no flavorings or colorings, just real cheddar cheese. But Sunshine is probably best known for its Hydrox, a carbon copy (except for the taste) of the Nabisco Oreo.

There are many other multimillion-dollar biscuit bakers to whom junk food addicts are loyal and grateful. Among them are Keebler, the second largest in national sales; Burry's, a division of Quaker Oats; and, perhaps the most worshipped of all, Pepperidge Farm, Margaret Rudkin's folksy baking company, now owned by Campbell's Soups.

In 1937 Margaret Rudkin, coaxed by friends and relatives, began baking her "specially formulated" bread for New England distribution. It was an instant success; other breads were added and they, too, proved to be moneymakers. Not until 1950 did Pepperidge Farm decide to enter the competitive cookie business. Mrs. Rudkin searched through Europe for unusual taste sensations. Her savvy eye and discriminating palate resulted in what is now called the Distinctive Cookie Line, which includes the easy-to-love Milano, Nassau, and Bordeaux cookies, among others.

But not everyone in the United States can afford PF's prestigious cookies. The quality of ingredients necessitates equally prestigious prices. Consequently, some parts of the country never even see the Distinctive Line. "Utah, for example," says the PF spokesman, "doesn't get as many chocolate cookies because the people there simply can't afford them."

Using quality ingredients and no preservatives creates numerous hassles for PF. It had to suspend the manufacture of the Geneva Cookie because it was too difficult and costly to apply a thick, tempting layer of chocolate on the thin

cookie without breaking it. When the price of chocolate hit the roof, PF also discontinued the Orleans Wafer. But in response to a flood of mail from distressed consumers, PF resumed manufacture—at a hefty (but who's complaining?) price increase.

The company, whose name still conjures up a small, home-kitchen operation, now provides our sweet tooth with a welcome assortment of cakes, pastries, and snack products, most of them baked from old European recipes.

Thank you, Pepperidge Farm.

10.
WHAT WE ALL SCREAM FOR

Ten percent of all milk "mooed" in America is used to make our favorite dessert —ice cream. Close to 800 million gallons of the stuff are now produced yearly. In case you don't have a calculator handy, that's about 20 gallons per person a year. Of course, ice cream comes in many forms—ice milk, sherbet, frappes, bars, sandwiches, Dixie cups, cakes—well over 300 different ways.

Although ice cream was one of the first specialty desserts served in the first years of the White House by Thomas Jefferson and James Madison (his wife, Dolley, was an expert ice cream maker), the first major ice cream business didn't open its doors until 1851, when Jacob Fussel began his Baltimore, Maryland, wholesale bulk ice cream operation.

Our forefathers didn't have the choice of flavors we enjoy today. Vanilla, chocolate, and a few fruit flavors were all that was offered. But as competition grew, so did an intense, almost ludicrous, hunt for novelty flavors. The rainbow assortment was an excellent sales gimmick, but America's first love has remained the immutable, old-faithful vanilla.

The frantic search for flavors, each more bizarre than the preceding one, has reached ridiculous proportions. The parade now includes apple strudel, banana daiquiri, borscht, bubble gum (lawsuits reportedly hit its manufacturer when people broke teeth on the rock-hard frozen gum), casaba melon, chili con carne, eggnog, iced tea, jelly bean, licorice, pineapple pecan, chocolate cheesecake, and a bicentennial favorite: Red, White and Blueberry.

The majority of these were invented and served by the Baskin-Robbins Ice Cream chain, which has more than 400 flavors to its credit. BR has even made the *Guinness Book of World Records* because of this dubious feat. (Bresler's Ice Cream, a smaller chain, has more than 200 flavors.)

The outrageous, wacky Baskin-Robbins flavor onslaught that still tickles our fancy, if not our tastebuds, is the result of an auspicious deal pulled off by a pair of GI morale officers during World War II on a South Seas island. Burton Baskin and Irving Robbins traded their jeep for a freezer and concocted exotic flavored ice cream to boost sinking wartime morale. Successful beyond their wildest expectations, the ice cream launched a thousand smiles—and an ice cream company when they returned to civilian life. Starting in California, the business quickly mushroomed to what is now a 1,400-store chain. By offering franchises to qualified entrepreneurs and creating zany flavors with top ingredients, Baskin and Robbins became legend. And rich.

Realizing that people would be wary of buying their strange ice creams if they didn't know how they tasted, they are still the only chain to offer customers samples of flavors on teeny plastic spoons.

Vanilla accounts for 51 percent of all ice cream sold in the United States, chocolate for 14 percent, strawberry for just 6 percent; other flavors make up the remaining 29 percent.

Among sherbets, orange is the leader, with pineapple, lime, lemon, and raspberry following.

Coffee ice cream is a New England passion while nutty flavors lead in the South. Alaska, surprisingly, eats more ice cream, proportionately, than the rest of the country.

Novelties—popsicles, cones, eskimo pies—account for a bewildering ten billion pieces or 25 percent of the industry's total gallonage.

Eskimo pies were born by accident. Their father was Christian Nelson, who in 1919 ran a candy store. One day a boy came in and had more than the normal amount of trouble making up his mind between an ice cream sandwich and a candy bar. Nelson decided to offer two in one. The first chocolate-covered ice cream bars *without* a stick appeared under the trademarked name Eskimo Pies in 1921. Within one year a million were sold daily. Today some 750 million are sold each year.

At about the same time the Good Humor Bar appeared on the scene. The bars with sticks became popular mainly because of their method of sale: the jolly Good Humor man.

And in 1924 Popsicles—water ices on sticks—were patented, and immediately sold 3 million a year.

Just over fifty years elapsed from the time Nancy Johnson invented the ice cream freezer in 1846 to the discovery of the ice cream cone, another accidental birth.

A Syrian immigrant named Ernest A. Hamwi was running a St. Louis World's Fair concession selling Zalabia, a waffle confection. When the neighboring concession selling ice cream ran out of dishes, Hamwi rolled one of his waffles into a cone as a replacement. Pretty soon other customers saw the waffle cone and clamored for the same.

Howard Johnson established his fame and fortune by hawking 28 flavors of high butter-fat ice cream (although any HoJo you go to today seems to stock only 11 flavors). In the process, he started the fast food franchise business which dominates the entire restaurant field today.

Whether it's Baskin-Robbins, Howard Johnson, Breyers, Dreyers, or A&P brand, the basic composition of ice cream remains uniform by federal and state legal standards which determine minimum—and sometimes maximum—percentages of the various ingredients.

MINIMUM & MAXIMUM STANDARDS FOR FROZEN DAIRY DESSERTS
(may vary by State Law)

		Plain	Bulk	Ice Milk	Sherbert	Water Ice
Milk Fat	Min %	10	8	2	1	
	Max %			7	2	
Milk Solids	Min %	20	16	11	5	
	Max %				5	
Food Solids (lb./gal)		1.60	1.60	1.30		
Weight (lb./gal.)		4.50	4.50	4.50	6.0	
Stabilizers	Max %	.50	.50	.50	.50	.50
Emulsifers	Max %	.30	.30	.30	.30	
Salts	Max %	.24	.24	.24		
Acidity					.35	.35

• Milk fat determines the richness and creaminess of ice cream. It is responsible for the smooth texture and full body that ice cream has or fails to have. It is the most expensive component and thus the higher the milk fat content, the more premium the product becomes.

• Milk solids round out the flavor, provide protein, and improve texture.

• Corn sweeteners impart a chewiness to the body of ice cream.

• Stabilizers bind water and produce smoothness of texture by reducing ice crystals. Gelatin was for years the most widely used stabilizer but now the scientists have found materials derived from seaweeds and plants that do the trick for less.

• Emulsifiers help ice cream accept air which is pumped into it. This air is important for increased bulk, especially in el cheapo supermarket brands.

• Air and water in frozen desserts are a fact of life. The air, incorporated as tiny bubbles hardly visible to the eye, and water, partially frozen into small crystals, give ice cream palatability, texture, and body.

• The increase in product volume resulting from the air content is referred to in dairy lingo as "overrun" and is defined as the volume of ice cream obtained in excess of the volume of the mix. Federal and state laws on the weight per gallon of the finished product determine the maximum allowable overrun.

REPRESENTATIVE FORMULAS
(varies by state laws)
Percentage of ingredients in frozen dairy desserts

	Premium I.C.	Bulk (brick)	Ice Milk	Sherbert	Softserve*
Milk/Butter Fat	16	10½	3	1½	6
Milk Solids	9	11	12	3½	12
Sucrose	16	12½	12	19	9
Corn Syrup Solids		5½	7	9	6
Stabilizers	.1	.3	.3	.5	.3
Emulsifiers		.1	.15		.2
Total Solids	41.1	39.9	34.45	33.50	33.50
Pounds per Gallon of Mix (draw from freezer)	9.17	9.36	9.46	9.48	9.30
% Overrun	65–70	95–100	90–95	50	41
Pounds per Gallon (finished product)	5.4	4.6	4.8	6.25	6.5

Each manufacturer prepares its ice cream to its own formula. This chart merely provides an approximation to those formulas.

* Soft ice cream has same ingredients as regular ice cream but is served in a semifrozen state. The industry produces 150 million gallons of softserve ice cream a year, all served over the counter from special machines.

II.
SNACKS FACTS

If there is one class of junk food whose sales show a definite trend in American food habits it is the crispy, crunchy, cracklin', salted snack: pretzels, corn chips, popcorn, cheese fries, and potato chips.

In 1964 Americans purchased $528 million worth of potato chips. Twelve years later that figure had climbed to a record $1.5 billion. Last year the 242 potato chip factories in the United States used approximately four billion pounds of potatoes.

Potato chippers—as the manufacturers like to call themselves—say that we average 4.5 pounds of chips per person in a year. It *must* be an average. I know I can zip through that much in less than a month. And I'm not alone. Potato chips are America's favorite snack food, whether they come with ridges or in sticks or the way George Crum originally made them in Saratoga Springs, New York, back in 1853.

George Crum was a chef at the Carey Moon Lake House, which had just opened as a lakeside resort for its first season. Crum was a proud man, and if any guest dared to return an order to the kitchen, that guest would receive a completely indigestible replacement from the chef.

One day in 1853 when a guest sent back his french fries to the kitchen with a request to have them sliced thinner and fried longer, Crum decided to teach him a lesson.

He sliced the potatoes as thin as toilet paper, and threw the shavings into a tub of nearby ice water. Then, after letting them soak for a while, he dropped them quickly into a vat of boiling grease. They came out curled and crisp. He put some salt on them and sent them to the diner. George was dumbfounded when the guest sent his compliments and an order for more. Other guests heard about the potatoes and within a day every table was served the new creation. Soon after, Crum was able to open his own restaurant. They say that when George Crum died many years later he "left a lot of money."

The potato chip industry has always been comprised of many diverse family-owned operations. Many have been successful enough to catch the eye of encroaching conglomerates, but for the most part each potato chip company has regional distribution at most. Only one snack maker has been able to distribute nationally: Frito-Lay, which is the marriage of two regional giants that merged in 1961. Herman Lay was an enterprising Sunshine Biscuit salesman who skillfully built up a franchise system to produce his unique potato chips. His company joined forces with the Dallas-based Frito Company, founded by Elmer

Doolin in 1932 as a corn chip manufacturer, to form the single largest snack producer in the world. PepsiCo merged with Frito-Lay in 1965.

Potato chips are a hypnotic food, habit forming, irresistible. They are roughly 60 to 65 percent potato and 35 to 40 percent oil, according to a potato chip technologist. The fundamental rule is: the thicker the slice, the less oil absorbed and the more potato taste. The type of oil used to fry potatoes also affects the flavor. Vegetable oil, because it is lighter in taste and texture, is best.

THE GREAT AMERICAN TENNIS BALL CAN WAR

Looking back on the donnybrook between the potato chip industry and Procter & Gamble, it's clear now that the potato chippers had nothing to worry about. Their concern at the time stemmed from the 1975 national introduction by P&G of its "potato chips in a can," Pringles. Unlike regular potato chips, Pringles are uniformly shaped and stacked in a tennis ball cannister. Also unlike real potato chips, Pringles are fabricated chips made from dehydrated potatoes that have been processed into mush, pressed, and fried. Additives bring the taste as close to genuine potato chips as possible.

The potato chippers' trade group, the Potato Chip/Snack Food Association, sued Procter & Gamble in 1969 to prevent P&G from calling its man-made creation potato chips. But the chippers lost. The Association came back for another skirmish in 1973 when they petitioned the Food and Drug Administration to issue a regulation about what could and could not be called potato chips. They declared, using surveys as proof, that most consumers were unaware that the molded chips were not prepared from fresh potatoes.

While the FDA plodded toward a decision, the potato chip companies watched P&G—the world's largest advertiser—launch a massive "air attack" with TV commercials and other media promotions for Pringles. At one point Pringles and a bunch of copycats including Planter's, Munchos, Chipos, and a refreshingly honest contribution from Pillsbury, French Frauds, were taking away 15 percent of real chip sales.

Finally, on November 24, 1975, the FDA ruled that any product not made from fresh potatoes would have to be clearly labeled "potato chips made from dried potatoes." The order, however, was stayed until after December 31, 1977.

So the chipsters mounted large advertising offensives to ward off the "Pringles attack," stressing the natural goodness of real chips versus the ersatz quality of Pringles.

The whole brouhaha would never have occurred if the potato chip makers had trusted us consumers more. We knew right away after the first sampling of fabricated chips that they were no match for the real thing. The only valid argument in favor of the fabricated chips was that they remain fresh for months.

As soon as the novelty—and the ad blitz—wore off, so did sales of fabricated chips, which are now down to a piddling $150 million, or 10 percent of what potato chips rack up yearly. They will no doubt plummet even more when their remaining fanciers realize the full perversity of eating food packed in a tennis ball can.

Corn chips are one crunchy example to show how America, the Melting Pot, has obtained many of its finest junk foods from its immigrants.

Corn chips evolved from the tortilla, a fried corn flour bread that has always been a staple in the Mexican and Mexican-American diet.

Today, with automation, corn chips are a $330 million enterprise, up from only $70 million in 1964. Two-thirds of this business is controlled by the vast Frito-Lay (PepsiCo) empire, which has the resources to market and advertise nationally.

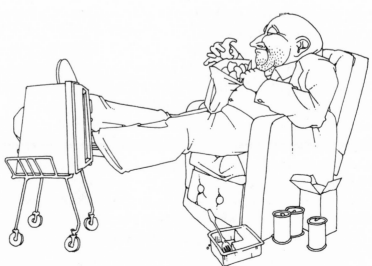

There are two types of corn chips, plain and tortilla. The plain variety remains our favorite but the tortilla is fast becoming a habit also, especially with its distinctive flavors: taco, cheese, nacho, etc.

Both types are prepared from wet corn meal (masa), which is flattened and cut into shape (rectangular for regular and triangular for tortilla) before frying. Tortilla chips, because they are highly seasoned, cannot be dumped directly into a frying vat. They would explode into tiny pieces. So they are seasoned and baked before meeting their fate in the fat.

Popcorn is the granddaddy of all snack nibbles in America. Indeed, it is the oldest existing snack in the world! Expeditions made in bat caves in west central New Mexico produced petrified ears of popcorn which, with radio carbon testing, proved to be 5,600 years old.

The Indians were the first known poppers in North America. Their method, according to the Popcorn Institute, was usually to toss kernels into the fire or hot ashes and letting the corn pop its way out. Others put the whole ear of corn on a stick and held it over the fire, for what must have been a remarkable fireworks display.

The Colonists were introduced to popcorn at the first Thanksgiving feast in Plymouth, Massachusetts by an Iroquois Indian. Today we munch 400 million pounds a year, for which we pay $260 million. Sixty percent of all this popcorn is consumed at home, 30 percent at movie theaters, amusement parks, and sports arenas. The remaining 10 percent is used as packaging effluvia and animal feed.

To guarantee that 99 percent of the popcorn we cook will pop, continuous research to find the "perfect pop" is carried on at the University of Iowa and Purdue University. According to the Popcorn Institute, the quality of popcorn is determined by its expansion rate—how large it will bloom—and moisture content. The best expansion rate is about 34 to 35 times the kernel size. Moisture content should be about 13.5 percent of the kernel.

The Indians thought there was a little demon imprisoned in the corn kernels and when the demon got angry enough, it would pop out. Actually, the demon is the inner moisture, which builds up pressure when the kernel is heated.

Suppose you find that your popcorn doesn't blow up into big fluffy kernels.

It probably means, says the Popcorn Institute, that the corn has lost its vital moisture. To recondition it, fill a quart jar three-quarters full with popcorn and add one tablespoon of water. Cover the jar and shake frequently at seven-minute intervals until all the water is absorbed. Set the jar aside. In two to four days the corn will be as good as new.

Popcorn is about 10 percent protein and only 3 percent fat, the other 80-plus percent consisting of a starchy carbohydrate and water. But when it's popped the fat content climbs because of the absorption of the cooking oil used to make it.

Popcorn is great for weight-conscious nibblers: when popped a cup has only 40 to 65 calories depending on the size of the kernels.

The Pennsylvania Dutch are the source of a legend-laden snack, the pretzel.

There are so many tales about the origin of the pretzel that I won't even bother sorting out the real ones from the fantasy. Suffice it to say that pretzels were introduced to America in Pennsylvania, where for the most part they have remained. Of the eighty-eight pretzel bakeries in the United States, sixty-six are in Pennsylvania. And why not? Consumption of pretzels in the Keystone State is roughly nine pounds per person a year, far above the national average. We plunked down $185 million in change for pretzels in 1975, and since sales figures have risen dramatically in the past twelve years there is definite reason to believe we will grow even more enamored of them as the years roll along.

Nabisco is the largest pretzel maker, with 25 percent of all production. Rold-Gold, owned by Frito-Lay, is next, followed by Bachman (General Cigar), and Quinlan (Ward Food). Dozens of other bakeries scattered around Pennsylvania (but only twenty-two bakeries outside that state) also make hard and soft "street vendor" pretzels.

Lay's Potato Chips created a commercial in the early 1960s which summed up the psychology of salted snacks. The great comic actor Bert Lahr dared us: "Betcha can't eat just one!" Of course we couldn't. Potato chips or any other snack food mesmerize our tastebuds. Whether it's the salt or other seasoning, whether it's the crunchy, crispy sound, or whether it's the oil or shortening they are prepared with, when we eat snacks we tend to eat a lot, and we do so without thinking.

Why do you think movie theaters have been selling popcorn steadily for the past fifty years? Snack food is entertaining and easy. We can let our hand move automatically back and forth from bag to mouth. What we are eating is hardly more than bulk, carbohydrate volume, a tranquilizing oral gratification. Party food. *Bas cuisine* that keeps us happy for a long time after we learn that life really *isn't* a cabaret.

Light, unassuming universally accepted, snack foods provide us with our mandatory fat fix, and for that alone we cherish them.

In fact, I think I'll have some Cheez-Doodles right now.

12.
BREAKFAST CEREALS:
THE <u>REAL</u> SUGAR BOWL

There is only one cereal on the market today that has 1 percent or less sugar (sucrose). Much of the nutrition in today's cereals has been added by the manufacturer to replace previously processed-out nutrients. Moreover, while it has been proved that the fortification of cereals with 100 percent of the recommended dietary allowance of vitamins costs less than one penny, you pay upwards of 18 cents for that 0.6 cents' worth of vitamins. To get these added nutrients, the kids who dote on these snappers, cracklers, and poppers must also plow through puffs, shreds, and flakes that are up to 68 percent sugar. In fact, many breakfast cereals clearly contain more sugar than actual cereal and more sugar than the amounts found in popular candy bars and cookies.

In the chart that follows, those cereals marked with an asterisk are cereal products in the top 20 of those advertised on network television in 1976. They are prime examples of *kiddie litter*.

.   .   .

CEREAL	SUGAR CONTENT (percent)
50% or more	
Super Orange Crisp	68.0
Sugar Smacks	61.3
King Vitamin	58.5
Fruit Pebbles	55.1*
Apple Jacks	55.0*
Cocoa Pebbles	53.5
Lucky Charms	50.4*
Cinnamon Crunch	50.3
40% or more	
Pink Panther	49.2
Honeycomb	48.8*
Froot Loops	47.4*
Trix	46.6*
Cocoa Crispies	45.9*
Baron Von Redberry	45.8
Vanilly Crunch	45.8
Boo Berry	45.7
Quisp	44.9
Orange Quangaroos	44.7
Count Chocula	44.2
Frosted Flakes	44.0
Frankenberry	44.0
Kaboom	43.8
Captain Crunch Crunchberry	43.4*
Captain Crunch	43.3*
Cocoa Puffs	43.0*
Super Sugar Crisp	40.7*
Sir Grapefellow	40.7
Alpha Bits	40.3*
25% or more	
Sugar Pops	37.8*
Frosted Mini Wheats	33.6
Sugar Sparkled Corn Flakes	32.2
Brand Buds	30.2
Sugar Frosted Flakes	29.0*

CEREAL	SUGAR CONTENT (percent)
10% or more	
Super Sugar Chex	24.5
Heartland (Natural)	23.1
Fortified Oat Flakes	22.2
Granola (w/almonds & filberts)	21.4
All Bran	20.0
100% Bran	18.4
Granola (natural)	16.6
40% Bran Flakes (Kellogg)	16.2
Brown Sugar-Cinnamon Frosted Mini Wheats	16.0
Team	15.9
40% Bran Flakes (Post)	15.8
Sugar Frosted Corn Flakes	15.6
Granola w/raisins	14.5
Granola w/dates	14.5
Life	14.5
Buck Wheat	13.6
Heartland w/raisins	13.5
Raisin Bran (Kellogg)	10.6*
Rice Krispies	10.0*

CEREAL	SUGAR CONTENT (percent)	CEREAL	SUGAR CONTENT (percent)
Less than 10%		Less than 10%	
Concentrate	9.9	Post Toasties	4.1
Raisin Bran (Post)	9.6	Alpen (Natural)	3.8
Crisp Rice	8.8	Puffed Wheat	3.5
Rice Chex	8.5	Grape Nut Flakes	3.3
Total	8.1	Wheat Chex	2.6
Corn Flakes (Kellogg)	8.1	Uncle Sam Cereal	2.4
Crispy Rice	7.3	Puffed Rice	2.4
Grape Nuts	6.6	Cheerios	2.2*
Corn Chex	5.5	Shredded Wheat (spoon size)	1.3 (per biscuit)
Peanut Butter	5.2	Shredded Wheat (large size)	1.0 (per biscuit)
Wheaties	4.7	NONE	
Special K	4.4		
Corn Total	4.4		
Product 19	4.1		

13.
BUCKETS AND BURGERS: FAST FOOD

- When nineteen-year-old Reenie Palmiere married Tom Kavano, twenty, they must have had a wedding reception that was prepared quickly enough to qualify for the *Guinness Book of World Records*. The two kids decided to hold their reception under the golden arches of a Westmont, New Jersey, McDonald's. They dressed in formal gown and tuxedo, but catered the affair with low-brow Big Macs and fries. The happy couple was also presented with a Ronald McDonald clock by the management.

- Mrs. Gloria Pitzer of Pearl Beach, Michigan, spent two painstaking years trying to duplicate the taste of Arthur Treacher's Fish and Chips and Colonel Sanders' Kentucky Fried Chicken in her own kitchen. She finally did crack the corporate recipe secrets and now produces a monthly newsletter describing homemade substitutes for a brigade of junk foods.

- When King Taufa'ahau Tupou IV, sovereign of Tonga, a Southwest Pacific island kingdom, arrived in Los Angeles, the first meal he ordered to be sent up to his Wilshire Hotel suite was not a gourmet specialty from Chasen's but a "snack" consisting of thirty Big Macs.

The burgeoning of the fast-food business has changed not only our eating habits but also our lifestyles. The spectacular rise of the fast-food restaurant, from a scattered assortment of drive-ins in the baby boom years after World War II into the mind-boggling $15 billion big business of today, is easily witnessed wherever you live or travel in America.

Drive along the labyrinth of interstate highways and more often than not the only choice of restaurant you will have is a franchise. Fast-food outlets have moved from the highly trafficked highways to the high-rises of the inner city, to posh suburban malls, to small country towns. They have saturated the countryside and festooned the cityscape with candycane-striped buildings, revolving oversized buckets, and golden arches. We can't ignore them, and we can hardly prevent ourselves from eating the junk food they serve up millions of times each day.

Government sources indicate that fast-food outlets are now over 47,000 strong. McDonald's, the largest chain, with 4,600 units nationwide, spent 14 years opening its initial 1,000 restaurants. During the next four years, from 1968 to 1972, it galloped to double that total. Since then it proudly announces that it averages at least one opening per day.

Kentucky Fried Chicken has lined the landscape with more than 4,000 of its red-and-white-striped buildings since Colonel Harland Sanders started his franchise operation in 1956. (He sold out to Heublein Inc. in 1964 after enlarging his one Kentucky restaurant into a 600-unit chain.)

Pizza Hut dishes out millions of Italian pies each day in the more than 2,500 restaurants it has established from humble beginnings in Wichita, Kansas, in 1958.

Dozens of similar chains have also developed devout followers of fast-food

cuisine. Obviously, they must be dishing out something we want.

In addition to the food, which is the bedrock of the industry, the quickie chains sell us speed, convenience, service, and, ostensibly, thrift.

And boy, are they selling it hard!

In 1970 McDonald's invested $18.5 million to advertise its burger bill of fare; by 1976 the ad budget—most of it devoted to TV—had expanded 450 percent to $100 million!

And what a payoff for that media deluge: after twenty years of burgering, McDonald's sales in 1976 were $2,470,000,000.

Kentucky Fried Chicken, not about to be left behind by some chopped meat outfit, also raised its TV and billboard ante 450 percent, to $55 million. Adding it up, the top fast-food chains spent $262 million on advertising in a single year.

The Agriculture Department informs us that we eat one of three meals away from home. (By 1980, we will feed ourselves one meal in a restaurant for every meal we eat at home.) And half of these restaurant meals are in fast-food joints.

With 47,000 restaurants you might think that there would be no place left to open yet another one.

Wrong.

The chains are moving from the boulevards and main streets into hotels, motels, universities—now even into public schools. The Benton, Arkansas, Public High School became the first to have its cafeteria converted into a McDonald's stand. Amazingly enough, there were no complaints from parents worried about the quality of the lunch their youngsters would get every day. The enterprising franchiser who took over the lunchroom, John Kosin, reports that he had only one complaint. "That was from a mother who wished we wouldn't serve McDonald's food at lunch because that's what she liked to serve her child for dinner."

When another chain, Hardee's, moved into a college student union hall, the only thing students objected to was the loss of their Hostess Twinkies. Their protests and campus paper editorials forced the return of the beloved sponge cakes.

From extensive, sophisticated market testing, McDonald's found out what it was that made fast-food franchises appeal to the populace. "People appeared to be seeking something more than a burger and fries—they come for a break from the routine."

Hence, "You deserve a break today," the remarkable catch phrase of McDonald's advertising, hits at a truth with which we can identify.

We also enjoy the speed with which we can consume a fast-food meal. The average meal in a fast-food restaurant lasts no more than ten minutes. (A number of coffee-shop-type chains extend this by twenty minutes.) If we are traveling, we want to get back on the road quickly, which explains the concentration of fast-food outlets along Interstates.

Families especially flock to these restaurants. McDonald's found that in 75 percent of all families the children decide where to eat. Accordingly, Big Mac ads focus on the child, as the path of least resistance to the consumer purse.

For every "You deserve a break today" there is a McDonaldland fantasy trip with Ronald McDonald, a happy-go-lucky burger-toting clown. The chain even has fifty live Ronald McDonald's on the payroll to make local appearances.

But let's face it, you can't eat advertising. We continue to patronize these plastic-roofed emporiums because *we like the food*. We love hamburgers, fried chicken, hot dogs, french fries, pancakes, tacos, and pizza. And we know we can get these favorites around practically *any* corner.

Fast food is essentially car food. The restaurants and their corresponding limited menus are specifically designed to meet the high-volume, heavy-turnover trade of passing motorists. The accent is on large parking lots and small inside seating space. Even the food is geared to be eaten in a car. If you choose to consume your meal within the confines of the limited seating area, the operator, whose profits depend on revolving-door turnover, has the built-in safeguard of uncomfortable stool-high tables, which prod his customers to wolf down their orders all the more hastily.

The chains are even returning to drive-in window service so customers never have to leave their cars. The Jack-in-the-Box restaurants (owned by Ralston Purina) have always had window service. Burger King has been installing this service in all its new units and adding "drive thrus" in busy existing locations. KFC and Gino's are among other major chains returning to this method.

The car provides us with our own private dining room away from the tumult and muzak of the restaurants' plastic inner sanctums. And eating in the car is quicker, sparing us valuable extra minutes so we can get on our way that much sooner.

We pay an average of $1.50 for a large meat sandwich (i.e., McDonald's Quarter Pounder, Burger King's Whopper, Jack-in-the-Box's Jumbo Jack), an order of fries, and a non-ice-cream ice cream shake. The average calories for the whole repast number 1,000 to 1,300, with 90% of that supplied in carbohydrates (sugar and starch) and fat.

Although the nutritional quality of the fast-food meal has always been a debatable issue, one prominent nutritionist, Dr. Laurence Finberg of New York's Montefiore Hospital, thinks an occasional fast-food meal may be of some value.

Finberg had been asked to give a speech to pediatricians on adolescent nutrition. He went to the fast-food chains where teenagers tend to congregate, ordered up a "prototype" meal, and checked out each item in the lab. He found that the prototype meal can be a "reasonable" part of a daily diet, although fast food can't be relied on for three meals a day.

"Fast food is not junk food," Finberg declared. Possibly not, but it certainly does resemble the assembly-line stuff processed in factories and bought in supermarkets. Hamburger buns have an average of three teaspoons of sugar in them. Chicken and burgers, as well as french fries, are loaded with grease. Shakes are made with large amounts of sugar and gelatin instead of milk and real ice cream.

And as with any junk food, we care more about the surface benefits than the nutritive value. We don't concern ourselves with the lack of substance if the food is filling, fits our preconditioned taste preferences, and is served in a glitzy package a minute after we order it.

Dr. George Christakis, former chief nutritionist at New York City's Mt. Sinai School of Medicine, eyeing this short-order trend, calls us "the McDonald's generation." We are raised to trust Ronald McDonald more than intrinsic common sense about our diet. If we restrict ourselves to the limited menus of fast-food chains in our youth, Dr. Christakis says, we run the risk of poor health as we grow older. "A limited diet tends to remain limited," he maintains.

In the last analysis, though, it is not the nutrients in our diets that the fast-

food giants are taking away. Instead, it is the unifying family home-cooked dinners that are being lost in the shuffle.

Restaurants that catered *bas cuisine* didn't always rush us this way. The last vestiges of these "restaurants"—the ancestors of the contemporary fast-food chains—can still be seen today. These are the roadside diners that emerged with the machine age of the late nineteenth century. The manufacturers selected a form, the railroad car, and turned it into the ultimate technological product in the factory process. At the time the railroad was the peak mode of transportation and the pullman-type cars evoked an explicit association with the sleek railroad image of speed, mobility, and efficiency.

Dining cars were tight, self-contained units that were able to produce the highest efficiency in the restaurant industry. Designed to operate at minimum overhead, diners could afford to serve wholesome food at lower prices than standard "regular" restaurants could. They achieved this by combining traditional technology, essentially carpentry and metalwork, with the latest materials, such as stainless steel, aluminum, formica, porcelain enamel, and bakelite in an assembly-line process.

Diner construction made gallant leaps forward from its humble beginnings in the 1880s when the old gray mare pulled the local lunchwagon to town. The 1930s and 1940s witnessed the golden age of diners, and by 1950 there were more than 6,000 of them across the United States.

But golden ages do not retain their glitter for very long. In the mid-fifties, forced by competition and superhighways, the diner had to appeal to a wider market—the mainstream of restaurant clientele. New, larger, glitzier prefab buildings were erected but to no avail.

The 1950s produced a nation more dependent than ever on—and in love with —the automobile. And, with this, grew a new type of eatery: the drive-in. The "American Graffiti"–type drive-in in turn evolved into the "drive-through" take-out-only restaurant.

With the rapid demise of the railroads, the diner became the *objet troúve*. As hurriedly as the diners started to disappear, the land was taken over by a rash of orange and turquoise roofs, screaming pink and puce neon signs, and obligatory golden arches. Not all of them were prefabricated like their diner forebears. Their food was, though. Every one of them beckoned the passing motorist on the new congressionally mandated Interstates to their "E-Z on, E-Z off," cookie-cutter-shaped buildings to buy their endless assembly-line caravan of Whoppers, Big Macs, Jumbo Jacks, and Buckets.

The assessment that got Howard Johnson started—that Americans prefer a meal that can be boringly repetitious and uniformly bland as long as it is dependable—worked now for all fast-fooders. We know *exactly* what we could expect before we trek into the stamped-out-box building: quick, impersonal service from little pixies with paper caps and Clearasil complexions who stand behind gleaming stainless-steel counters where indistinguishable burgers and computerized fries are ground out.

We like the food—it seems innocuous enough and it lets us get in and out in a minute. Back on the road. And what does the panorama hold in store? From sea to shining sea: golden yellow arches, plastic purple roofs, and the forever flashing nemesis: 20 *billion sold*.

Heartened by the roaring success of McDonald's and Kentucky Fried Chicken, dozens of other copycats got into the act with franchises of every conceivable origin. The trend into the early 60s—the height of franchising—was to use the name of any "personality" who was recognizable.

Blooming out of nowhere came Roy Rogers' Roast Beef Sandwiches, Minnie Pearl Fried Chicken, Broadway Joe's (Namath) nightspots, Al Hirt's Sandwich Saloons, Rocky Graziano's Pizza Ring, Tony Bennett's spaghetti mills, Fats Domino's New Orleans Style Chicken, Mahalia Jackson's Glori-Fried Chicken —all of them with their names emblazoned in neon reading more like a line up for an Ed Sullivan Show than an excuse to start a business.

On the average, an individual franchise restaurant today will gross from $300,000 to $750,000 a year. Now the parent companies are realizing that they can profit more by not selling franchises. They are opening new units themselves. Company-owned stores also help to maintain quality control, which varies drastically among the franchisers. One licensed owner who doesn't take pride in the food or cleanliness of the restaurant can give the entire chain a bad reputation.

So chains are buying back old franchises or refusing to sell new ones. McDonald's, Burger King, KFC, Denny's, Sambo's, and many other chains are more than ever corporate machines. This means not only more profits for the companies but also better, more standardized and reliable products for the consumer.

14.

FAST FOOD CHAINS: A TRAVELER'S GUIDE TO EATING ACROSS AMERICA

You have to get your pocket calculator out to add up the spiraling number of restaurants operated by fast-food chains throughout the nation. Right now there are approximately 47,000 separate units and, according to *Hospitality* Magazine, this will have increased by 50 percent in 1980, to 70,000. Furthermore, before 1980 dollar volume at the chains will double.

Hospitality, the merchandising magazine for hotels and restaurants, lists some 137 major fast food/chain restaurants. *The Complete Junk Food Book* has rated about 40 of them on the quality of the food they provide, how they dish it out, the cleanliness of the location, the atmosphere, and the price value.

I visited different locations of each chain, in various cities and towns in different states. I wanted to get as diverse a sampling as possible (frequently chains in one area are operated under a single franchise or by the same regional manager). I visited each one once at an off-peak time and again during a rush hour, usually lunch.

You might suppose from the advertisements that each unit of a given chain, from building design to food and service, would be dependably and unwaveringly similar. I used to think when a location was poorly operated or served bad

food, that this must be fairly typical of the chain's other units. But when I purposely ate at different units to check consistency in service, food, and other cri-
teria, I often found that the particular franchise-holder or company manager
was doing a slipshod job which reflected unfairly on the chain as a whole.

My expectation upon entering a fast-food restaurant was to receive quick
clockwork service and well-prepared food. The public deserves to have what it
is paying for—whether junk or a cut above junk—served exactly as described in
the menu or in the pictures the company uses.

The ratings are a composite of opinions from various judges who accom-
panied me to the restaurants included here. *These are subjective unscientifi-
cally arrived-at opinions.*

A number of the restaurants are included here only because they are large

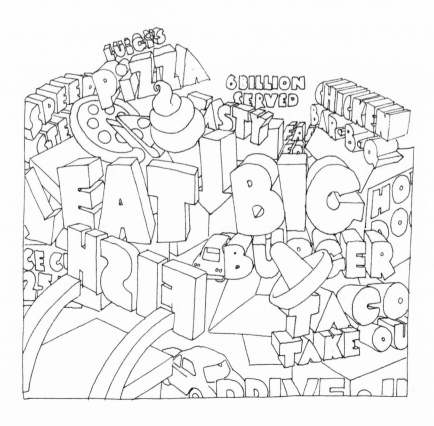

chains. While some do not serve junk food per se, their fast-food menus are typified by junk food's high fat and/or sugar content.

KEY TO ABBREVIATIONS AND DESCRIPTIVE PHRASES

CO: company-owned restaurant   FR: franchise locations
Menu: B(reakfast) L(unch) D(inner)
Drive-In: server comes to your car window for order
Drive-Thru: you drive up to window in building to order
Grease quotient: presence of frying oil (taste and feel)
    Top rating: Hard to notice
      Average: Only an aftertaste
        Poor: Slippery
Prices: Top rating: Good buy   Average: Acceptable   Poor: Rip-off

======== "THE WORLD'S FASTEST RESTAURANT"

I guess many of us have become so accustomed to or jaded by the relatively quick pace of fast-food restaurants that we now consider *real* efficiency to be even speedier. In answer to this a Kansas based chain called "Chutes" is claiming that it is the world's fastest (and most gimmicky) restaurant. It wants to be listed in the Guinness Book, too. A patron at Chutes drives up to one of three lanes, much like the drive-in window at a bank. There, he places an order, puts his money into an 8-inch cylinder and drops the cylinder into a pneumatic tube. Change is returned via the same route in seconds. The customer then drives to another console where the food—also delivered in a pneumatic tube—awaits him. Maximum waiting time: one minute.

The menu, on color transparencies illuminated on an overhead board, offers fried chicken, pizza, and submarine sandwiches. The chain is spreading rapidly through Kansas and advertises that it is just the place "for people who can't wait to eat."

A & W (ROOT BEER) INTERNATIONAL

Main Office: Santa Monica, Ca. / **2,000**+ units nationwide (**95**% FR; **5**% CO)

MENU	L/D
QUALITY OF SERVICE	Excellent
TIME TO BE SERVED	Less than 5 minutes
	Drive-In (Some locations have no inside seating)
CLEANLINESS	Acceptable to poor (depending on location)
GREASE QUOTIENT	Poor
AMBIENCE	Friendly, cheerful, generally well managed
QUALITY OF FOOD	Arrived hot, tastes cooked-to-order, well wrapped, blandly spiced, soft drinks excellent.
PRICES	Average ($**1.50** for a filling meal)

A & W is one of the oldest chains in the country and is built upon the franchise method it helped to start. Quality varies according to the owner-manager. Most A&Ws are drive-ins but the company is modernizing with urban sit-down "restaurants." In last few years A&W has purged more than 100 inferior units in an effort to get away from the root-beer-stand image. Eighty-five percent of its units are still in towns of about 25,000 people, and 50% of these are seasonal operations. Their root beer is tops, comes appropriately in a mug with the frothy foam brimming at the top. When A&W is good, it's great; when it's bad, it is downright rotten.

ARBY'S INTERNATIONAL

Main Office: Youngstown, Ohio / **600**+ units (**85**% FR; **15**% CO)

MENU	L/D
QUALITY OF SERVICE	Good
TIME TO BE SERVED	Less than 5 minutes
CLEANLINESS	Acceptable
GREASE QUOTIENT	Average
AMBIENCE	Friendly, cheerful
QUALITY OF FOOD	Arrived hot to lukewarm, cooked-to-order taste, acceptably wrapped, moderately spiced, soft drinks oversyruped.
PRICES	Average ($**1.50**–$**1.95** for a filling meal)

Arby's is the nation's largest roast beef sandwich chain and now has a larger choice of sandwiches "on a bun" from which to choose. The company is definitely housecleaning, with new, better designed buildings popping up everywhere. Consumer suggestion/complaint cards are found at most locations and a larger selection of condiments to put on your sandwich are now provided.

―――――――――――――――

ARTHUR TREACHER'S FISH AND CHIPS
Main Office: Columbus, Ohio / 500 units nationwide (50% FR; 50% CO)

MENU	L/D
QUALITY OF SERVICE	Poor
TIME TO BE SERVED	10 minutes
CLEANLINESS	At one location the server ran her blue fingernails through her hair and then served the food.
GREASE QUOTIENT	Poor
AMBIENCE	Noisy, mismanaged
QUALITY OF FOOD	Lukewarm, holding-table taste, blandly spiced, soft drinks overwatered, poorly wrapped.
PRICES	Poor. ($2–$3 for a filling meal)

Fish chains are dealing with a highly perishable product and one that can be exceptionally fishy. Since the entire meal is fried, grease is ever present. It cannot be reused too often before it will impart an undesirable oily taste in the food. Treacher's seems to lack rigid quality control, at least in the trio of locations I went to. Once, in Wichita, the food was served promptly, but I was the only customer in the place.

BASKIN-ROBBINS ICE CREAM STORES
Main Office: Burbank, Ca. / 1600 stores (90% FR; 10% CO)

MENU	Ice cream and soda fountain specialties
QUALITY OF SERVICE	Excellent
TIME TO BE SERVED	Less than 5 minutes
AMBIENCE	Friendly
QUALITY OF FOOD	With thirty-one flavors plus standard chocolate, vanilla, and strawberry, quality varies from one flavor to the next. In some hokey flavors the chemical taste is apparent, but most are good. Soda fountain specialties are generally well made.
PRICES	Average—for ice cream that is considered premium (about $1.00 per pint)

Baskin-Robbins started during World War II and has been built into an ever-expanding business, now worldwide. BR is the only chain that allows a customer to test-taste any flavor of ice cream before actual purchase. Their ice cream is high in butterfat and the sherbets are especially fruity, with authentic flavor.

BIG BOY ENTERPRISES (SHONEY'S)
Main Office: Nashville, Tenn. / 300+ units (50% FR; 50% CO)
(JB's Big Boy Family Restaurants operates approximately 75 units in Western states)

MENU	B/L/D
QUALITY OF SERVICE	Excellent
TIME TO BE SERVED	Less than 5 minutes
CLEANLINESS	Exceptional
GREASE QUOTIENT	Top rating
AMBIENCE	Friendly, pleasing
QUALITY OF FOOD	Served hot, hamburger had holding-table taste, well presented, blandly seasoned, soft drinks overiced.
PRICES	Average (Full meal for less than $2.50)

There was a line at whatever Big Boy Restaurant I went to, but it was efficiently cleared within minutes each time. The waitresses seem to go out of their way to please the customers. The food was standard, unexceptional fare but was welcomed by a hungry traveler. The chain is centered, as Shoney's, in the southeastern portion of the country and, under other names (JB, Bob's, etc.), in the West. Big Boy has yet to penetrate the northern states.

BURGER CHEF
Main Office: White Plains, New York (Division General Foods) / 1,000+ Units (25% CO; 75% FR)

MENU	L/D
QUALITY OF SERVICE	Good
TIME TO BE SERVED	Less than five minutes
CLEANLINESS	Excellent
GREASE QUOTIENT	Excellent
AMBIENCE	Friendly
QUALITY OF FOOD	Served cooked to order tasting, acceptably wrapped, blandly spiced (has do-it-yourself condiment counter); soft drinks overwatered.
PRICES	Average ($1.50–$2)

Burger Chef would be no different from any of the myriad burger pavilions except for their inventive gimmick: the Burger Chef Works Bar, offering free condiments. Since you can add these to any burger, order the cheapest. You pay for the "works" already put on the more expensive ones. The bottomless Salad Bar offers as many refills as you want. Adult platters (the Rancher and the Mariner) are more expensive but worth the price. Avoid the Thick Shakes unless you are a gelatin freak. Burger Chef is found in 41 of the 48 contiguous states.

BURGER KING (PILLSBURY)
Main Office: Miami, Fl. / **2,000**+ units (**70**% FR; **30**% CO)

MENU	L/D
QUALITY OF SERVICE	Good
TIME TO BE SERVED	Less than **5** minutes
	Drive-Thru service at some units
CLEANLINESS	Acceptable
GREASE QUOTIENT	Average
AMBIENCE	Noisy
QUALITY OF FOOD	Served lukewarm to hot, holding-table taste, acceptably wrapped, blandly seasoned, soft drinks overwatered and overiced.
PRICES	Average ($**1.50** for most meals)

Burger King seems to be the most inventive of the burger chains in competition with McDonald's. They have added crunchy onion rings, different sandwiches, and other good tasting items to the limited menu and they stand up to their advertised pitch of preparing your burgers "your way." The Whopper is the original messy burger and seems like a better value than a Big Mac. Lettuce and tomato are piled on along with the "special sauce." When you get "your" burger hot the Whopper can't be beat but in the numerous locations where I ordered a Whopper, it came out lukewarm and somewhat soggy. Burger King is striving to reign over burgerdom and have even signed up some former McDonald executives. When a chain's fries become less soggy, you know it's improving. And Burger King's fries get crisper all the time.

CARVEL CORP.
Main Office: Yonkers, N.Y. / 650+ units (99% FR)

MENU	Ice cream
QUALITY OF SERVICE	Good
TIME TO BE SERVED	Less than 5 minutes
CLEANLINESS	Good
AMBIENCE	Friendly
QUALITY OF FOOD	Poor
PRICES	Average

Carvel has stores along the east coast, two-thirds of them within a 50-mile radius of New York. Since 1960, the stores have been walk-in instead of walk-up-to. In addition to the soft ice cream, there are hard ice creams, novelties (sandwiches, cones, cakes), shakes, and soft drinks. Carvel claims to have a secret to their ice cream formula. It's one they can keep, too. You can taste the thickener, the sugar, all blended into the cold-cream texture of the machine-dispensed ice cream. Chocolate flavor is slightly better than vanilla. The kiddies will like it but depending on your threshold, you may not accept the saccharin sweetness of the stuff. Waffle cones are supplied normally; you have to request a sugar cone.

CHURCH'S FRIED CHICKEN
Main Office: San Antonio, Texas / **700**+ units (**90% CO; 10% FR**)

MENU	L/D
QUALITY OF SERVICE	Good
TIME TO BE SERVED	Less than 5 minutes
	Seating available but mostly drive-in/take-out locations
CLEANLINESS	Acceptable
GREASE QUOTIENT	Only an aftertaste (and even that's rare)
AMBIENCE	Friendly
QUALITY OF FOOD	Served hot to lukewarm, cooked-to-order taste, acceptably wrapped, well seasoned, soft drinks acceptable.
PRICES	Average ($1.50 average per person tab)

This rapidly growing fried chicken take-out restaurant has found a keen enough competitive edge to make the Colonel shake his bucket. Church's offers remarkably tasty fried chicken that is neither dry nor greasy. The pieces seem to by much larger than Kentucky Fried's and on the whole the service and atmosphere seem less impersonal. Located in the midwest and south, Church's is widening its market faster than a chicken lays eggs. And why not? Fried chicken is an American favorite and the company, with its finely honed quality control, prepares it crisp and pleasantly seasoned. The french fries are crisp and usually not greasy and the coleslaw seems to rely more on salad seasoning and less on sugar. The company has developed a sound management system and enjoys high employee morale—and with that, can't fail.

DAIRY QUEEN/BRAZIER FOODS
Main Office: Minneapolis, Minn. / **4,700**+ units (**99% FR**)

MENU	L/D
QUALITY OF SERVICE	Good
TIME TO BE SERVED	Less than 5 minutes
CLEANLINESS	Acceptable
GREASE QUOTIENT	Average
AMBIENCE	Friendly

QUALITY OF FOOD	Brazier food served hot, cooked-to-order taste, well wrapped, blandly seasoned, soft drinks overwatered and overiced.
PRICES	Average ($1.50–$1.75 for a filling meal)

The first Dairy Queen store opened in 1940 in Joliet, Illinois, when its founder, J. F. McCullough, decided that ice cream would taste better if served at 24°F instead of the customary −10 to 20°F. Soft ice cream was a hit and franchises were sold nationally. While many of the DQ stores still only carry ice cream and related products, even more are selling Brazier hamburgers, hot dogs, fries, onion rings, and chicken. Because DQ/Brazier is so highly franchised the quality of each unit varies drastically. Some offer thick shakes that are rich and luxurious; others dole out ones that taste plastic. Some offer burgers that are char-broiled while others are content to make soggy ones. Because of these wide differences I can only say that this chain at best is adequate but uninspired.

DENNY'S
Main Office: La Mirada, Calif. / 600+ units (93% CO; 7% FR)

MENU	B/L/D
QUALITY OF SERVICE	Good
TIME TO BE SERVED	5–10 minutes
CLEANLINESS	Acceptable (bathrooms poor)
GREASE QUOTIENT	Poor
AMBIENCE	Friendly, cheerful, generally well managed
QUALITY OF FOOD	Served hot to lukewarm, cooked-to-order taste, acceptably presented, blandly seasoned, soft drinks acceptable.
PRICES	Poor (Much higher than similar chains: average check $2.50 or more)

Denny's is a coffeeshop chain that extends from coast to coast, although not in every state. Clustered mainly in California, along Interstate 5, along the West Coast, in the north central states and in Florida, it serves travelers twenty-four hours a day. Most of the restaurants seat at least 106 people at their counters and tables. The menu is varied to meet the needs of families, especially those with finicky children. What you are served is dependable, standard, convenience fare: prefrozen meats with mashed potatoes dispensed from a machine, sandwiches, and breakfasts.

DER WIENERSCHNITZEL INTERNATIONAL
Main Office: Torrance, Ga. / 250 units (100% CO)

MENU	L/D
QUALITY OF SERVICE	Poor
TIME TO BE SERVED	10 minutes
	Some units with seating, most with walk-up windows or drive-thrus
CLEANLINESS	Poor
GREASE QUOTIENT	Poor
AMBIENCE	Noisy, mismanaged
QUALITY OF FOOD	Served cold, holding-table taste, poorly wrapped, blandly seasoned, soft drinks overwatered and overiced (beware of orange soda—yecch!)
PRICES	Average

Repeatedly this proved to be the worst chain I endured. At one location many items on the menu were out of stock. The only soda was a flat-tasting orange flavor ("Sorry, that's all we got today.") The hot dogs were hardly ever hot; lukewarm if you were lucky. After consuming—or attempting to anyway—one of their charming hamburgers, I developed a personal philosophy which meant the best way to approach their burgers in the future would be with a cattle prod. The elastic fries might make good suspenders. The prices are low but so is the service and food quality.

=====

DUNKIN' DONUTS
Main Office: Randolph, Mass. / 850 units in 41 states and abroad (93% FR; 7% CO)

MENU	Donuts, beverages, and, most recently, soup.
QUALITY OF SERVICE	Good
TIME TO BE SERVED	Less than 5 minutes
CLEANLINESS	Acceptable
GREASE QUOTIENT	Average or better
AMBIENCE	Friendly, well managed
QUALITY OF FOOD	Doughnuts made two to four times daily; the closer to baking time, the better the quality. Some doughnuts are too sweet; the variety is best early in the morning
PRICES	Poor (20 cents or more per doughnut)

This chain has built its hefty profits and worldwide expansion exclusively on doughnuts. Most operate twenty-four hours a day but bake less often than they used to; consequently quality has slipped while prices have skyrocketed. Their coffee is great, and the Munchkins, originally created for kids, are popular adult snacks too. (Munchkins are the doughnut hole leftovers, made into little balls of cake.) Mr. Donut, DD's chief competitor, is one reason DD has extended its menu from coffee and doughnuts to soups. Now you can have snacks and quasi-lunches, too. Most stores are found in the East and Midwest.

=====

FRIENDLY ICE CREAM SHOPS
Main Office: Wilbraham, Mass. / 600 units (100% CO)

MENU	B/L/D
QUALITY OF SERVICE	Excellent
TIME TO BE SERVED	5–10 minutes
CLEANLINESS	Exceptional
GREASE QUOTIENT	Top rating
AMBIENCE	Friendly (!)
QUALITY OF FOOD	Served hot, cooked-to-order, well presented, spiced pleasingly, soft drinks acceptable.
PRICES	Top rating

Around since 1935, this venerable chain, located in the northeast and north central states, is a perfect illustration of the quality that can be maintained by a company-owned chain. Each year the company sells over 8 million gallons of its own ice cream in some 20 flavors. Its food is prepared fresh and tastes it. Counters and booths for informal meals and snacks are extremely efficient, served by hard-working waiters and waitresses. The quality is revealed by the growth rate: approximately one new unit every 110 hours, says the company. Prices are surprisingly modest for what you get, so this is a good place for a family meal or a fast snack. One of the few chains with remarkably unpretentious ("Georgian Colonial") architecture.

H. SALT SEAFOOD GALLEYS/H. SALT FISH & CHIPS (KENTUCKY FRIED CHICKEN)

Main Office: Louisville, Ky. / 300 units (67% FR; 33% CO)

MENU	L/D
QUALITY OF SERVICE	Fair
TIME TO BE SERVED	Less than five minutes
	Seating available at some units; drive-thru at others
CLEANLINESS	Acceptable
GREASE QUOTIENT	Poor
AMBIENCE	Friendly, sometimes noisy
QUALITY OF FOOD	Served lukewarm, hold-table taste; acceptably wrapped; properly seasoned; soft drinks overiced.
PRICES	Average ($1.50–$2 for a filling meal)

What I originally had to say about H. Salt was libelous, the publisher tells me. I think that gives a clear indication that what I had to say wasn't very complimentary. Let's just leave it at that. The less said here the better.

HARDEE'S
Main Office: Rocky Mount, S.C. / 950 units (63% FR; 37% CO)

MENU	L/D
QUALITY OF SERVICE	Good
TIME TO BE SERVED	Less than 5 minutes
CLEANLINESS	Poor to fair
GREASE QUOTIENT	Poor
AMBIENCE	Disorderly
QUALITY OF FOOD	Served lukewarm, holding-table taste, acceptably wrapped, blandly seasoned, soft drinks acceptable.
PRICES	Average ($1.50–$2)

A vastly expanded menu to fit all mealtimes and snacks, an award-winning new building design, and abstinence in the use of plastic are the first signs that this chain intends to grow with quality in the foreground. A few years back, I used to patronize the Ithaca, New York, branch of Hardee's because their burgers, unlike other chains, were charcoal broiled. But, alas, modernization has done away with this. Right now Hardee's seems like just another chain, but this could change at any time. Meanwhile, Hardee's is worth a try.

HOWARD JOHNSON'S
Main Office: Braintree, Mass. / 1,000+ units (30% FR; 70% CO)

MENU	B/L/D
QUALITY OF SERVICE	Poor
TIME TO BE SERVED	15 minutes
CLEANLINESS	Acceptable
GREASE QUOTIENT	Average
AMBIENCE	Noisy, disorderly, mismanaged
QUALITY OF FOOD	Served lukewarm to cold; holding-table taste; acceptably presented, blandly seasoned, soft drinks overiced.
PRICES	Average to poor.

HoJo's can be found in about forty-two states, Washington D.C., Puerto Rico, Canada, and the Bahamas. Located in the States usually on or near Interstate expressways, the restaurants (many with motor lodges) seat 112–320 people, but that doesn't mean it can serve them all well. I think the chain's lackluster service and its TV-dinner style meals (all prefrozen) are now common knowledge. The ice cream seems to have gone downhill in recent years, too. But because HoJo serves full menu meals and many are open twenty-four hours a day, travelers pour in by the thousands daily. If its swiftness you want, stay away. But if you crave a mediocre meal served at a snail's pace in a perfunctory style, this orange-roofed inn is often made to order.

INTERNATIONAL HOUSE OF PANCAKES
Main Office: Los Angeles, Ca. / 500 units (25% FR; 75% CO)

MENU	B/L/D
QUALITY OF SERVICE	Good
TIME TO BE SERVED	10 minutes
CLEANLINESS	Acceptable
GREASE QUOTIENT	Average
AMBIENCE	Varied radically from unit to unit; generally noisy
QUALITY OF FOOD	Served hot, cooked-to-order taste, acceptably presented, blandly seasoned, soft drinks acceptable.
PRICES	Poor ($2.00 or more, usually)

Their reputation is linked to their name. A large variety of pancakes and sugary syrups to put on them are offered throughout the day, along with a large menu of other items. Each table (no counter service) comes with a pitcher of coffee. The high ceilinged A-frame restaurant has a cold sterile atmosphere, though, and service, depending on the management of the particular unit, can be dreadfully slow. Invariably crowded at breakfast, especially on weekends, IHOP is usually packed with families with screaming children, but during non-rush hours it can be found practically deserted. The prices, compared to other fast-food coffeeshop chains, seem way out of line. But if its novelty pancakes you want (and good ones at that) you can endure the high prices. The food in general, otherwise, is lackluster. You can't miss IHOP on the road, it's the building with the hideous turquoise A-frame roof—the neo-alpine look.

JACK-IN-THE-BOX
Main Office: c/o Ralston Purina Co., St. Louis, Mo. / **1,000** units (**98**+% CO)

MENU	B/L/D
QUALITY OF SERVICE	Poor
	Seating available; drive-thru service
CLEANLINESS	Poor
GREASE QUOTIENT	Poor
AMBIENCE	Noisy, disorderly, mismanaged
QUALITY OF FOOD	Served lukewarm; holding-table taste, acceptably wrapped, blandly seasoned, soft drinks overwatered and overiced.
PRICES	Average ($1.50–$2)

This is one of the few twenty-four-hour fast-food operations. JITB is located mainly in the West but Ralston Purina, famous for feed chows for animals, is mounting an expansion program into areas not yet covered. The name of the chain suggests that it is designed for the kiddies, and the food is the type that only their undiscriminating palates would readily approve. Beyond the three-napkin-messy Jumbo Jack burgers, there is a wider than usual assortment on the menu. The service at all locations I went to was horrible. Attentive service is a coveted selling point for chains of this sort, and without it, their food had better be topnotch. JITB's isn't. The drive-thru service (you give your order through a mike in a clown statue) is well run. The brilliant Stiller & Meara TV commercials add a welcome touch of class.

KENTUCKY FRIED CHICKEN
Main Office: Louisville, Ky. / **4,000**+ units (**25**% FR; **75**% CO)

MENU	L/D
QUALITY OF SERVICE	Excellent
TIME TO BE SERVED	Less than **3** minutes
	Seating and/or drive-thru windows available in some units
CLEANLINESS	Acceptable
GREASE QUOTIENT	Poor (but Top rating on extra-crispy)
AMBIENCE	Friendly

QUALITY OF FOOD	Served hot; cooked-to-order taste; acceptably wrapped; blandly seasoned (extra crispy), just right (original style); soft drinks acceptable.
PRICES	Poor (look for weekday and other specials)

You'll soon be looking through windows at KFC, as tests showed that drive-thru service boosted sales 30 percent or more. The company has been buying back franchises to increase its control and profits. Additions to the poultry-based menu are continuously being tested and some locations are offering the old standby hamburgers. Since fried chicken is the number one favorite food in America, and Colonel Sander's unique idea of pressure cooking the birds gives them a zesty taste, KFC has done well for its parent company, Heublein (producer of cocktail mixes and Smirnoff vodka). Chicken prices average 50–60 cents per piece which doesn't seem high if you think of the time and mess you save by not making it yourself.

McDONALD'S
Main Office: Oak Brook, Ill. / 4,200+ units (30% CO; 70% FR)

MENU	B/L/D
QUALITY OF SERVICE	Good to excellent
TIME TO BE SERVED	Less than 5 minutes
CLEANLINESS	Exceptional
GREASE QUOTIENT	Top rating (occasional lapses)
AMBIENCE	Businesslike
QUALITY OF FOOD	Served hot to lukewarm, holding-table taste, wrapped ready for placement in a time capsule, blandly seasoned, soft drinks overiced.
PRICES	Average ($1.50–$2)

The high-paced efficiency behind the counter is one reason this chain has become the leading fast-fooder in the world. All food is produced with the mathemathical exactness of computers, but who cares? The french fries are still the best, firm and crispy. The Big Mac is a work of art and can satisfy any junk food attack that comes over you. Quality control is high so that even a lukewarm McDonald's burger tastes good. Each store averages $750,000 in business a year, so they must be doing something right. Although it ruins their routine, McD will make a burger to your specifications, but alas, you have to wait for it. With so many units, McD is bound to vary from one to the next but most are meticulously maintained. The McMachine keeps grinding, with drive-up windows being added to new units, and McSundaes, McHoagies, McFeasts being added periodically to the McMenu, after consumer testing (McTesting?).

ORANGE JULIUS OF AMERICA
Main Office: Santa Monica, Ca.

MENU	L/D
QUALITY OF SERVICE	Good
TIME TO BE SERVED	Less than 5 minutes
	Some locations permit take-outs or standup consumption only
CLEANLINESS	Acceptable
GREASE QUOTIENT	Average
AMBIENCE	Noisy, disorderly, with some exceptions
QUALITY OF FOOD	Served lukewarm, holding-table taste, poorly wrapped, blandly seasoned; soft drinks acceptable.
PRICES	Average ($1.50 or less)

The orange juice drink is the thing here. What's in it besides the juice has remained a secret with the company, whose stands are located largely in suburban malls and near tourist areas. Whatever it is that makes the orange juice frothy and creamy, it's great. The food that many of the Orange Julius stands now turn out is another story. Adequate would be the most diplomatic word to use. This is your basic amusement park fare (hot dogs, burgers, fries). Forget them—go for the orange drink. If there isn't one in your area here is a recipe for "Almost" Orange Julius: 8 ounces fresh orange juice; 1 tablespoon simple syrup; 1 egg; crushed ice. Mix all ingredients in a blender until foamy. (Simple syrup is one part water to 2 parts sugar boiled for 5 minutes.) Store in a bottle in the refrigerator.

========

PIZZA HUT
Main Office: Wichita, Kansas/ **2,600** units (**45**% CO; **55**% FR)

QUALITY OF SERVICE	Good
TIME TO BE SERVED	Less than 5 minutes
CLEANLINESS	Acceptable to poor
GREASE QUOTIENT	Top rating
AMBIENCE	Friendly, ordinarily well managed
QUALITY OF FOOD	Served hot, cooked-to-order taste, well wrapped or presented, blandly seasoned, soft drinks acceptable.
PRICES	Average ($1.75–$2.50 per person in groups of two or more)

Pizza Hut took from 1958 to 1972 to open its first 1,000 units and just five more to expand to 2,600. The management is devoutly concerned with immaculate quality control and has scolded and threatened its franchise-holders and company managers to maintain it. However, there is nothing they can do with the basic recipe, which is remarkably unremarkable pizza. The thin n' crispy is slightly seasoned tomato sauce on cardboard. The thick 'n chewy is at least mediocre. Dough is prepared fresh daily and all pizza pies are made to order. Your best bet here is the Pizza Hut Supreme. It may be the most expensive on the menu, but it is definitely the best, with cheese, pork, mushrooms, pepperoni, onions, and green peppers piled on heartily. The restaurant continues to improve, and various testings show that its food has the best nutritional qualities of any fast-food outfit. Give 'em a try.

RED BARN (SERVOMATION CORP.)
Main Office: McLean, Va. / **300** units (**100% CO**)

MENU	L/D (Breakfast at some)
QUALITY OF SERVICE	Excellent
TIME TO BE SERVED	Less than **3** minutes
CLEANLINESS	Acceptable
GREASE QUOTIENT	Poor
AMBIENCE	Friendly
QUALITY OF FOOD	Served hot, cooked-to-order taste, well wrapped, seasoned just enough, soft drinks acceptable.
PRICES	Top rating ($**1.50**–$**2.25**)

Currently located in half the states and Canada, Red Barn offers the full gamut of fast-food favorites—burgers, chicken, fish, and a well-stocked salad bar for unlimited helpings. Ice cream sundaes you make yourself with all the toppings is a feature no other chain offers and is a welcome junk food feast. The Barn-buster is a Big Mac take-off, not as messy, and slightly more wholesome in taste in which you can identify each component. The soft drinks, as with every other chain, are from bottled syrup, but mixed well. Root beer is the best bet, since too much water or syrup can't harm a solid root beer flavor. Orange is more or less colored water. The prices are comparable with those of competing chains, but you seem to get more for your money here. Well run, Red Barn is worth a visit.

SAMBO'S RESTAURANT
Main Office: Santa Barbara, Ca. / **750**+ units (**100% CO**)

MENU	B/L/D
QUALITY OF SERVICE	Acceptable
TIME TO BE SERVED	Less than **5** minutes
CLEANLINESS	Acceptable
GREASE QUOTIENT	Average
AMBIENCE	Friendly

QUALITY OF FOOD	Served hot, cooked-to-order taste, well presented, blandly seasoned, soft drinks acceptable.
PRICES	Top rating ($2.oo)

Found coast to coast, Sambo's is a counter-and-booth, family-type coffeeshop chain which features pancakes and a full menu of luncheon and dinner items. The service is *usually* prompt and efficient, and features a bottomless cup of coffee. Generous portions for your money and well-prepared food is the rule here. Many of the units are open twenty-four hours a day, with breakfast, particularly on weekends, being the most crowded. Expect a line then. A kiddie menu and tacky Sambo murals should keep the little ones happy, also. Recommended. Fully company owned means that if you have a complaint it will be heard and acted upon by a young, energetic, consumer-conscious, president.

━━━━━━━━━━━━━━━━━━━

TACO BELL
Main Office: Torrance, Ca. / 750+ units (60% FR; 40% CO)

MENU	L/D
QUALITY OF SERVICE	Excellent
TIME TO BE SERVED	Less than 3 minutes
	Some locations permit only take-out service
CLEANLINESS	Exceptional
GREASE QUOTIENT	Average
AMBIENCE	Friendly
QUALITY OF FOOD	Served hot, cooked-to-order taste, acceptably wrapped (Beef Tostada extremely messy), soft drinks acceptable (except for orange soda).
PRICES	Top rating (a meal for under $2.00)

The fastest-growing Mexican fast-food chain, Taco Bell has nowhere to go but up, considering the increasing popularity of this type of food among Americans. The first unit opened in 1962 in California, and has since entrenched itself from coast to coast. The food is blandly seasoned, but hot varieties are available, as is a special "Taco sauce" to liven things up. Seating capacity is extremely limited but it's worth the wait for their tacos, tostados, frijoles, burritos, and other specialties, all well made—to order. Highly recommended.

━━━━━━━━━━━━━━━━━━━

WENDY'S INTERNATIONAL (WENDY'S OLD FASHIONED HAMBURGERS)
Main Office: Columbus, Ohio / 950+ units (75% FR; 25% CO)

MENU	L/D
QUALITY OF SERVICE	Good
TIME TO BE SERVED	Less than 5 minutes
	Drive-in service and seating at most locations
CLEANLINESS	Acceptable
GREASE QUOTIENT	Average
AMBIENCE	Friendly

QUALITY OF FOOD   Served lukewarm, holding-table taste, acceptably presented, blandly seasoned, soft drinks overiced.

PRICES   Average (meals for under $1.75)

This fast growing burger chain features burgers made to your specification. Condiments are kept behind the counter and added to your order. Chili (tastes like beans in Campbell's Tomato Soup) and a few other items are on the limited menu. The burger may be old fashioned, but it is completely and utterly tasteless and should be smothered in whatever is available. The fries are stringy and soggy and the batches I got at two locations were encrusted with salt. Wendy's has nevertheless proved popular because of its drive-in window and made-to-order fixings on the burger. Wendy's doesn't plan to expand the menu beyond the chili and burgers fare because they feel they can't train people effectively to make too many dishes. From the results they're getting now, I suspect they're right.

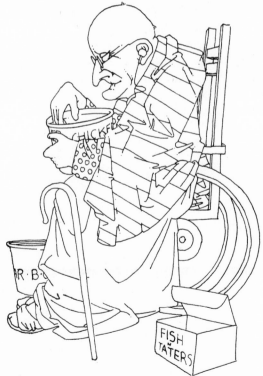

WINCHELL'S DONUT SHOPS (DENNY'S)
Main Office: La Mirada, Ca. / 700+ units (100% CO)

MENU	Doughnuts
QUALITY OF SERVICE	Good
TIME TO BE SERVED	Less than 3 minutes
	Take-out only in some locations
CLEANLINESS	Acceptable
GREASE QUOTIENT	Average (more noticeable in cake type donuts)
AMBIENCE	Friendly
QUALITY OF FOOD	Doughnuts made twice daily, best at midnight and in the morning, soft drinks acceptable.
PRICES	Average (about 15 cents each)

A wide variety of doughnuts is always available, but to avoid sinkers buy them only up to two hours after bake time. Inquire about bake times before making a purchase. Winchell's fresh donuts are delicious but ones that have sat around too long are no better than day-old ones from a supermarket. The honeydip or glazed donuts are slightly oversugared, but still light and tasty. Stores stay open twenty-four hours in almost all locations. A welcome oasis for the long-distance traveler.

LEAVING WELL ENOUGH ALONE:
OTHER FAST-FOOD RESTAURANTS

A number of other major fast-food franchise operators—large enough for inclusion here but for which enough up-to-date accurate information could not be gathered—are listed below. The fare they offer can be considered standardized and commonplace and unless noted are unexceptional (neither better nor worse than average).

Gino's (King of Prussia, Pa.) offers pizza and fried chicken in well over 500 company-owned locations, mostly in the east.

Long John Silver's (Hermitage, Tenn.) has some 500 units, 60 percent of which are franchised, offering some rather raunchy fried fish. The only identifiable fish on the menu seems to be the shrimp and clam dinners. Others are merely referred to in the generic "fish" jargon. Mostly located in the East and Midwest. Training activities are conducted at the LJS Management Academy located on the campus of Transylvania University. Isn't that where Dracula studied?

Pizza Inn (Dallas, Tx.) is increasing its piece of the (pizza) pie in the close to 500 units spread around 32 states, mainly in the midwest. Its primary type of pizza is the cardboard thin crust but a thicker variety is also offered. Sixty percent of the restaurants are franchised and the firm, born in 1959, continues its expansion with company-owned stores from coast to coast.

Shakey's Pizza whose motto is "Others feed you fat, we feed you fun," is currently undergoing change. The former mess hall-type structures are giving way to more personalized, warmer buildings. The pizzas are not extraordinary but well above average fare. About 20 percent of the more than 500 units, found mainly in the Western states, are company owned.

Tastee Freez is a purveyor of soft and hard ice creams at well over 2,500 units scattered nationwide. Some of these include Big T Family Restaurants which serve hamburgers, chicken, and hot dogs. Company is based in Des Plains, Ill.

THE CHEAPO STEAK JOINTS

Bonanza Sirloin Pits (Dallas), **Ponderosa** (Dayton, Ohio), **Rustler Steak Houses** (King of Prussia, Pa.), and **Sizzler Family Steak Houses** (Los Angeles) are found in profusion around the United States. Each offers identical type food—tenderized steaks at low prices. A fifth chain, **Mr. Steak** (Denver) offers the same at higher than average prices (average $4.95 and up). With the exception of Mr. Steak, all follow the cafeteria style rigamarole and provide a good selection of cuts (although they all seem to taste the same) of meat with baked potato, large slice of bread, and salad. Except for an occasional gimmick, one is no different from the next, but all offer a wholesome family meal for the budget-minded.

PART THREE

NOW THAT YOU KNOW WHY YOU EAT JUNK FOOD AND HOW MUCH, CHOOSE CAREFULLY FROM THE RATINGS IN THIS SELECTIVE COMPENDIUM.

After sampling hundreds of junk foods, I have selected the most popular national and regional favorites for inclusion in the following compendium.

Because there are literally thousands of junk food products flooding the market, your own favorite may not be among those listed here. If so, I apologize.

Each food is reviewed as to its ingredients, its sugar and oil content, how many calories it has, its quality, taste, and price. The *Sugar Quotient* is found by comparing the amount of refined sugar and sugar products to the amount of other ingredients in the food, according to information supplied by the manufacturer, or the ingredient label on the package. (Ingredients are listed on all packages in descending order, according to the quantity used in the product.) The *Oil Quotient* was arrived at in the same way. It shows the amount of oil, fat, shortening, etc. compared to the amount of other ingredients.

The *Dental Checkup* is the author's judgment based on published dental information and consultation with dental experts. A food listed as a *Tooth Rotter* is one whose ingredients, texture, and composition is highly cariogenic (cavity-inducing). Less cariogenic foods are rated either *Average* or *Low*.

The *Nutrient Level* is arrived at by comparing the amount of nutrients a food provides in comparison to the amount of sugar and oil you will have to consume simultaneously to get those nutrients. For example, if a candy bar has enough peanuts to provide some protein or other nutrients, but is also swimming in sugar and oil, the food is rated as "Empty calories." If the product has less sugar with those peanuts, the rating goes up to read "Minimal—some fortification present."

If an unusual chemical additive is included in the ingredients a word of explanation is offered in the description of the product.

The descriptions of each food are the author's subjective opinion. I have tried to provide the reader with an indication of what he or she might expect before buying and eating each item.

Those junk foods considered by the author to be superior, although not necessarily nutritious, in taste, appeal, and ingredients are listed as A MEMBER OF THE JUNK FOOD BOOK HALL OF FAME. This exclusive group of foods are the ones I would want in lifetime supplies if I were marooned on a desert (dessert?) island.

CANDY

PRODUCT	**ALMOND JOY**
MANUFACTURER	Peter Paul
INGREDIENTS	Corn syrup, milk chocolate (sugar, cocoa butter, chocolate, milk, emulsifier and vanillin), coconut, sugar, almonds, hydrogenated vegetable oil, salt, cocoa powder, non-fat dry milk, whey powder, vanilla, chocolate, egg white solids, lecithin, and artificial flavors.
SUGAR QUOTIENT	High
DENTAL CHECKUP	Tooth rotter
OIL QUOTIENT	High
NUTRIENT LEVEL	Empty calories
CALORIE COUNT	141/oz.

What superlatives could be applied to a candy named after its fifth largest ingredient. In an average Almond Joy, you get the same gooey coconut and corn syrup base as in a Peter Paul's Mounds bar, plus two to four measly almonds.

The coconut candy center coupled with the sweet chocolate may be too much for some folks, but for devout junk food junkies, A. J. has the sugar jolt they crave. Peter Paul is one of the pioneers in price hikes so this is almost premium priced. Whether or not this seems a rip-off depends upon how much you love coconut flavored candy.

PRODUCT	**ALMOND ROCA**
MANUFACTURER	**Brown & Haley**
INGREDIENTS	**Sugar, almonds, milk chocolate (sugar, cocoa butter, whole milk solids, chocolate, soya lecithin, natural flavor), fresh butter, coconut oil, salt, soya lecithin, and natural flavors.**
SUGAR QUOTIENT	**High**
DENTAL CHECKUP	**Tooth rotter**
OIL QUOTIENT	**High**
NUTRIENT LEVEL	**Empty calories**
CALORIE COUNT	**160/piece**

A buttercrunch-style candy with brittle butterscotch-type nuggets coated with chocolate and almond bits. Usually found in expensive candy shops, where you get a hair less than an ounce for 20 cents. About two bites worth. The price is rather steep and the candy is overly sweet. Good try, but no cigar.

PRODUCT	**BABY RUTH**
MANUFACTURER	**Planters/Curtiss Confectionery (Standard Brands)**
INGREDIENTS	**Sugar, roasted peanuts, corn syrup, hydrogenated vegetable oil, sweetened condensed skim milk, dextrose, cocoa, soy flour, dairy whey, salt, glycerin, lecithin, sodium caseinate, artificial flavor, dipotassium phosphate, and artificial color.**
SUGAR QUOTIENT	**High**
DENTAL CHECKUP	**Tooth rotter**

OIL QUOTIENT	**High**
NUTRIENT LEVEL	**Minimal—peanuts supply some nutrition.**
CALORIE COUNT	**141/oz.**

Whenever they start adding sodium caseinate, a major ingredient of non-dairy creamer, the candy begins to taste ersatz or stretched. This classic candybar of chocolate covered peanuts and caramel has a whitish semisoft center. Something about that center makes the whole bar taste "instant." Baby Ruth was not named after baseball's legendary hero, but the oldest daughter of President Grover Cleveland.

PRODUCT	**BIT-O-HONEY**
MANUFACTURER	**Ward Johnston**
INGREDIENTS	**Corn syrup, sugar, sweetened condensed skim milk, sweetened condensed whey, hydrogenated coconut oil, almonds, modified food starch, honey, cashews, peanuts, salt, dried egg whites, soya protein, filberts, sodium acetate, and artificial flavor.**
SUGAR QUOTIENT	**High**
DENTAL CHECKUP	**Tooth rotter**
OIL QUOTIENT	**Moderate**
NUTRIENT LEVEL	**Empty calories**
CALORIE COUNT	**141/oz.**

A delightful surprise, this is a taffy candy for adults. Each "bit" is a blend of honey, almonds, cashews, peanuts and filberts. You get the real color of the ingredients (beige) and a subtly sweet nutty flavor. The taffy consistency can be chewed, like any taffy, or held in the mouth while the flavor is released slowly. Clever wax paper packaging keeps each piece separate and unstuck from the next.

PRODUCT	**BONOMO TURKISH TAFFY**
	(Vanilla, chocolate, strawberry, banana)
MANUFACTURER	**Tootsie Roll Industries**
INGREDIENTS	Corn syrup, sugar, egg albumen, hydrolyzed cereal solids, monoglycerides, artificial flavors, and artificial colors. (Third ingredient in chocolate flavor is cocoa and vanilla flavor has natural flavors added and no artificial colors.)
SUGAR QUOTIENT	**High**
DENTAL CHECKUP	**Tooth rotter**
OIL QUOTIENT	**None**
NUTRIENT LEVEL	**Empty calories**
CALORIE COUNT	**104**/oz. (chocolate); **106**/oz. (flavors)

The chewy, get-stuck-in-your-teeth texture sells this candy. It has very little else to offer. The chocolate flavor has a slight raw cocoa aftertaste. The strawberry tastes like a perfumed strawberry-cherry. Banana has no resemblance to that fruit at all. Vanilla has a bland sugary-smooth flavor. Taffy is dangerous for teeth; it not only gets stuck between them (where its sugar goes to work forming potholes) but it can pull old fillings right out of their cemented homes.

PRODUCT	**BOSTON BAKED BEANS**
MANUFACTURER	**Ferrara Pan Candy Co.**
INGREDIENTS	Sugar, peanuts, dextrose, corn syrup, corn starch, gum arabic, flour, carnauba wax, artificial flavors, and U.S. certified colors.
SUGAR QUOTIENT	**High**
DENTAL CHECKUP	**Tooth rotter**
OIL QUOTIENT	**None**
NUTRIENT LEVEL	**Empty calories**
CALORIE COUNT	**125**/oz.

If you like soggy peanuts surrounded by an overbearingly sweet capsule, then BBBs are for you. You can practically feel the sugar granules on your tongue.

They do resemble slightly Boston real bean dish, but this kiddie litter is otherwise pure schlock. The taste provides about as much pleasure as the end product of real beans does.

PRODUCT **BRACH'S CHOCOLATES**
MANUFACTURER **E. J. Brach & Sons**
INGREDIENTS **Varies with each product.**

The company makes approximately twenty-seven different chocolate covered items with seven different blends of real chocolate (five milk chocolates and two dark chocolates). One typical milk chocolate, found in their pan-coated raisins, includes sugar, cocoa butter, chocolate, powdered milk, corn syrup solids, dextrose, soya lecithin, salt, vanillin, and ethyl vanillin. That's a "blend" all right, yet it tastes surprisingly good. Below is a list of Brach's candies. The number following the name is the rating (from 0 to 10) it received from a panel of six junk food addicts crazed by too many nutritious foods. If an item scored low (4 or less) it was usually because the candy was too sweet or too artificial in its taste. All items below are chocolate covered:

Raisins (7); Peanut Clusters (7); Malted Milk Balls (7); Bridge Mix (6); Mints (7); Peanut Caramel Clusters (8); Stars (5); Cashew Clusters (7); Peanuts (7); Almonds (8); Miniature Milk Chocolates (5); Caramels (7); Peanut Butter Chips (7); Standard Cream Drops (3); Orange Sticks (3); Candy-coated Jots (5); Raisin Clusters (9); Molasses Chews (8); Dark Chocolate Bingmont Cherries (7).

PRODUCT **BRACH'S NON-CHOCOLATE CANDY**
MANUFACTURER **E. J. Brach & Sons**
INGREDIENTS **Varies with each product.**

The company manufactures about six dozen different types of "general line" candies. They are packaged in large plastic bags, offered as pick-a-mix single pieces placed in bins for self-service selection, or sold in small bags, hung from display racks. As with the chocolate candies, all are high in sugar quotient, but unlike the chocolates are low to zero in oil quotient. All Brach's candy is tooth rotter on the dental checkup and is nonexistent in nutrients. A panel of six rated a random selection of Brach's non-chocolate candies as follows: Candy Corn (10); Spearmint Leaves (10); Jelly Beans (8); Cinnamon Imperials (8); Milk Maid Caramels (9); Circus Peanuts (8); Kentucky Mints (7); Licorice Bullies (2); Butterscotch Disks (5); Spicettes Gumdrops (6); French Burnt Peanuts (3); Cinnamon Balls (Great Balls of Fire) (9); Peppermint Lozenges (like Canada Mints) (6); Licorice Twists (7); Lemon Drops (7); Sunbeam Kisses (3); Jordon Almonds (5); Maple Nut Goodies (1); Jelly Nougats (4).

PRODUCT	**BUTTERFINGER**
MANUFACTURER	**Planters /Curtiss Confectionery (Standard Brands)**
INGREDIENTS	**Sugar, corn syrup, peanut butter, hydrogenated vegetable oil, soy flour, cocoa, dairy whey, molasses, lecithin, salt, artificial color, and artificial flavor.**
SUGAR QUOTIENT	**High**
DENTAL CHECKUP	**Tooth rotter**
OIL QUOTIENT	**High**
NUTRIENT LEVEL	**Minimal—peanut butter supplies some nutrition**
CALORIE COUNT	**136/oz.**

A real peanut butter taste, combined with molasses, makes this a worthwhile candy. Soft with a crunchy, brittle texture, the bar is covered in chocolate. But they "fudged" a bit; there is no real chocolate. Cocoa is mixed with other ingredients. This isn't so unusual—many candies are made this way. But combined with this blend of candy the taste is a bit too sweet and not "chocolatey" enough.

PRODUCT	**BUTTERNUT**
MANUFACTURER	Hollywood Brands
INGREDIENTS	Sugar, corn syrup, peanuts, hydrogenated vegetable oil, water, skim milk solids, non-fat dry milk, whey solids, cocoa, chocolate, salt, lecithin, and mono- and diglycerides.
SUGAR QUOTIENT	High
DENTAL CHECKUP	Tooth rotter
OIL QUOTIENT	High
NUTRIENT LEVEL	Empty calories
CALORIE COUNT	Not available

A chewy, peanut buttery, caramel smooth filling, covered with just the right sweetness of chocolate makes this Hollywood bar uncommonly tasty. As with all Hollywood candy bars you get a generous sized portion for your money.

PRODUCT	**CADBURY CHOCOLATES** (various)
MANUFACTURER	Cadbury Corp.
INGREDIENTS	*Coconut filled:* sweet chocolate (sugar, chocolate, cocoa butter, milk, butterfat) with added emulsifier, sugar, dextrose, corn syrup, coconut, and artificial natural flavors.
	Peppermint filled: sweet chocolate (sugar, chocolate, cocoa butter), sugar, glucose, invert sugar, butter fat, water, hydrogenated coconut oil, soya lecithin, salt, natural flavors, vanillin and artificial colors.
SUGAR QUOTIENT	High
DENTAL CHECKUP	Tooth rotter
OIL QUOTIENT	High
NUTRIENT LEVEL	Empty calories
CALORIE COUNT	Not available

This leading candy maker in England and Canada has now launched an all-out attack on America's sweet tooth. It is the first battle between the English and the Colonists which the English are winning. Cadbury's chocolate covered coconut, peppermint, caramel, and others are made of well-blended chocolate and wonderfully gooey fillings. While the Canadian import Peppermint lists absolutely no oil of peppermint, the pale green filling is properly mint flavored and the coconut bar may give Peter Paul's Mounds some competition. Cadbury's are premium chocolate bars at candy counter prices. Bravo!

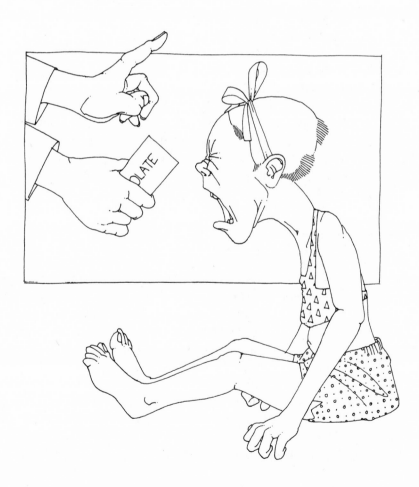

PRODUCT	**CARAVELLE**
MANUFACTURER	**Peter Paul**
INGREDIENTS	**Milk chocolate (sugar, cocoa butter, chocolate, milk, emulsifier and vanillin), corn syrup, sugar, hydrogenated vegetable oil, whey powder, crisped rice, non-fat dry milk, defatted soy, cocoa powder, salt, stabilized wheat germ, sodium caseinate, egg white solids, artificial flavor and color, chocolate, glycerol monostearate, sodium bicarbonate, and lecithin.**
SUGAR QUOTIENT	**High**
DENTAL CHECKUP	**Tooth rotter**
OIL QUOTIENT	**High**
NUTRIENT LEVEL	**Empty calories**
CALORIE COUNT	**136/oz.**

The chewy Caravelle is similar to Nestle's $100,000 Bar—chocolate-covered caramel and crisped rice. But the comparison ends there. The sweet taste does not overwhelm, the caramel and chocolate flavors aren't flaunted, and the crisped rice adds a crunchy "mouthfeel." The one drawback is the football field of additives used—at least they include sodium bicarbonate (an antiacid) to buffer the gut from the rest of the junk in the bar. Two two-bite bars in a pack.

PRODUCT	**CHARLESTON CHEW**
MANUFACTURER	**Fox Cross**
INGREDIENTS	**Corn syrup, sugar, vegetable oil, non-fat milk solids, cocoa, egg albumen, sorbitan monostearate, glycerol lacto palmitate, artificial flavor, lecithin, vegetable protein, and salt.**
SUGAR QUOTIENT	**High**
DENTAL CHECKUP	**Tooth rotter**
OIL QUOTIENT	**High**
NUTRIENT LEVEL	**Empty calories**
CALORIE COUNT	**125/oz.**

Nauseatingly sweet ersatz chocolate covers a taffy-textured marshmallow-type filling. Many candy bars that taste fake are at least tolerable—this one is strictly bad news. Some people like to eat CC frozen. They would do better to let some Elmer's Glu-All congeal and eat that. It might even taste better.

PRODUCT	**CHARMS (Fruit Squares and Lollipops)**
MANUFACTURER	**Charms Co.**
INGREDIENTS	**Sugar, corn syrup or cream of tartar, citric acid, natural and artificial flavor, and U.S. certified colors.**
SUGAR QUOTIENT	**High**
DENTAL CHECKUP	**Tooth rotter**
OIL QUOTIENT	**None**
NUTRIENT LEVEL	**Empty calories**
CALORIE COUNT	**110/oz. average**

Individually wrapped, square hard candies in a rainbow array of colors and fruit flavors. The sour variety is a bit more tolerable than the syrupy-sweet plain. Charms lollipops are available in a variety of one-hour suckers. The ice cream flavors nearly duplicate vanilla and chocolate ice cream. The half-sour/half-sweet pops are unusual and taste great at least half the time. The best flavor is sour cherry: tart and lipsmacking good. These lollipops came close to relieving a sore throat which hadn't responded to lozenges.

PRODUCT	**CHARMS BLOW POPS (Candies and Lollipops)**
MANUFACTURER	**Charms Co.**
INGREDIENTS	**Sugar, corn syrup, gum base, starch, citric acid, glycerine, artificial flavors, artificial colors, and BHT.**
SUGAR QUOTIENT	**High**
DENTAL CHECKUP	**Tooth rotter**
OIL QUOTIENT	**None**
NUTRIENT LEVEL	**Empty calories**
CALORIE COUNT	**120/oz. average**

Insidious little monsters. Hard candy surrounds a wad of bubble gum that is harder than the candy. People tend to chomp away at the hard candy in their eagerness to get to the mother lode: the bubble gum. When they do, there isn't enough acorn-hard gum to create a good-sized bubble. The candy is the same syrupy sweet stuff found in regular Charms.

PRODUCT	**CHOCO' LITE (Whipped Milk Chocolate with Crispy Crisps)**
MANUFACTURER	**Nestlé**
INGREDIENTS	**Milk chocolate (sugar, fresh whole milk, cocoa butter, chocolate liquor, lecithin, vanillin), sugar, corn syrup solids, honey, and artificial flavor.**
SUGAR QUOTIENT	**High**
DENTAL CHECKUP	**Tooth rotter**
OIL QUOTIENT	**High**
NUTRIENT LEVEL	**Empty calories**
CALORIE COUNT	**120/oz.**

One of the few major candies which uses honey as a basic ingredient. I still haven't figured out exactly what the "crisps" are, but they blend well in the mocha-colored hard sponge center. Choco' lite is aerated and solidified by the stretched Nestlé Chocolate which covers it—slightly oversweet but not cloying. Not unlike Nestlé's Crunch, this is a cross between a hardened nougat and a rice crisped candy. But this has no rice.

PRODUCT	**CHUNKY (original style—Peanut and Plain also available)**
MANUFACTURER	**Ward Johnston**
INGREDIENTS	**Milk chocolate (sugar, whole milk, cocoa butter, and chocolate), raisins, cashews, peanuts, soya lecithin, and vanillin.**
SUGAR QUOTIENT	**High**

DENTAL CHECKUP	Tooth rotter
OIL QUOTIENT	High
NUTRIENT LEVEL	Minimal—raisins, cashews, peanuts supply some nutrition.
CALORIE COUNT	145/oz.

A one-half-inch-thick wedge of chocolate loaded with raisins and chopped nuts —a delicious, if small, indulgence. Most other bars provide 50 percent more candy; with Chunky you get thickness instead. There is something divinely obscene about sinking your teeth into a thick hunk of chocolate—which may explain why Chunky has a legion of devotees. The original silver wrapped version remains the best.

PRODUCT	**CLARK BAR**
MANUFACTURER	D. L. Clark Co.
INGREDIENTS	Sugar, corn syrup, peanut butter, molasses, wheat bran, hydrogenated vegetable oil, cocoa, non-fat dry milk, chocolate liquor, salt, natural and artificial flavor, acetyl, tartaric esters of mono- and diglycerides, soya lecithin, and artificial color.
SUGAR QUOTIENT	High
DENTAL CHECKUP	Tooth rotter
OIL QUOTIENT	High
NUTRIENT LEVEL	Minimal—peanut butter adds some nutrition.
CALORIE COUNT	133/oz.

This molasses-crunch and peanut butter bar is surrounded by chocolate— somewhat like a Butterfinger. The semi-hard, gritty texture inside seems to be both oily and rather dry at the same time. The taste is modestly sweet but the overall flavor is weak. The competition ranks better, but Clark goes down fighting valiantly, if artificially.

PRODUCT	**CRACKER JACK**
MANUFACTURER	Cracker Jack (Borden Inc.)
INGREDIENTS	Sugar, corn syrup, popcorn, peanuts, molasses, vegetable oil, salt, and soya lecithin.
SUGAR QUOTIENT	High
DENTAL CHECKUP	Tooth rotter
OIL QUOTIENT	Moderate
NUTRIENT LEVEL	Empty calories
CALORIE COUNT	151/oz.

Combine our love of sweets with our love of the crunch of popcorn and peanuts and you've got Cracker Jacks. Still the best of the caramelized popcorns, it is nevertheless disturbing to find more sugar than popcorn here. The popcorn may take up most of the package, but sugar and corn syrup are the largest ingredients. Borden's advertising pitch says Cracker Jacks aren't like other additive-filled snacks—they are completely natural. Natural *what?* I don't deny they taste good. They do. And you still get a toy prize in each box—worth ½ cent and chintzier than ever. But some of the fun and magic is taken away when you become aware that this classic confection is even more junky than you thought.

PRODUCT	**CRUNCHOLA (Peanut Butter with or without Chocolate Chips)**
MANUFACTURER	Sunfield Foods
INGREDIENTS	Rolled oats, chopped and ground peanuts, hydrogenated vegetable oil, corn sweeteners, sugar, sweet diary whey solids, sodium and calcium caseinate, soy flour, wheat flour, defatted wheat germ, brown sugar, vegetable oil, lecithin, salt, U.S. certified color, and vanilla with other natural flavors. (The chocolate chips style uses peanut butter in place of peanuts plus components for chocolate.)
SUGAR QUOTIENT	High

DENTAL CHECKUP	Tooth rotter
OIL QUOTIENT	High
NUTRIENT LEVEL	Minimal—some fortification present
CALORIE COUNT	16o/each

This allegedly nutritious granola-peanut butter bar is a tasty blend of peanuts, wheat germ and the other garbage put in "natural" candy these days. Admittedly, there is more protein here than in most bars. But their claims to wholesomeness should be ignored. The flavor is peanut buttery, but not indulgently sweet. The plain peanut butter bar holds up better (and has more nutrients) than the chocolate chip variety, which also has an ersatz aftertaste.

PRODUCT	CUP-O-GOLD
MANUFACTURER	Hoffman Candy
INGREDIENTS	Sugar, vegetable fat, corn syrup, milk solids, coconut, chocolate liquore, almonds, vegetable lecithin, salt, albumen, vanillin, and other artificial flavors.
SUGAR QUOTIENT	High
DENTAL CHECKUP	Tooth rotter
OIL QUOTIENT	High
NUTRIENT LEVEL	Empty calories
CALORIE COUNT	Not available

This chocolate patty in a paper shell contains gooey coconut, a blob-like creme concoction left over from some Grade B horror movie. The "creme" reminds me of hardened non-diary creamer. The almond bits in the chocolate coating don't help. They call it Cup-O-Gold because of the yellow slimy syrup that oozes out with the first bite. Sugar and vegetable fat (not oil) are the two largest ingredients. Oh, yes—this is a messy snack, as well.

========

PRODUCT	**FIFTH AVENUE**
MANUFACTURER	Luden's
INGREDIENTS	Milk chocolate with artificial flavor and lecithin, peanuts, sugar, corn syrup, almonds, molasses, hydrogenated vegetable oil, demineralized whey, cocoa, salt, artificial flavor, BHA, and BHT.
SUGAR QUOTIENT	High
DENTAL CHECKUP	Tooth rotter
OIL QUOTIENT	Moderate
NUTRIENT LEVEL	Minimal—peanuts and almonds supply some nutrition.
CALORIE COUNT	160/1.2 oz.

Peanut butter and molasses candy bars are numerous, but this one has a gimmick: almonds. There are two to three almonds in each bar, and, like the peanut butter and molasses, they are covered by a milk chocolate stretched with artificial flavoring. The texture is gritty—like pastry dough meeting peanut brittle. The tastes of fake chocolate, molasses, and almonds collide.

========

PRODUCT	**FOREVER YOURS**
MANUFACTURER	M&M/Mars
INGREDIENTS	Milk chocolate (sugar, chocolate, cocoa butter, milk, butter, oil, emulsifier, natural and artificial flavors), corn syrup, sweetened condensed milk, hydrogenated vegetable oil, nonfat dry milk, butter, salt, vanilla, egg whites, vegetable protein, and artificial flavor.
SUGAR QUOTIENT	High
DENTAL CHECKUP	Tooth rotter
OIL QUOTIENT	High
NUTRIENT LEVEL	Empty calories
CALORIE COUNT	121/oz.

Distributed only regionally by one of the world's largest candy companies,

this bar was probably the most difficult to locate. I finally found one at a Chicago airport newsstand. It was worth the search. A vanilla hybrid, of Milky Way and Three Musketeers, this is a fluffy white mix of caramel nougat and dairy-flavored vanilla dough, covered by sweet chocolate. The dough has a meringue airiness; the result: a candy that tastes light and rich at the same time. With a splashy new package, M&M is stepping up its revival of this candy; it should ease its way into your area soon—hopefully.

PRODUCT	**GHIRADELLI (MINT) CHOCOLATE**
MANUFACTURER	**Ghiradelli Chocolate Co. (Golden Grain Macaroni)**
INGREDIENTS	**Sweet chocolate (sugar, unsweetened chocolate, cocoa butter and whole milk powder), soya lecithin, and oil of peppermint.**
SUGAR QUOTIENT	**High**
DENTAL CHECKUP	**Tooth rotter**
OIL QUOTIENT	**High**

NUTRIENT LEVEL	Empty calories
CALORIE COUNT	175/1.2 OZ.

This quality chocolate has been around the San Francisco Bay area for nearly a century. Creamy smooth with a well-balanced sweetness and flavor, these premium bars (at candy counter prices) are mostly found in the Pacific Northwest. The mint chocolate is the best and is reminiscent of how Girl Scout Mint Cookies *used* to taste. Although many other varieties are available, don't miss this one. For chocolate and mint lovers, this is paradise. Say: GEAR-AR-DELLY.

PRODUCT	**GOETZE'S CARAMEL CREAMS**
MANUFACTURER	Goetze's (pronounced *Getses*)
INGREDIENTS	Dextrose, flour, sugar, corn syrup, vegetable oil, condensed milk (not fat), sorbitol, salt, and artificial flavor.
SUGAR QUOTIENT	High
DENTAL CHECKUP	Tooth rotter
OIL QUOTIENT	Moderate
NUTRIENT LEVEL	Empty calories
CALORIE COUNT	Not available

Caramels should be chewy and smooth. These are hard, dry, chalky crumbs. The "creme" center is almost tasteless. This candy reveals the desperate lengths we will go to for a caramel fix. There are three different sugars in this concoction and that may be the problem. Good caramel requires only plain white refined sugar. These candies do look tempting in their package—they should probably be kept there.

PRODUCT	**GOOBERS** (Milk Chocolate Covered Peanuts)
MANUFACTURER	**Ward Johnston**
INGREDIENTS	**Peanuts, milk chocolate (sugar, whole milk, cocoa butter and chocolate), sugar, soya lecithin, vanillin, salt, tapioca dextrin, and resinous glaze.**
SUGAR QUOTIENT	**High**
DENTAL CHECKUP	**Tooth rotter**
OIL QUOTIENT	**High**
NUTRIENT LEVEL	**Minimal—peanuts supply some nutrition.**
CALORIE COUNT	**153/ounce**

The rip-off price (about $2.40/lb.) doesn't stop our indulging in these peanuts covered with sugary chocolate. Goobers are peanuts by definition, and now that Ward Johnston has trademarked the name, maybe they can make the chocolate taste like chocolate—not a syrup-sweet glaze. A good product that needs a little improvement.

PRODUCT	**GOOD N'PLENTY/GOOD N'FRUITY**
MANUFACTURER	**American Chicle**
INGREDIENTS	**Dextrose, sugar, corn syrup, molasses, starch, dextrin, wheat flour, artificial and natural flavor, guar gum, sodium carbonate, confectioners glaze, carnauba wax, vegetable oils, and artificial colors.**
SUGAR QUOTIENT	**High**
DENTAL CHECKUP	**Tooth rotter**
OIL QUOTIENT	**Low**
NUTRIENT LEVEL	**Empty calories**
CALORIE COUNT	**164 (Plenty); 172 (Fruity)/oz.**

The first four ingredients in this candy are sugar-based. That's a lot of sugar for such a small candy. Good N' Plenty has a weak licorice flavor in white and pink pellets. To get the flavor you practically have to break your teeth on the outer candy coating. Then, as you chew, the candy forms a gummy mass not unlike cement. Good N' Fruity is the offspring of Plenty. The allegedly fruity flavors come in rainbow-colored candy you have to gnaw like a beaver to get through.

PRODUCT	**HALVAH** (Marble, Vanilla, Chocolate)
MANUFACTURER	Joyva
INGREDIENTS	Crushed sesame, glucose, sugar, vegetable shortening, cocoa, chocolate, dried egg albumen, and artificial and natural flavor.
SUGAR QUOTIENT	High
DENTAL CHECKUP	Tooth rotter
OIL QUOTIENT	High
NUTRIENT LEVEL	Empty calories
CALORIE COUNT	Not available

Halvah is a cross between sandpaper and wet chalk. This block of crushed sesame seeds in a sugar and shortening base is available in Jewish delis and supermarket dairy cases (it should be refrigerated for lengthy storage). It is oily to the touch and gritty to the taste. Perhaps crushed sesames are somewhat "healthy," but the wallop of glucose and sugar in this candy cancels out any benefits. Yet once the taste is acquired there is something permanently habit-forming about Halvah.

PRODUCT	**HEATH ENGLISH TOFFEE**
MANUFACTURER	Heath Candy Co.
INGREDIENTS	Milk chocolate with lecithin, salt, and vanillin, hydrogenated vegetable oil, sugar, corn syrup, almonds, salt, non-fat dry milk, lecithin, mono- and diglycerides, artificial flavor, and Beta carotene (coloring).

SUGAR QUOTIENT	High
DENTAL CHECKUP	Tooth rotter
OIL QUOTIENT	High
NUTRIENT LEVEL	Empty calories
CALORIE COUNT	153/oz.

A crunchy and semi-chewy blend of toffee-caramel and almonds smothered in rich milk chocolate. Pleasantly sweet, the toffee taste blends well with the chocolate. The crunchy texture of the almond bits and the semi-firm toffee makes this a unique confection and a dandy junk food for adults as well as kids. Beware: Heath Bars tend to become habit-forming. This candy was the inspiration for the Heath Ice Cream Bar.

PRODUCT	**HERSHEY'S ALMOND**
MANUFACTURER	Hershey Foods
INGREDIENTS	Sugar, milk, cocoa butter, chocolate, almonds, soya lecithin, and vanillin.
SUGAR QUOTIENT	High
DENTAL CHECKUP	Tooth rotter
OIL QUOTIENT	High
NUTRIENT LEVEL	Empty calories
CALORIE COUNT	200/1.3 oz.

The point of this chocolate bar is its almonds. But some bars have lots of almonds, while others have hardly any. This is sloppy quality control. Hershey's generally has a fine reputation for quality, and they even grow their own almonds in California. They are the largest almond-users in the world. To paraphrase Mae West: When they are good, they are very good, but when they are bad, they're the pits.

PRODUCT	**HERSHEY'S KRACKLE**
MANUFACTURER	**Hershey Foods**
INGREDIENTS	**Sugar, cocoa butter, milk, chocolate, crisped rice, salt, soya lecithin, malt, and vanillin.**
SUGAR QUOTIENT	**High**
DENTAL CHECKUP	**Tooth rotter**
OIL QUOTIENT	**High**
NUTRIENT LEVEL	**Empty calories**
CALORIE COUNT	**210/1.4 OZ.**

This malt and crisped rice chocolate bar tastes fake, like chemicals. The rice makes the candy feel as if it were infused with ashes. The rice and the malt do add a crunchy quality, but this copy of Nestlé's Crunch doesn't make the grade.

PRODUCT	**HERSHEY'S SPECIAL DARK**
MANUFACTURER	**Hershey Foods**
INGREDIENTS	**Sugar, chocolate, cocoa butter, soya lecithin, and vanillin.**
SUGAR QUOTIENT	**High**
DENTAL CHECKUP	**Tooth rotter**
OIL QUOTIENT	**High**
NUTRIENT LEVEL	**Empty calories**
CALORIE COUNT	**220/1.4 OZ.**

Hershey states on the label that this is "mildly sweet chocolate," and it is much less sweet than Hershey's regular milk chocolate. But it still assaults the tongue with cloying richness and a slight, not altogether unpleasant, bitter aftertaste remains.

=====

PRODUCT	**HEYDAY CARAMEL PEANUT LOGS**
MANUFACTURER	**Nabisco**
INGREDIENTS	**Peanuts, corn syrup, sugar, shortening, enriched wheat flour, rye flour, non-fat milk solids, whey solids, cocoa (processed with alkali), sorbitan monostearate, lecithin and polysorbate 60 emulsifiers, pure creamery butter, salt, leavening, and artificial flavors and color.**
SUGAR QUOTIENT	**High**
DENTAL CHECKUP	**Tooth rotter**
OIL QUOTIENT	**High**
NUTRIENT LEVEL	**Empty calories**
CALORIE COUNT	**128/each**

Excellent junk, this! Not really a cookie, it's a candy bar in disguise. Caramel, chocolate, and peanuts are poured onto a thin cookie wafer. With fourteen logs in each 10-ounce package, the weight and price are comparable to a family pack of candy. The ingredients work well with each other and the blend, while rich, is not cloying. Definite guilt inducers—but who cares! (Found in the cookie section of most supermarkets and groceries.)

=====

PRODUCT	**HOLLYWOOD**
MANUFACTURER	**Hollywood Brands**
INGREDIENTS	**Sugar, corn syrup, hydrogenated vegetable oil, peanuts, water, cocoa, skim milk solids, chocolate, salt, egg white solids, vegetable protein, lecithin, artificial flavor and mono- and diglycerides.**
INGREDIENTS	**High**
SUGAR QUOTIENT	**Tooth rotter**
OIL QUOTIENT	**High**
NUTRIENT LEVEL	**Empty calories**
CALORIE COUNT	**Not available**

According to Robert C. Evans, Manager of Hollywood Brands, Quality Assurance, the company "makes no nutritional claims with respect to our products, but we do feel they are as nutritional as similar items." I'll let my mother answer Mr. Evans: "Two wrongs don't make a right." Hollywood is a bar of nougat, caramel, and peanuts, covered by compound chocolate. Its sweetness is so heavy it's almost sickening. An immediate rumbling in the gut is followed by a lingering aftertaste. According to the company, of its six candy bars, this one is fifth in sales. If only Neilsen could have rated this candy: by next year it would have been canceled.

PRODUCT	**JUJUBES**
MANUFACTURER	**Henry Heide**
INGREDIENTS	**Sugar, natural gum, malto dextrins, corn syrup and starch, gelatin, emulsifier, and artificial flavors and colors.**
SUGAR QUOTIENT	**High**
DENTAL CHECKUP	**Tooth rotter**
OIL QUOTIENT	**High**
NUTRIENT LEVEL	**Empty calories**
CALORIE COUNT	**Ten = 134**

Heide says in fine print that these are "genuine gum candies." I never doubted that they were genuine—but that doesn't make them taste or look any better. They bear a close resemblance to the colored gravel used in the botton of fish-tanks. A tough resilient gum- and gelatin-based candy, these pits have little flavor and are practically indestructible, unlike the human molar. Great as ammunition for a slingshot.

PRODUCT	**JUJYFRUITS**
MANUFACTURER	**Henry Heide**
INGREDIENTS	**Corn syrup, sugar, dextrose, licorice, corn starch, citric acid,**

and artificial flavors and colors, coated with confectioners glaze.

SUGAR QUOTIENT	High
DENTAL CHECKUP	Tooth rotter
OIL QUOTIENT	High
NUTRIENT LEVEL	Empty calories
CALORIE COUNT	Ten = 150

Similar to Mason Dots, these gum drops have a consistency capable of pulling the fillings in your teeth. Jujyfruits are shaped like the fruits each color supposedly represents. The similarity to fruit ends there. The flavor is subdued, faintly perfumed, and not all that sweet. If you enjoy playing tug o'war with your teeth, this is the candy for you.

PRODUCT	**JUNIOR MINTS**
MANUFACTURER	**Nabisco Confections**
INGREDIENTS	Sugar, chocolate with vegetable lecithin, corn syrup, peppermint oil, confectioners glaze, gum arabic, concentrated non-fat milk, vegetable protein, and invertase.
SUGAR QUOTIENT	High
DENTAL CHECKUP	Tooth rotter
OIL QUOTIENT	Low
NUTRIENT LEVEL	Empty calories
CALORIE COUNT	Ten = 104

A shiny glaze covers each button-shaped, soft chocolate mint. The flavoring is on the sweet side but the peppermint seems to balance this. These make good, though small, after dinner mints. They tend to become habit-forming.

PRODUCT	**KIT KAT**
MANUFACTURER	Reese Candy Co. (Hershey Foods)
INGREDIENTS	Sugar, whole dry milk, cocoa butter, flour, chocolate, vege-

table oil, butter, soya lecithin, yeast, sodium bicarbonate, and vanillin.

SUGAR QUOTIENT	High
DENTAL CHECKUP	Tooth rotter
OIL QUOTIENT	High
NUTRIENT LEVEL	Empty calories
CALORIE COUNT	180 each

Made from a British recipe, Kit Kat is a chocolate-covered sugar wafer cooky. It is highly overpriced for what you get. Nabisco, for example, makes a Creme Wafer Stick, quite similar, at a much lower price. The cookie wafer is crisp and on the dry side. The chocolate covering is oversweet. They went all the way to England just to get this? With Hershey's confectionery know-how, surely they could have stayed home and dreamed up a better one themselves.

PRODUCT	**KRAFT CARAMELS** (Regular or Chocolate)
MANUFACTURER	**Kraft Foods**
INGREDIENTS	Condensed sweet milk, corn syrup, sugar, hydrogenated vegetable oil, cream, whey solids, salt, and artificial and natural flavor. (In chocolate caramels the fourth ingredient is chocolate, the fifth is cream.)
SUGAR QUOTIENT	High
DENTAL CHECKUP	Tooth rotter
OIL QUOTIENT	High
NUTRIENT LEVEL	Empty calories
CALORIE COUNT	118/oz.

Many junk food junkies who eat candy on a regular basis adore caramel and dream of separating it from whatever candy it's contained in. Kraft came to our rescue with packages of chewy plain and chocolate caramels. The plain variety is a sweet candy with little character. Although it doesn't appear to have been shot with air, it does have an aerated texture. The chocolate caramel is richer and more satisfying, with a chocolate fudge texture and flavor, no doubt from the added cream. Kraft suggests using the caramels as cooking ingredients. You should.

PRODUCT	**LIFE SAVERS** (Fruit-Flavored)
MANUFACTURER	**Life Savers**
INGREDIENTS	**Fancy Fruits: Sugar, corn syrup, artificial flavors and colors. Tropical Fruits: Sugar, corn syrup, artificial and natural flavors, artificial colors. Five Flavor: Sugar, corn syrup, artificial and natural flavors, and artificial colors.**
SUGAR QUOTIENT	**High**
DENTAL CHECKUP	**Tooth rotter**
OIL QUOTIENT	**None**
NUTRIENT LEVEL	**Empty calories**
CALORIE COUNT	**9 each**

The Life Savers Company has always produced a quality product. Fancy Fruits are artificially flavored apple, black raspberry, pear, and grapefruit candies. Although the first three don't live up to their real life counterparts, the grapefruit tastes uncannily similar. Tropical Fruits hit the mark with artificially flavored tangerine, mango, melon, banana, pineapple, and coconut. I conducted a blind test with six people; all were able to distinguish which flavor was which. The Five Flavor selection is the original lemon, lime, cherry, orange, and pineapple package. The taste is too sweet and doesn't match the fruits at all. Eleven candies to a pack.

PRODUCT	**LIFE SAVERS** (Butter-Flavored)
MANUFACTURER	**Life Savers**
INGREDIENTS	*Butter Rum:* **Sugar, corn syrup, molasses, salt, vinegar, artificial flavors and colors and hydrogenated vegetable oil.** *Butterscotch:* **Sugar, corn syrup, salt, butter, and artificial flavors and colors.**
SUGAR QUOTIENT	**High**
DENTAL CHECKUP	**Tooth rotter**
OIL QUOTIENT	**Low to zero**
NUTRIENT LEVEL	**Empty calories**
CALORIE COUNT	**9 each**

Salt and vinegar in candy? It may sound like salad dressing but these are surprisingly pleasant, butter-smooth, modestly sweet, butterscotch-flavored candies. The Butterscotch tastes like caramel with butter added. The Butter Rum is a notch better; it has an extra snap and a lingering tart aftertaste. Eleven candies to a roll.

PRODUCT	**MALLO CUP**
MANUFACTURER	Boyer Bros.
INGREDIENTS	Milk chocolate, corn syrup, sugar, dextrose, coconut, cornflake, egg whites, vegetable stabilizers, salt, natural and artificial flavors, and potassium sorbate.
SUGAR QUOTIENT	High
DENTAL CHECKUP	Tooth rotter
OIL QUOTIENT	Moderate
NUTRIENT LEVEL	Empty calories
CALORIE COUNT	Not available

Bite into this cupcake-shaped chocolate-covered candy and a whitish-yellow slime oozes out. And is this glop ever sweet! They seem to have added extra sugar to make up for the lack of flavor enhancers. Coconut creme surrounded by milk chocolate is generally a winning combination—but not here.

PRODUCT	**MARATHON**
MANUFACTURER	M&M/Mars
INGREDIENTS	Milk chocolate (sugar, milk, cocoa butter, chocolate, emulsifier, natural and artificial flavors), corn syrup, sweetened condensed milk, sugar, hydrogenated vegetable oil, salt, and artificial flavor.
SUGAR QUOTIENT	High
DENTAL CHECKUP	Tooth rotter

OIL QUOTIENT	**High**
NUTRIENT LEVEL	**Empty calories**
CALORIE COUNT	**130/oz.**

Marathon is a foot-long, thin, pretzel-shaped bar of chocolate-covered cara-mel. The name "Marathon" ostensibly comes from the length. Eating stringy caramel and chocolate is not unlike consuming a coat hanger, but the choco-late and caramel meet your craving, and the bar does seem to last longer even if there's no additional volume. A clever novelty.

PRODUCT	**MARS ALMOND BAR**
MANUFACTURER	**M&M/Mars**
INGREDIENTS	**Milk chocolate (sugar, milk, cocoa butter, chocolate, emulsi-fier, natural and artificial flavors), sugar, corn syrup, al-monds, hydrogenated vegetable oil, honey, salt, egg whites, and vegetable protein.**
SUGAR QUOTIENT	**High**
DENTAL CHECKUP	**Tooth rotter**
OIL QUOTIENT	**High**
NUTRIENT LEVEL	**Empty calories.**
CALORIE COUNT	**135/oz.**

One of the company's premium products, Mars' Almond Bar has rich velvety nougat and whole almonds with a chocolate coating. The honey may make this a trifle too sweet. The nougat, made from egg whites, is similar to that found in Three Musketeers. Consistency in the quality of this bar, like all Mars candies, is high and Mars is one of the few candy companies to put an expiration or freshness date prominently on the outer wrapper. The rest of the confectionery business could learn a lesson from this candy giant.

PRODUCT	**MARY JANE**
MANUFACTURER	Charles N. Miller Co.
INGREDIENTS	Corn syrup, sugar, peanut butter, molasses, hydrogenated vegetable oil, salt, glyceryl monostearate, and lecithin.
SUGAR QUOTIENT	High
DENTAL CHECKUP	Tooth rotter
OIL QUOTIENT	High
NUTRIENT LEVEL	Empty calories
CALORIE COUNT	Not available

Another molasses and peanut butter bar, but in taffy form. Mary Jane used to be a popular, ubiquitous candy; now it is somewhat hard to find. It is a clever combination, as the molasses adds a spicy flavor to the peanut butter's nutty one, all in a smooth, slick sheen of pliable taffy. The consistency does stick to your teeth and the sugar, unfortunately, makes Mary Jane sweeter than it has to be.

PRODUCT | **MASON CROWS**
MANUFACTURER | **Tootsie Roll Industries**
INGREDIENTS | **Corn syrup, sugar, starch, licorice extract, molasses, natural and artificial flavors, and artificial color.**
SUGAR QUOTIENT | **High**
DENTAL CHECKUP | **Tooth rotter**
OIL QUOTIENT | **None**
NUTRIENT LEVEL | **Empty calories**
CALORIE COUNT | **95/oz.**

There must be other ways to get your licorice fix which don't come close to ruining your teeth. The taste is a genuine licorice flavor—but it's no great shakes. These are gumdrops: smooth glossy black pieces with a hardened gummy texture. Crows, however, are better than Mason Dots.

PRODUCT | **MASON DOTS**
MANUFACTURER | **Tootsie Roll Industries**
INGREDIENTS | **Corn syrup, sugar, starch, malic acid, natural and artificial flavors, and artificial colors.**
SUGAR QUOTIENT | **High**
DENTAL CHECKUP | **Tooth rotter—extra dangerous**
OIL QUOTIENT | **None**
NUTRIENT LEVEL | **Empty calories**
CALORIE COUNT | **95/oz.**

This is a dental hazard. Be warned. These gumdrops can pull fillings out and coat teeth with a gummy, hard to clean, sugary gel. The colors are the most unattractive of any candy rated in this book: pale and unappetizing at best. The taste: undistinguished.

PRODUCT	**MELLOMINT PATTIES**
MANUFACTURER	**Luden's**
INGREDIENTS	**Sweet chocolate (chocolate liquor, sugar, and cocoa butter), lecithin, artificial flavoring, sugar, invert sugar, corn syrup, egg whites, oil of peppermint, and invertase.**
SUGAR QUOTIENT	**High**
DENTAL CHECKUP	**Tooth rotter**
OIL QUOTIENT	**High**
NUTRIENT LEVEL	**Empty calories**
CALORIE COUNT	**135/oz.**

They've gone overboard on the mint flavoring placed in a corn-syrup/egg-white base and covered with chocolate. It reminds me of soda pop when too much syrup has been used. Peppermint should be added subtly. Too much results in a cheap taste that lingers long after it's wanted. That's what happened here.

PRODUCT	**MILK DUDS**
MANUFACTURER	**M. J. Holloway (Beatrice Foods)**
INGREDIENTS	**Sugar, corn syrup, hydrogenated vegetable oil (soybean and cottonseed), non-fat dry milk, dextrose, whey, mono- and diglycerides, cocoa, salt, sodium caseinate, vegetable lecithin, and artificial flavors.**
SUGAR QUOTIENT	**High**
DENTAL CHECKUP	**Tooth rotter**
OIL QUOTIENT	**High**
NUTRIENT LEVEL	**Empty calories**
CALORIE COUNT	**165/dozen average**

Sodium caseinate lurks in this chocolate-flavored caramel candy. The strange flavor is like fake chocolate but real caramel. You get about fifteen of these pebble-shaped balls in a 20-cent box. I'm afraid Holloway exercises solid judgment when they named this candy Milk Duds—at least they believe in truth in labeling.

PRODUCT	**MILK SHAKE**
MANUFACTURER	Hollywood Brands
INGREDIENTS	Sugar, corn syrup, hydrogenated vegetable oil, water, skim milk solids, malted milk, salt, chocolate, egg-white solids, vegetable protein, lecithin, artificial flavor, and mono- and diglycerides.
SUGAR QUOTIENT	High
DENTAL CHECKUP	Tooth rotter
OIL QUOTIENT	High
NUTRIENT LEVEL	Empty calories
CALORIE COUNT	Not available

Hollywood manufactures some really topflight candy bars. This is not one of them. Milk Shake is the kind of candy bar that suckers you by its name. The only milk in this oblong bar is dehydrated solids. The topping is made from a compound chocolate (cocoa and saturated fat) and the resulting taste is a poor counterfeit of a Milky Way. The nougat is nauseatingly sweet and the thin layer of caramel is almost undetectable. Worth eating—if you were stranded on a desert island and this was the only food.

PRODUCT	**MILKY WAY**
MANUFACTURER	M&M/Mars
INGREDIENTS	Milk chocolate (sugar, milk, cocoa butter, chocolate, emulsifier, natural and artificial flavors), corn syrup, sugar, milk, salt, malt, egg whites, vegetable protein, and artificial flavor.
SUGAR QUOTIENT	High
DENTAL CHECKUP	Tooth rotter
OIL QUOTIENT	High
NUTRIENT LEVEL	Minimal—some fortification present.
CALORIE COUNT	130/oz.

There are real ingredients among the artificial ones in this king of American candies. A perennial bestseller, Milky Way is a combination of caramel, nougat, and diary-fresh milk and butter covered by a good-tasting chocolate. Good either frozen or at room temperature, Milky Ways are excellent junk. They rank second and third as regional favorites and are number one in the North Central States. Attempts to get information about this product, however, were met with a cold reception. While Mars is willing to pass information on to consumers, they do not like to publicize their products, no matter how delicious, as junk food.

A MEMBER OF THE JUNK FOOD BOOK HALL OF FAME.

PRODUCT	**MISTER GOODBAR**
MANUFACTURER	**Hershey Foods**
INGREDIENTS	**Sugar, peanuts, cocoa butter, milk, chocolate, soya lecithin, and vanillin.**
SUGAR QUOTIENT	**High**
DENTAL CHECKUP	**Tooth rotter**
OIL QUOTIENT	**High**
NUTRIENT LEVEL	**Minimal—some fortification from peanuts is present.**
CALORIE COUNT	**280/1.8 OZ.**

It hardly seems possible, but there is more sugar than peanuts packed into this bar. This habit-forming candy certainly is as sweet as many others, but the sugar is mitigated by all those peanuts. The candy is delicious, without the cloying aftertaste peanut-based candies sometimes give. One of Hershey's Best.

A MEMBER OF THE JUNK FOOD BOOK HALL OF FAME.

PRODUCT	**M&M'S PLAIN/M&M'S PEANUT**
MANUFACTURER	**M&M/Mars**
INGREDIENTS	**Milk chocolate (sugar, milk, chocolate, cocoa butter, peanuts, emulsifier, salt, and artificial flavor), sugar, corn starch and syrup, dextrin, and artificial colors. (In Peanut, the third ingredient is peanuts.)**
SUGAR QUOTIENT	**High**
DENTAL CHECKUP	**Tooth rotter**
OIL QUOTIENT	**High**
NUTRIENT LEVEL	**Empty calories**
CALORIE COUNT	**140 (plain); 145 (peanut)/oz.**

These thin-shelled, button-shaped, chocolate-filled candies are a perennial American favorite. The plain has mystique, the peanut variety is clearly *déclassé*. Once you're an M&M devotee you learn to suck gently on the outer candy until your tongue feels the little 'M' imprinted on each shell. The secret of the unique chocolate taste is a subtle blend of peanuts in the chocolate itself. M&Ms are supposed to "melt in your mouth, not in your hand." This is difficult to prove; as soon as I get hold of M&Ms I put them immediately into my mouth. There's no lollygagging when M&Ms are around.

A MEMBER OF THE JUNK FOOD BOOK HALL OF FAME.

PRODUCT	**MOUNDS**
MANUFACTURER	**Peter Paul**
INGREDIENTS	**Corn syrup, semi-sweet chocolate (chocolate, sugar, cocoa butter, emulsifier, and vanillin), coconut, sugar, salt, vanilla, and egg-white solids.**
SUGAR QUOTIENT	**High**
DENTAL CHECKUP	**Tooth rotter**
OIL QUOTIENT	**High**
NUTRIENT LEVEL	**Empty calories**
CALORIE COUNT	**142/oz.**

The dark chocolate makes the difference, complementing the gooey coconut middle, making it all taste great. An auspicious way to introduce greenhorns to coconut. Dark Chocolate Mounds makes being a junk food junkie seem worthwhile. Amen.

A MEMBER OF THE JUNK FOOD BOOK HALL OF FAME.

PRODUCT	**MUNCH BAR**
MANUFACTURER	**M&M/Mars**
INGREDIENTS	**Peanuts, sugar, corn syrup, butter, salt, baking soda, emulsifier, BHA, and BHT.**
SUGAR QUOTIENT	**High**
DENTAL CHECKUP	**Tooth rotter**
OIL QUOTIENT	**High**
NUTRIENT LEVEL	**Minimal—some fortification from peanuts is present.**
CALORIE COUNT	**155/oz.**

Good peanut brittle for the price. There is enough in one bar to please the palate; any more would be cloying. Loaded with peanuts in a corn syrup base, Munch Bar is crunchy like its name, with a flavor enhancer—salt—taking some of the edge off the sweetness.

PRODUCT	**NECCO WAFERS**
MANUFACTURER	New England Confection Co.
INGREDIENTS	Sugar, corn syrup, K-gelatin, artificial and natural flavors, gum tragacanth, chocolate, citric acid, artificial colors, carbon black, propylene glycol, and K-glycerine.
SUGAR QUOTIENT	High
DENTAL CHECKUP	Tooth rotter
OIL QUOTIENT	High
NUTRIENT LEVEL	Empty calories
CALORIE COUNT	4 per wafer

Quarter-sized, pastel-colored chips which offer little flavor and have a chalky consistency shouldn't be popular. But NECCO wafers continue to charm kids. I think the illusion of getting a lot for your money attracts youngsters to these sugar disks. But this is the type of candy that gives all junk food a bad name. Definitely garbage.

NECCO comes from the name of the company: New England Confection COmpany.

PRODUCT	**NESTLÉ'S CRUNCH**
MANUFACTURER	Nestlé
INGREDIENTS	Milk chocolate (sugar, fresh whole milk, cocoa butter, chocolate liquor, lecithin, vanillin), and crisped rice.
SUGAR QUOTIENT	High
DENTAL CHECKUP	Tooth rotter
OIL QUOTIENT	High
NUTRIENT LEVEL	Empty calories
CALORIE COUNT	140/oz.

Better than Hershey's Krackle, Crunch is still only an average candybar. The real chocolate is stretched with globs of sugar until it is supersweet, no doubt so that it will appeal to children as well as adults (who normally prefer a less sweet chocolate). The generous portions of crisped rice save this candy from tasting as ersatz as Hershey's crisped rice bar.

═══════════════════════

PRODUCT	**NIBS**
MANUFACTURER	**Y&S Candies**
INGREDIENTS	**Corn syrup, sugar, flour, molasses, starch, licorice extract, vegetable shortening, salt, artificial color, natural flavor, and potassium sorbate.**
SUGAR QUOTIENT	**High**
DENTAL CHECKUP	**Tooth rotter**
OIL QUOTIENT	**Low**
NUTRIENT LEVEL	**Empty calories**
CALORIE COUNT	**100/oz.**

Maybe because more corn syrup is used than molasses, Nibs have a more genuine flavor than other licorice items. They are little tooth-sized black licorice gum drops that are fun to eat. You don't seem to get all that much for the price, though.

═══════════════════════

PRODUCT	**NUT GOODIE**
MANUFACTURER	**Pearson Candy**
INGREDIENTS	**Milk chocolate, peanuts, sugar, corn syrup, egg albumen, soya protein, salt, cream of tartar, invertase, artificial maple flavoring, soya lecithin, and artificial color.**
SUGAR QUOTIENT	**High**
DENTAL CHECKUP	**Tooth rotter**
OIL QUOTIENT	**High**
NUTRIENT LEVEL	**Empty calories**
CALORIE COUNT	**136/1.4 oz.**

A cluster of chocolate and peanuts surrounds a highly artificial maple cream. The nuts and chocolate taste good together, almost like Mr. Goodbar, but the ersatz maple flavor of the cream reduces the quality.

PRODUCT	**OH! HENRY!**
MANUFACTURER	Ward Johnston
INGREDIENTS	Roasted peanuts, corn syrup, sugar, vegetable oil, cocoa powder, skimmed condensed milk, invert sugar, dextrose, sorbitol, soya flour, corn starch, salt, soya protein, natural and artificial flavors, and soya lecithin.
SUGAR QUOTIENT	High
DENTAL CHECKUP	Tooth rotter
OIL QUOTIENT	High
NUTRIENT LEVEL	Minimal—peanuts add some fortification.
CALORIE COUNT	**140**/ounce

"Tons" of peanuts and just enough caramel all covered in chocolate. The peanuts prevent oversweetness, making this a genuinely great candy bar.

A MEMBER OF THE JUNK FOOD BOOK HALL OF FAME.

PRODUCT	**$100,000 BAR**
MANUFACTURER	Nestlé
INGREDIENTS	Milk chocolate (sugar, fresh whole milk, cocoa butter, chocolate liquor, lecithin, vanillin), corn syrup, sweetened condensed milk (sugar, milk), crisped rice, vegetable oil, sugar, mono- and diglycerides, lecithin, salt, and artificial flavors.
SUGAR QUOTIENT	High
DENTAL CHECKUP	Tooth rotter
OIL QUOTIENT	High
NUTRIENT LEVEL	Empty calories
CALORIE COUNT	**130**/ounce

Crisped rice and caramel, covered by milk chocolate—although a teeny bit cloying, it works well. Two two-bite bars in each pack. The delirious child on the label indicates the target audience for this candy.

PRODUCT	**PAYDAY**
MANUFACTURER	Hollywood Brands (Consolidated Foods Co.)
INGREDIENTS	Peanuts, sugar, corn syrup, water, skim milk solids, hydrogenated vegetable oil, salt, egg-white solids, artificial flavor, mono- and diglycerides, and vegetable protein.
SUGAR QUOTIENT	High
DENTAL CHECKUP	Tooth rotter
OIL QUOTIENT	High
NUTRIENT LEVEL	Minimal—peanuts supply some fortification.
CALORIE COUNT	Not available

Payday is a delicious blend of peanuts, caramel, and salt clustered together. Lots of peanuts add that popular crunch, the caramel and nougat make it chewy, and the salt balances the sweet. A filling candybar, and by far the company's best seller.

A MEMBER OF THE JUNK FOOD BOOK HALL OF FAME.

PRODUCT	**PEANUT BUTTER** *with no jelly*
MANUFACTURER	Peter Paul
INGREDIENTS	Peanut butter, milk chocolate (sugar, cocoa butter, chocolate, milk, emulsifier, and vanillin), sugar, dextrose, crisped rice, whey powder, and salt.
SUGAR QUOTIENT	High
DENTAL CHECKUP	Tooth rotter
OIL QUOTIENT	High
NUTRIENT LEVEL	Empty calories
CALORIE COUNT	153/oz.

Peter Paul boasts that their candy is "indescribably delicious." This bar is. Milk chocolate covers a peanut butter bar, with crisped rice added for consistency. Happily, the first ingredient is peanut butter; the obligatory sugar and dextrose follow. The solid p.b. flavor mixes well with chocolate. Despite the gritty texture and noticeable but not objectionable aftertaste, it is one of the best peanut butter candy bars now available. Two pieces per package.

PRODUCT	**PEANUT BUTTER OOMPAS (WILLY WONKA'S)**
MANUFACTURER	**Concorde Confections**
INGREDIENTS	**Sugar, vegetable oil, peanut butter, non-fat dry milk, malto-dextrin, cocoa processed with alkalin, artificial coloring, dextrin, salt, lecithin, artificial flavor, hydroxypropyl cellulose, carnauba wax, BHA and propyl gallate, and citric acid.**
SUGAR QUOTIENT	**High**
DENTAL CHECKUP	**Tooth rotter**
OIL QUOTIENT	**High**
NUTRIENT LEVEL	**Empty calories**
CALORIE COUNT	**140/oz.**

A gross imitation of M&Ms, this has peanut butter rather than real peanuts. These are obnoxiously sweetened dayglo-colored, mothball-size clumps. Six of the ingredients are chemicals, half of them preservatives, but there's not much to preserve. Willy Wonka wouldn't have made—or wanted—it this way.

PRODUCT	**POM-POMS**
MANUFACTURER	**Nabisco Confections**
INGREDIENTS	**Sugar, corn syrup, hydrogenated vegetable oil, concentrated non-fat and whole milk, invert sugar, cocoa, artificial flavor, confectioners glaze, salt, sorbitan monostearate, tapioca dextrin, and vegetable lecithin.**

SUGAR QUOTIENT	High
DENTAL CHECKUP	Tooth rotter
OIL QUOTIENT	High
NUTRIENT LEVEL	Empty calories
CALORIE COUNT	172/dozen

Like Milk Duds, these are caramel balls covered with a chocolate-flavored glaze. Even though there are few additives, both the chocolate and the caramel taste chemical. There are fourteen pieces or so in each 15-cent box, guaranteed to leave remnants on your teeth. You'd better have strong molars—you'll have to fight this candy all the way.

===

PRODUCT	**POWERHOUSE**
MANUFACTURER	Peter Paul
INGREDIENTS	Sugar, corn syrup, hydrogenated vegetable oil, peanuts, non-fat dry milk, whey powder, cocoa powder, defatted soy, chocolate, salt, glycerol monostearate, sorbitol, lecithin, artificial flavor, and sodium bicarbonate.
SUGAR QUOTIENT	High
DENTAL CHECKUP	Tooth rotter
OIL QUOTIENT	High
NUTRIENT LEVEL	Empty calories
CALORIE COUNT	126/oz.

A poor man's version of Oh! Henry!, the label claims this is fudge candy. Fudge? I didn't taste any. Nor do I know what that gooey white stuff is. Pretty boring and not what one expects from Peter Paul.

This candy bar does not live up to the promise of its name.

PRODUCT	**RAISINETS**
MANUFACTURER	**Ward Johnston**
INGREDIENTS	**Raisins, milk chocolate (sugar, whole milk, cocoa butter, and chocolate), sugar, soya lecithin, vanillin, salt, tapioca dextrin, and resinous glaze.**
SUGAR QUOTIENT	**High**
DENTAL CHECKUP	**Tooth rotter**
OIL QUOTIENT	**High**
NUTRIENT LEVEL	**Minimum—some fortification present.**
CALORIE COUNT	**100/ounce**

Mel Brooks loves these, proclaiming his passion in Blazing Saddles. You get the taste of raisins, and milk chocolate; two flavors blended into a third. Because of the high cost of raisins, you get just a small mouthful in each candy counter box. Despite funnyman Brooks' endorsement of this old standby, it seems overpriced. For incurable raisin hounds only.

PRODUCT	**RALLY**
MANUFACTURER	**Hershey Foods**
INGREDIENTS	**Sugar, peanuts, corn syrup, cocoa butter, milk, chocolate, invert sugar, vegetable oil, sorbitol, salt, vanillin and other artificial flavors, soya lecithin, and sodium bicarbonate.**
SUGAR QUOTIENT	**High**
DENTAL CHECKUP	**Tooth rotter**
OIL QUOTIENT	**High**
NUTRIENT LEVEL	**Empty calories**
CALORIE COUNT	**260/1.8 oz.**

The label may boast "brown sugar" but the ingredient panel doesn't. The quality of this chocolate-covered nutroll seems excellent. The salt and peanuts make the taste properly sweet, and the middle has an authentic dairy taste. A fine piece of junk food.

=======

PRODUCT	**RED HOTS**
MANUFACTURER	**Ferrara Pan Candy**
INGREDIENTS	**Sugar, corn syrup, dextrose, corn starch, gum arabic, carnauba wax, artificial flavors, and U.S. certified colors**
SUGAR QUOTIENT	**High**
DENTAL CHECKUP	**Tooth rotter**
OIL QUOTIENT	**None**
NUTRIENT LEVEL	**Empty calories**
CALORIE COUNT	**106/oz.**

As we grow our tastes change—and so, it seems, does candy. Red Hots used to burn my tongue out—they were that hot. And that's why kids liked them. Today these little red candy imperials seem tame, with the bark of a basenji dog. The cinnamon flavor is, as with all candy cinnamon, artificially induced. The packaging gives one an image of fireballs and bombs in the night. Actually Red Hots as they are now wouldn't be hot if you ate them in a pizza oven.

=======

PRODUCT	**REED'S (Candies and Mints)**
MANUFACTURER	**Reed**
INGREDIENTS	**Sugar, corn syrup, and artificial flavor and color.**
SUGAR QUOTIENT	**High**
DENTAL CHECKUP	**Tooth rotter**
OIL QUOTIENT	**None**
NUTRIENT LEVEL	**Empty calories**
CALORIE COUNT	**Unavailable**

These individually wrapped cinnamon, spearmint, butterscotch, peppermint, root beer, and wintergreen candies have been around for ages. The cinnamon is hot—almost burning your mouth. The mint flavors seem to have endless staying power. The butterscotch and root beer are tasty. Delicious hard candies, not too sweet, shaped like a filled-in life preserver. Just right.

=======

PRODUCT	**REESE PEANUT BUTTER CUPS**
MANUFACTURER	Hershey Foods
INGREDIENTS	Sugar, peanuts, cocoa butter, milk, chocolate, dextrose, salt, and soya lecithin.
SUGAR QUOTIENT	High
DENTAL CHECKUP	Tooth rotter
OIL QUOTIENT	High
NUTRIENT LEVEL	Minimal—some fortification present.
CALORIE COUNT	135 per cup

This is the most popular candybar in America—our Number One Bestseller. It combines our passion for chocolate with our love of peanut butter. Each cupcake-shaped candy has a thick layer of chocolate surrounding a center of peanut butter. The chocolate comes across too sweet; the peanut butter too salty, gritty, and oily. Which goes to show you there is just no accounting for taste.

=======

PRODUCT	**ROCKY ROAD**
MANUFACTURER	Annabelle Candy
INGREDIENTS	Milk chocolate, sugar, corn syrup, hydrogenated vegetable oil, cashews, whey powder, sorbitol, malted milk gelatin, cocoa, artificial flavoring, glycerine, salt, sodium benzoate, lecithin, and vanillin.
SUGAR QUOTIENT	High
DENTAL CHECKUP	Tooth rotter
OIL QUOTIENT	High
NUTRIENT LEVEL	Empty calories
CALORIE COUNT	Not available

The name Rocky Road, whether for candy or ice cream, usually indicates nuts and marshmallow in chocolate. Here cashews, instead of the more common peanut, are embedded in lots of Pollyanna-sweet marshmallow. All this is covered in milk chocolate which runs through the middle of the marshmallow as well.

PRODUCT	**ROLO**
MANUFACTURER	**Hershey Foods**
INGREDIENTS	**Sugar, glucose, syrup, invert sugar, cocoa butter, milk, chocolate, vegetable fat, non-fat dry milk, butter, salt, soya lecithin, and vanillin.**
SUGAR QUOTIENT	**High**
DENTAL CHECKUP	**Tooth rotter**
OIL QUOTIENT	**High**
NUTRIENT LEVEL	**Empty calories**
CALORIE COUNT	**Not available**

Made in England where toffee caramel production is an art, this Hershey import is really chocolate-flavored sugar. If you like caramel *and* chocolate, there are many better than this. For 20 cents you get a handful of bite-size chocolate covered caramels. The British like their candy supersweet which may be the reason these are so dreadfully sugary. Did Hershey really have to import them?

PRODUCT	**SCREAMING YELLOW ZONKERS**
MANUFACTURER	**Ovaltine Products**
INGREDIENTS	**Sugar, corn syrup, popcorn, hydrogenated vegetable oil, margarine, salt, artificial flavor, artificial color, and TBHQ to preserve freshness.**
SUGAR QUOTIENT	**High**
DENTAL CHECKUP	**Tooth rotter**
OIL QUOTIENT	**High**
NUTRIENT LEVEL	**Empty calories**
CALORIE COUNT	**121/oz.**

The name, the product, the taste and the slick packaging exude corporate venality at its height. An imitation of *Cracker Jack*, aimed at the kiddie litter set. Touted as a "cripsy light sweet glazed popcorn snack," SYZ relies on fake flavors and colors to produce an inferior, soggy-tasting, candied popcorn. Even in the world of junk food, where tolerance of manufacturers' chemical follies is profuse, this is an insult. Furthermore, the price is out of sight. Instead of crispy, hardened kernels of corn like those in *Cracker Jack*, we get cotton candy light ghosts of oversized popcorn. The texture is disconcertingly chewy.

PRODUCT	**SEVEN UP**
MANUFACTURER	**Pearson Candy Co.**
INGREDIENTS	**Chocolate, sugar, corn syrup, hydrogenated vegetable oil, whey solids, sodium caseinate, coconut, salt, anhydrous milk fat, egg albumen, soya protein, invertase, soya lecithin, cream of tartar, natural and artificial flavor, and artificial colors.**
SUGAR QUOTIENT	**High**
DENTAL CHECKUP	**Tooth rotter**
OIL QUOTIENT	**High**
NUTRIENT LEVEL	**Empty calories**
CALORIE COUNT	**1.5/oz.**

Like a sampler box of candies in just one bar, Seven Up is divided into seven compartments, all covered in chocolate. Each section is a different flavor: mint, nougat, butterscotch, fudge, coconut, buttercream, and caramel. You can eat each one separately or in combo, for new and surprisingly satisfying flavors. Each section weighs about .17 ounces. (In case you're wondering, the soft drink company did license the use of its name.) Available in dark or milk chocolate, both properly sweetened.

══════════

PRODUCT	**SNICKERS**
MANUFACTURER	**M&M/Mars**
INGREDIENTS	**Milk chocolate (sugar, milk, cocoa butter, chocolate, emulsifier, and natural and artificial flavors), peanuts, corn syrup, sugar, sweetened condensed milk, butter, salt, egg whites, vegetable protein, artificial flavor, BHA, and BHT.**
SUGAR QUOTIENT	**High**
DENTAL CHECKUP	**Tooth rotter**
OIL QUOTIENT	**High**
NUTRIENT LEVEL	**Empty calories**
CALORIE COUNT	**130/oz.**

The best way to describe this totally delicious mixture of caramel, nougat, peanuts, and chocolate would be to call it a Milky Way with peanuts. Thank Frank Mars himself for this creation; he and his wife actually made this candy bar by hand in the early 1920s. Milky Way, Snickers, and Three Musketeers made his small candy company a $30 million business within a decade. This is junk food you eat joyfully, with a "who-cares-about-calories" attitude.

A MEMBER OF THE JUNK FOOD BOOK HALL OF FAME.

══════════

PRODUCT	**STARBURST FRUITCHEWS**
MANUFACTURER	**M&M/Mars**
INGREDIENTS	**Sugar, corn syrup, hydrogenated vegetable oil, citric acid, dextrin, food starch—modified, natural and artificial flavors, gelatin, artificial colors, and emulsifier.**
SUGAR QUOTIENT	**High**
DENTAL CHECKUP	**Tooth rotter**
OIL QUOTIENT	**High**
NUTRIENT LEVEL	**Empty calories**
CALORIE COUNT	**112/oz.**

Made in England for the Mars Company, these soft taffy-like pastel candies allegedly represent lemon, orange, lime, and strawberry flavors. Kids love 'em for their easily chewable texture. The flavors are somewhat on the sour side, and taste downright ersatz. Expect an aftertaste, too.

PRODUCT	**SUGAR BABIES/SUGAR DADDY**
MANUFACTURER	**Nabisco Confections**
INGREDIENTS	**Sugar, corn syrup, invert sugar, hydrogenated vegetable oil, nonfat milk, whey, calcium caseinate, gum arabic, salt, artificial flavors and colors, lecithin, confectioners' glaze.**
SUGAR QUOTIENT	**High**
DENTAL CHECKUP	**Tooth rotter**
OIL QUOTIENT	**High**
NUTRIENT LEVEL	**Empty calories**
CALORIE COUNT	**Babies—74/dozen**
	Daddy—133/ounce

Nabisco labels these "delicious milk caramel tidbits." You may be more apt to consider them bird droppings. Approximately two dozen of these small ununiform egg-shaped pellets are included in each yellow-and-red bag—more than enough to satisfy any yen for sugar you have during the next century. With a little effort the seemingly hard "tidbits" are chewable. The flavor is hardly caramel but more a flavored sugar and corn syrup. The first four ingredients (not to mention the ones that follow) are sugar and saturated fat—all junk. The same can be said for Sugar Daddy, the hardened all-day sucker on a stick which uses the same formula without the softening agents of Babies. Because *its* high sugar content stays in the mouth for a long period, it can be considered a number one enemy of the teeth.

PRODUCT	**SUPER SKRUNCH (WILLY WONKA'S PEANUT BUTTER)**
MANUFACTURER	Concorde Confections
INGREDIENTS	Sugar, vegetable oil, crisp rice, peanut butter, dextrose, whey, cocoa, salt, lecithin, artificial flavor and color, and BHT.
SUGAR QUOTIENT	High
DENTAL CHECKUP	Tooth rotter
OIL QUOTIENT	High
NUTRIENT LEVEL	Empty calories
CALORIE COUNT	215/1.5 OZ.

Aerated peanut butter shot with crisped rice, all covered in chocolate, a Reese cup cum Nestle's Crunch. Although aeration reduces the sweetness to an acceptable level, it does take some of the flavor away (air was never very tasty). The texture has an oily quality, as can be expected with any peanut butter candy.

PRODUCT	**SWEETARTS**
MANUFACTURER	Sunline Brands
INGREDIENTS	Dextrose, malto-dextrin, malic acid, magnesium stearate, and artificial flavors and colors.
SUGAR QUOTIENT	High
OIL QUOTIENT	None
DENTAL CHECKUP	Tooth rotter
NUTRIENT LEVEL	Empty calories
CALORIE COUNT	Not available

If the ingredient list was not right in front of me, I'd be sure this was pure alum. These button-sized tablets wash your mouth with the tartest flavor in candy-dom. Guaranteed to make you blink and wink your eyes and moan, this is a deliciously masochistic, tangy candy. Three dozen per pencil-long roll, they come in four flavors. But as these are so tart, don't try to discern each flavor. And look! No refined sugar—just dextrose. A unique candy.

=====

PRODUCT	**SWITZER LICORICE**
MANUFACTURER	**Switzer Candy (Beatrice Foods)**
INGREDIENTS	**Water, flour, sugar, corn syrup, molasses, licorice mass, burnt coloring, salt, and sodium propionate.**
SUGAR QUOTIENT	**High**
DENTAL CHECKUP	**Tooth rotter**
OIL QUOTIENT	**None**
NUTRIENT LEVEL	**Empty calories**
CALORIE COUNT	**Black 63/ounce**
	Strawberry 83/ounce

"Pasty" is a good word to describe the consistency of the water-and-flour mix in this strip of black licorice. Among junk food addicts, Licorice freaks are legion, but this isn't the licorice they are freaking out over. Switzer is a major producer of American licorice candy, but because licorice is only the sixth ingredient in their licorice bar, they aren't makers of *quality* licorice.

=====

PRODUCT	**THREE MUSKETEERS**
MANUFACTURER	**M&M/Mars**
INGREDIENTS	**Milk chocolate (sugar, milk, cocoa butter, chocolate, emulsifiers, natural and artificial flavors), sugar, corn syrup, hydrogenated vegetable oil, cocoa, salt, egg whites, vegetable protein, and artificial flavor.**
SUGAR QUOTIENT	**High**
DENTAL CHECKUP	**Tooth rotter**
OIL QUOTIENT	**High**
NUTRIENT LEVEL	**Empty calories**
CALORIE COUNT	**120/oz.**

Why does this chocolate-covered nougat bar, a favorite of young and old, taste great? Three Musketeers is air-bloated, mocha-colored nougat, covered with sweet chocolate. The aeration makes the bar *look* larger than others, but it really isn't. And when you think about it, TM is a plain jane candy. Yet since the sales are so high, Mars must be doing something right.

PRODUCT	**TOOTSIE ROLLS**
MANUFACTURER	Tootsie Roll Industries
INGREDIENTS	Sugar, corn syrup, condensed skim milk, vegetable oil, cocoa, invert sugar, whey powder, salt, vegetable lecithin, natural and artificial flavors, and artificial color.
SUGAR QUOTIENT	High
DENTAL CHECKUP	Tooth rotter
OIL QUOTIENT	High
NUTRIENT LEVEL	Empty calories
CALORIE COUNT	112/oz. Flavors: 117/oz.

Austrian candy manufacturer Leo Hershfield named this long cylindrical roll of chocolate-flavored chewy taffy for his girl friend, Tootsie. An appealing name and a fun candy for generations. Both kids and adults love the soft texture and cocoa-ish flavor, but when you analyze this candy, you find there's not much to it. Tootsie Rolls look like solidified brownie batter, too bad they don't taste that way. They have a weak flavor and an oily blandness. The texture is what sells this candy, and why not? Tootsie Rolls do it best.

PRODUCT	**TOOTSIE ROLLS POP DROPS/TOOTSIE ROLL POPS**
MANUFACTURER	Tootsie Roll Industries
INGREDIENTS	Sugar, corn syrup, vegetable oil, cocoa, condensed skim milk, whey powder, citric acid, salt, vegetable lecithin, natural and artificial flavors, and artificial colors. (Caramel pops also contain partially saturated soy or coconut oil)

SUGAR QUOTIENT	High
DENTAL CHECKUP	Tooth rotter
OIL QUOTIENT	High
NUTRIENT LEVEL	Empty calories
CALORIE COUNT	111/oz.

At the turn of the century George Smith, a humble but enterprising employee of a small candy company, put candy on a stick so people could take it out of their mouth for a rest. He called his invention the Lolly Pop. Tootsie Roll took the lolly pop one step further when they put their famous tootsie roll candy in the middle. The ordinary hard candy outside is transformed by the chocolatey Tootsie in the middle. Flavors include cherry, grape, lemon, chocolate, caramel, raspberry.

========

PRODUCT	**TWIZZLER**
MANUFACTURER	**Y & S Candies**
INGREDIENTS	**Molasses, flour, corn syrup, sugar, starch, licorice extract, vegetable shortening, glycerine, salt, artificial color, lecithin, natural flavor, mono- and diglycerides, and potassium sorbate.**
SUGAR QUOTIENT	**High**
DENTAL CHECKUP	**Tooth rotter**
OIL QUOTIENT	**Moderate**
NUTRIENT LEVEL	**Empty calories**
CALORIE COUNT	**100/OZ.**

Not unlike tough, resilient telephone cable, Twizzlers are strips of midnight black, licorice-flavored, rope-shaped candy. They don't have enough licorice taste to earn a high rating. As licorice extract is only the sixth ingredient, this is flavored, not real, licorice candy.

========

PRODUCT	**WAYNE BUN**
MANUFACTURER	**Wayne Candies (Planters/Curtiss)**
INGREDIENTS	**Sugar, peanuts, corn syrup, hydrogenated vegetable oil, non-fat milk solids, chocolate, whole milk solids, dairy whey, cocoa, salt, soy lecithin, and artificial flavor.**
SUGAR QUOTIENT	**High**
DENTAL CHECKUP	**Tooth rotter**
OIL QUOTIENT	**High**
NUTRIENT LEVEL	**Empty calories**
CALORIE COUNT	**148/OZ.**

Here is yet another oversweetened goo-oozer: a cupcake-shaped, chocolate-covered peanuty "bun." This may indeed be a step up from similar candies, but a step up from the pits won't get you out of the basement. C'mon, guys, this thing is dreadful! And what an aftertaste! You feel like an entire year's output of refined sugar is in your mouth.

PRODUCT	**WHITMAN'S SAMPLER: CHOCOLATES & CONFECTIONS**
MANUFACTURER	**Whitman's Chocolates (Pet Inc.)**
INGREDIENTS	**Sugar, milk chocolate and sweet chocolate with emulsifier and artificial flavoring, corn syrup, sweetened condensed skim milk, hardened vegetable fats, desiccated coconut, brazils, cashews, almonds, cherries, malted milk powder, dairy butter, powdered skim milk, cocoa, orange peel, peanut butter, cocoa butter, invert sugar, pecans, salt, pineapple, whole milk powder, bitter chocolate, raisins, oat flour, invertase, almond paste with potassium sorbate and polysorbate 80, peanuts, pectin, dried egg whites, citric acid, wheat flour, molasses, gelatin, corn syrup solids, gum arabic, soya lecithin, benzoate of soda, BHA, artificial flavors, natural flavors, and artificial colors.**
SUGAR QUOTIENT	**High**
DENTAL CHECKUP	**Tooth rotter**
OIL QUOTIENT	**High**
NUTRIENT LEVEL	**Empty calories**

A pound box of wonderful chocolates. An elaborate chart reveals the location of each filling so you don't have to poke your finger in the candy. You'll find nuts, fudge centers, caramels, chews, creams, coconuts, fruits and more in a festive box. (About $3.50 per box.)

PRODUCT	**WHOPPERS**
MANUFACTURER	**Leaf Confections**
INGREDIENTS	**Sugar, corn syrup, vegetable shortening, whey powder,**

malted milk, cocoa powder, soy lecithin, artificial flavor, salt, vegetable gum, and confectioners glaze.

SUGAR QUOTIENT	High
DENTAL CHECKUP	Tooth rotter
OIL QUOTIENT	High
NUTRIENT LEVEL	Empty calories
CALORIE COUNT	Ten = 35

Everyone seems to love these chocolate-covered candies with their "genuine malted milk" flavor. Gumball-sized, crunchy, and loaded with flavor, they brim with sugar. Those who can stand the sweetness must also cope with a saturation problem. Whoppers come in large packages just like milk containers, adding to the mystique of these bite-size morsels. Oversweet but fun!

PRODUCT	**ZERO**
MANUFACTURER	Hollywood Brands
INGREDIENTS	Sugar, corn syrup, hydrogenated vegetable oil, water, soya, non-fat dry milk, whey solids, almonds, cocoa, skim milk solids, malted milk, salt, egg white solids, lecithin, vegetable protein, artificial flavor, and mono- and diglycerides.
SUGAR QUOTIENT	High
DENTAL CHECKUP	Tooth rotter
OIL QUOTIENT	High
NUTRIENT LEVEL	Empty calories
CALORIE COUNT	Not available

Hollywood has covered this oblong nougat, caramel and almond bar with a white sugar-colored icing so that it looks like a block of Ivory Soap. The almonds and paper thin line of caramel are hard to find in the nougat. The sugar crystallization in either the icing or the filling tastes decidedly sweet and leaves a faint grittiness in your mouth. On a scale of one to ten, the name might well represent the score of this bar.

CAKES, PIES, PUDDINGS, AND ICE CREAM

BATTER UP! – A WORD OR TWO ABOUT CAKE MIXES

Hardly a day goes by without the introduction of yet another convenient, easy-to-make cake mix. Since the original basic yellow mix in a box, the manufacturers have developed a slew of fanciful flavors and teasing textures to woo our sweet tooth. The mixes leave out some basic ingredients which you then add (eggs, milk, nuts, etc.). I'm just a junk food addict, not the Pillsbury Dough-boy, so I declined to make any of these cakes. I did however check out those mixes which require little preparation and only the addition of water to the mix.

Most noteworthy of this bunch are the Duncan Hines (Procter & Gamble) Moist 'N' Easy Cakes offered in a variety of flavors (Apple Raisin, Chocolate Nut, Banana, etc.). P&G has done everything—you even use the same pan to mix the water and the powder, to bake the cake, and to serve. The Chocolate

Nut was moist and quite chocolatey, if a bit phoney, and of a fudge brownie consistency. The Apple Raisin was a disaster. It tasted ersatz (not apple-like at all), smelled even worse, and was so wet it stuck both to the pan and to my fingers when I was eating it.

Betty Crocker's (General Mills) Stir 'N' Frost comes complete with frosting and its own pan, and while not phony in its flavor, was an unexceptional institutional-type cake. Quaker Oats Instant Oatmeal Cookie Mix and Nestlé's Toll House Chocolate Chip Cookie Mix were both disappointments. The cookies are more cake-like than crispy or chewy. This is no doubt due to additives such as cellulose gum which are required to compensate for the instant, dehydrated, just-add-water nature of the product and the anticipation of a long shelf life. Betty Crocker's Snackin' Cake is a close duplicate of the Duncan Hines Moist 'N' Easy mixes. As with DH, BC's chocolate flavor is the best; the others, to be diplomatic, are not the cake you'd serve at a wedding. Or to a close friend. Pillsbury's Refrigerated Cookie Doughs are considerably better for baking and tasting, yet seem inordinately expensive (about $1). Both the chocolate chip and the sugar cookies tasted like fresh, home baked cookies and had a pleasing consistency.

The average price for a regular cake mix (plus the additionally required ingredients) is $1.50 to $2.00. This is considerably less than you'd pay for a cake in a local bake shop, or for one you prepared from scratch.

SARA LEE

Sara Lee makes dozens of different types of cakes, pies, and pastries, each one better than the next. Only the best and freshest dairy ingredients go into Sara Lee products and you can taste the difference immediately. Because I am partial to excellence my ratings of Sara Lee cakes and pies are invariably high. Some people, though, have questioned whether Sara Lee belongs in a book of "junk food" at all.

Well, if a Cheese Cake or an Apple Crunch Roll is not junk food, then what is it? A junk food may be better made, using highest quality ingredients, but it is still *bas cuisine*. We are so inured to what other manufacturers serve and call "quality" that when as fine a class of products as Sara Lee's comes along, we forget what these confections basically are. Similarly, a cake baked from scratch in grandma's oven is, nevertheless, loaded down in sugar and fat. It is still junk.

Sara Lee is high class stuff. Just the name "Sara Lee" conjures up images of rich desserts, wide smiles and more salivation than a Pavlov dog.

SUGAR QUOTIENT—High for all Sara Lee products.

DENTAL CHECKUP—Tooth rotter, except where noted.

NUTRIENT LEVEL—Minimal—some fortification present.

OIL QUOTIENT—High for all Sara Lee cakes.

PRODUCT	**APPLE CRUNCH ROLLS**
MANUFACTURER	**Kitchens of Sara Lee**
INGREDIENTS	**Enriched flour, sugar, vegetable shortening, water, dried apples, corn syrup, fresh whole eggs, skim milk, modified food starch, mono- and diglycerides, yeast, salt, cinnamon, lemon juice, vegetable gum, milk protein, citric acid, and baking soda.**
CALORIE COUNT	**105 per roll**

The pastry dough is light and delicate, with a crunchy texture. Large portions of apples are interspersed throughout. Sweet, but not cloying as many apple cakes can be, Crunch Rolls are a nice way to start the day. There is no butter in this product, but eggs and vegetable shortening make this a typically rich Sara Lee cake.

PRODUCT	**APPLE PIE**
MANUFACTURER	**Kitchens of Sara Lee**
INGREDIENTS	Apples, enriched flour, vegetable shortening, sugar, corn syrup, water, butter, modified food starch, salt, lemon juice, non-fat dry milk, dextrose, dried apples, cinnamon, baking soda, and citric acid.
CALORIE COUNT	**103 per ⅙ pie**

In direct competition with Mrs. Smith's, the leader in the pie world, Sara Lee offers a delicious, delicately seasoned apple pie. The crust is as light and flaky as you would want if you made it yourself. As with any frozen pie, bake for 30 to 60 minutes and, although the instructions are to let it cool, it really should be served warm. Leftovers are slightly gummy and hardened. A good dessert.

PRODUCT	**BANANA NUT POUND CAKE**
MANUFACTURER	**Kitchens of Sara Lee**
INGREDIENTS	Bananas, sugar, enriched flour, fresh whole eggs, butter, walnuts, mono- and diglycerides, baking powder, non-fat dry milk, salt, and baking soda.
CALORIE COUNT	**104 per ¹⁄₁₀ cake**

A rich, moist, flavorful cake bountiful in its supply of banana and walnuts. The bananas do make this a bit too sweet but that's in the nature of the beast.

PRODUCT **BROWNIES**
MANUFACTURER **Kitchens of Sara Lee**
INGREDIENTS Sugar, corn syrup, enriched flour, butter, chocolate, fresh whole eggs, walnuts, water, corn starch, salt, vanilla, lecithin, gelatin, vegetable gum, and baking soda.
CALORIE COUNT **195** per ⅛ cake

Sara Lee can't make brownies. The icing is as thick as latex house paint, and prevents us from tasting the brownie below. That may be intentional. Without the icing the cake isn't as chewy or fudgey as those made from boxed mixes. Well, nobody's perfect.

PRODUCT **BUTTER STREUSEL COFFEE CAKE**
MANUFACTURER **Kitchens of Sara Lee**
INGREDIENTS Enriched flour, butter, sugar, fresh whole eggs, corn syrup, fresh whole milk, yeast, mono- and diglycerides, salt, vanilla, corn starch, baking powder, and honey
CALORIE COUNT **160** per ⅛ cake

Not even local bakeries can produce a coffee cake as delicious as this one. A light and delicate pastry which melts in your mouth is blended with sugar, honey, and dynamite crumbbun chewies on top in a streusel swirl. Rich and satisfying, it may be too sweet for some. But the way it sells, many folks obviously think it's just right.

PRODUCT **SARA LEE'S ORIGINAL CHEESE CAKE**
MANUFACTURER **Kitchens of Sara Lee**
INGREDIENTS Cream cheese, sugar, bakers' cheese, sour cream, whole eggs,

enriched flour, vegetable shortening, fresh whole milk, non-fat dry milk, graham flour, corn syrup, water, modified food starch, vegetable gum, honey, salt, vanilla, baking powder, gelatin, baking soda, cinnamon, and citric acid.

CALORIE COUNT   **240** per ⅙ cake

A BEST BUY. This is the *pièce de résistance* of the junk food world. It is a nonpareil. Food of the Gods. Probably the best reason to gain weight. On a scale of ten, it rates an eleven. Into a seven-inch aluminum pie shell go a specially prepared graham cracker and lemon oil crust, then a velvety smooth cheese-based filling. This is topped with a sour cream icing. A new religion could be dedicated to the goddess who created this sublime food. (Strawberry Cheese Cake is the same cake with a strawberry topping. It is oversweet and the red fruit topping in gooey, blanketing the masterful flavor of the cheese cake.)

A MEMBER OF THE JUNK FOOD BOOK HALL OF FAME.

========

PRODUCT	**CAKE CART DESSERTS: BLACK FOREST CAKE**
MANUFACTURER	**Kitchens of Sara Lee**
INGREDIENTS	**Cherries, sugar, modified whey, corn syrup, enriched flour, fresh whole milk, fresh whole eggs, vegetable shortening, heavy whipping cream, butter, chocolate, cocoa, mono- and diglycerides, baking powder, modified food starch, vegetable gum, vanilla, salt, gelatin, ascorbic acid, skim milk, lecithin, and vegetable color.**
CALORIE COUNT	**135 per ⅛ cake**

Sara Lee services many restaurants in the U.S. with its well-made baked goods. It "Cake Cart Dessert" line, from which this comes, is now sold directly to the consumer at about $2.00 a cake (versus a buck or more a *slice* in the eateries). Black Forest Cake is fabulously fattening with two buttery layers of chocolate cake smothered in real velvety whipping cream and a horde of tart cherries and then decorated with a "lacy drizzle of chocolate." Other varieties include Strawberry Shortcake, Mandarin Orange, et al.

========

PRODUCT	**DEVIL'S FOOD CAKE WITH BUTTER CREAM FROSTING**
MANUFACTURER	**Kitchens of Sara Lee**
INGREDIENTS	**Sugar, butter, enriched flour, fresh whole milk, fresh whole eggs, corn syrup, sour cream, mono- and diglycerides, skim milk, cocoa, vegetable shortening, chocolate, baking powder, corn starch, vanilla, U.S. certified food color, citric acid, and spices.**
CALORIE COUNT	**189 per ⅛ cake**

Devil's Food is noted for its slightly reddish color, the result of food colorings added to the deep brown chocolate. This is a cake that's easy to O.D. on. As yummy as it is, it is an atom-bomb blast of sugar. Spongy and damp in texture, it is enhanced with a thick butter cream frosting. I think I broke out within half an hour after eating a quarter of the 14-ounce cake but every zit was worth it.

—————————————

PRODUCT	**FRUIT 'N' DANISH**
MANUFACTURER	**Kitchens of Sara Lee**
INGREDIENTS	**Apples, enriched flour, butter, sugar, fresh whole milk, fresh whole eggs, corn syrup, yeast, mono- and diglycerides, water, modified food starch, salt, lemon juice, cinnamon, citric acid, vegetable gum, vanilla, gelatin, and honey.**
CALORIE COUNT	**146 per ⅛ cake**

Similar to Apple Crunch Rolls, this is sweeter and comes in an oblong rectangular strip. The plentiful apples are layered on top of a danish pastry dough similar to coffee cake. Tastes light and just-baked. The added butter improves the overall taste. If you like apples, you'll like Fruit 'N' Danish.

—————————————

PRODUCT	**POUND CAKE**
MANUFACTURER	**Kitchens of Sara Lee**
INGREDIENTS	**Fresh whole eggs, enriched flour, sugar, butter, corn syrup, fresh whole milk, mono- and diglycerides, vanilla, salt, and baking powder.**
SUGAR QUOTIENT	**High**
DENTAL CHECKUP	**Average**
OIL QUOTIENT	**High**
NUTRIENT LEVEL	**Minimal**
CALORIE COUNT	**126 per ¹⁄₁₀ cake**

True to its name, this is a heavy, rich cake. Even when eaten plain, it makes a satisfying cake with coffee or tea or an uncomplicated dessert. Adding strawberries and cream is probably one of the best ways to eat it. Now this delicious cake is available in a chocolate blend which will bliss you out.

PRODUCT	**AMERICANA RICE PUDDING**
MANUFACTURER	**General Foods**
INGREDIENTS	Sugar, enriched rice, cornstarch, salt, calcium, carrageenan, polysorbate **6o**, artificial and natural flavor, and artificial color.
SUGAR QUOTIENT	**High**
DENTAL CHECKUP	**Tooth rotter**
OIL QUOTIENT	**Moderate**
NUTRIENT LEVEL	**Empty calories**
CALORIE COUNT	**1oo/4** ounces; **18o**/with milk

For rice pudding fans who don't want to endure the two-hour process of preparing the rice and then baking the pudding, General Foods has come to the rescue with this swell-tasting, convenient rice pudding. Simply add milk and in a short time you have a "just-like-home-made" thick and creamy dessert. Count on 1oo calories to a portion (one-half cup) without milk; 8o more with milk. Most of the calories come from the sugar content. The price is $1.6o a pound for rice and sugar; so you could prepare this dessert from scratch for much less money. You are paying for the convenience. Drawback: if you store this in the refrigerator for over a day, the pudding starts to separate and gets runny. (Tapioca pudding also available.)

PRODUCT	**COOL WHIP** (Non-Dairy Whipped Topping)
MANUFACTURER	**General Foods**
INGREDIENTS	Water, hydrogenated coconut and palm kernel oils, sugar, corn syrup solids, sodium caseinate, dextrose, polysorbate **6o**, natural and artificial flavors, sorbitan monostearate, carrageenan, guar gum, and artificial color.
SUGAR QUOTIENT	**High**
DENTAL CHECKUP	**Low**
OIL QUOTIENT	**High**

NUTRIENT LEVEL	**Empty calories**
CALORIE COUNT	**14/tablespoon**

At 14 calories per tablespoon and one gram each of fat and sugar (carbohydrate), Cool Whip seems innocuous enough. Basically used as a fake whipped cream topping for puddings, Jello, and other desserts, there are some junkies who eat CW as if it were a pudding itself. A light, modestly sweet taste enhancer, its consistency allows you to create swirls and shapes and provides "mouthfeel" to an otherwise vacuous substance. Cool Whip has all the proper attributes of a dependable substitute—it can be refrigerated for two weeks, frozen and refrozen, yet still will blend like the real thing. It even tastes good. However, it is more saturated in fats than real whipped cream.

PRODUCT	**DEVIL DOGS**
MANUFACTURER	**Drake's (Borden Foods)**
INGREDIENTS	**Flour, corn syrup, water, vegetable shortening, cane sugar dextrose, soya flour, non-fat dry milk, leavening, skim milk and whey protein, salt, dried whole eggs, rye flour, sorbitan monostearate, monoglycerides, polysorbate 60, whey powder, buttermilk powder, natural flavor, artificial flavors, sorbic acid (added in summer months), ferric orthophosphate, niacin, thiamine, and riboflavin.**
SUGAR QUOTIENT	**High**
DENTAL CHECKUP	**Tooth rotter**
OIL QUOTIENT	**High**
NUTRIENT LEVEL	**Empty calories**
CALORIE COUNT	**180 each**

Shaped like a hot dog in a bun with the bun cocoa flavored, the hot dog made of sugar creme filling, Devil Dogs are *de rigeur* for any true junk food fiend. I was practically weaned on them. Whenever I get a bittersweet nostalgic pang, I down one or two Devil Dogs to maintain the pleasant memories. Though DD's are sold only in the eastern half of the United States, other local commercial bakeries have their own versions of this perpetual lunch box favorite. Drake's still is the best despite all the recent cost shortcutting. Of dubious wholesomeness, Devil Dog is a 180 calorie depth-charge of fabulous junk food.

PRODUCT	**DING DONGS**
MANUFACTURER	Hostess (ITT Continental Baking)
INGREDIENTS	Sugar, shortening, water, enriched flour, corn sweetener, cocoa, eggs, whey leavening, skim milk, modified food starch, salt, sorbitan monostearate, polysorbate 60, mono- and diglycerides and lecithin, natural and artificial flavor, and sorbic acid.
SUGAR QUOTIENT	High
DENTAL CHECKUP	Tooth rotter
OIL QUOTIENT	High
NUTRIENT LEVEL	Empty calories
CALORIE COUNT	160 each

Similar in concept to a Devil Dog, Hostess Ding Dongs are round cakes covered with chocolate flavored icing. Inside the frosting is chocolate-flavored cake with a creme filling. The icing has a glaze and tastes notably sweeter than the frosting on Hostess creme-filled cupcakes, although it has a chocolatier taste. Not terrific, but not terrible either, Ding Dongs are acceptable junk food: if you come across one, eat it, but they're not worth going out of your way to find. I'd sure like to meet the turkey that named this creation. Ding Dongs, indeed!

PRODUCT	**DRAKE'S COFFEE CAKES**
MANUFACTURER	Drake's (Borden Foods)
INGREDIENTS	Flour, vegetable shortening, skim milk, brown sugar, sugar, dextrose, eggs, corn syrup, whey, soya flour, spices, salt, buttermilk, rye flour, leavening, egg whites, sodium propionate (added to retard spoilage), artificial color with vegetable colors, artificial flavors, ferric orthophosphate, niacin, natural flavor, thiamine, and riboflavin.
SUGAR QUOTIENT	High
DENTAL CHECKUP	Tooth rotter

OIL QUOTIENT	**High**
NUTRIENT LEVEL	**Empty calories**
CALORIE COUNT	**270/2¼ ounces**

Unless you consider the rising cost of sponges, this is a junk food rip-off. Drake's is rather proud of the vegetable shortening they use, listing it as a highlight on the label. But they've gone overboard here. Sure we want moist, fresh cake, but this tastes sopping wet. The sugar crumbs on top help dry the cake out somewhat. This is a trainer coffee cake for kids and junk food addicts who haven't yet graduated to Sara Lee.

PRODUCT	**HOSTESS FILLED CUPCAKES**
MANUFACTURER	**Hostess (ITT Continental Baking)**
INGREDIENTS	**Sugar, water, enriched flour, corn sweetener, shortening, cocoa, whey, leavening, skim milk, chocolate, corn starch, salt, modified food starch, mono- and diglycerides, gelatin, agar, artificial flavor, and sorbic acid.**
SUGAR QUOTIENT	**High**
DENTAL CHECKUP	**Tooth rotter**
OIL QUOTIENT	**High**
NUTRIENT LEVEL	**Empty calories**
CALORIE COUNT	**160 each**

Chocolate icing with a white swiggle, over chocolate flavored cake with a sugar creme filling—that's what Hostess Cupcakes are all about. Each weighs in at slightly over an ounce and a half, or about the size of an average candy bar. However it costs slightly less. The combination of rich devil's food with creme filling makes the cake sickeningly sweet. But not sweet enough to stop you from eating them. Found in virtually every grocery store, superette, and supermarket in the United States, Hostess Cupcakes are an American tradition. As the company's television ads say, "Hostess and Kids—they go together." The cupcakes are just the reverse of an acquired taste. You eventually lose your interest in them. Say, by the age of Clearasil.

PRODUCT	**HOSTESS FRUIT PIES**
MANUFACTURER	Hostess (ITT-Continental Baking)
INGREDIENTS	Apple: Apple, enriched flour, water, shortening, sugar, corn sweetener, modified food starch, salt, soy flour, skim milk, citric acid, calcium sulfate, calcium carbonate, spice, agar, mono- and diglycerides, natural and artificial flavor and color, sodium propionate, and sodium benzoate.
SUGAR QUOTIENT	High
DENTAL CHECKUP	Tooth rotter
OIL QUOTIENT	High
NUTRIENT LEVEL	Empty calories
CALORIE COUNT	Approximately **350** each

Shaped like a turnover or a pastry, Hostess mini fruit pies are surprisingly tasty. This quarter pound, self-enclosed slice of pie costs about 30 cents. The apple pie has a real apple flavor but the filling is basically small bits of apple rather

than large chunks. The sauce has a thick, gelatinous texture to it, filling the entire shell. There is apple flavor in each bite, but the crust is a disappointment. It is a cardboardy container for the fillings, and has a slick-and-thick cane sugar topping. When you consider how sweet the filling is, this is unnecessary. Other flavors worthy of attention: blueberry, lemon.

PRODUCT	**HUNT'S SNACK PACK PUDDINGS** (Chocolate and Chocolate Fudge Flavors)
MANUFACTURER	**Hunt-Wesson Foods**
INGREDIENTS	**Skim milk, water, sugar, hydrogenated vegetable oil, modified food starch, cocoa, salt, sodium stearoyl-2-lactylate, artificial flavors, BHA, and BHT. (In the Chocolate Fudge flavor water is the first ingredient, milk is second, and artificial colors are added.)**
SUGAR QUOTIENT	**High**
DENTAL CHECKUP	**Average**
OIL QUOTIENT	**High**
NUTRIENT LEVEL	**Empty calories**
CALORIE COUNT	**239 per can average**

These are creamy textured puddings packed in cute little 5-ounce tins. Moderately sweet and quite chocolatey in flavor, they leave behind a slight aftertaste which might be from the sodium stearoyl-2-lactylate or from the artificial flavors. Both chocolate puddings are made from cocoa, not real chocolate. However, the fudge variety is labeled "artificially flavored," although its only additional ingredient is artificial color and less skim milk. You figure it out. As it happens, the regular chocolate does taste richer and more authentic than the fudge. Both are as thick as Hunt's Tomato Paste—the one that doesn't fall off a spoon turned upside down.

PRODUCT	**JELLO**
MANUFACTURER	**General Foods**
INGREDIENTS	**Sugar, gelatin, adipic acid, disodium phosphate, fumaric acid, artificial color, and artificial flavor.**
SUGAR QUOTIENT	**High**
DENTAL CHECKUP	**Tooth rotter**
OIL QUOTIENT	**None**
NUTRIENT LEVEL	**Empty calories**
CALORIE COUNT	**320 per package**

The 160 calories per cup come from the mountains of sugar in this "light" dessert. Jello is basically Kool Aid (also from General Foods) with gelatin. The ads preach "There's always room for Jello." At 320 calories per package, who wants to *find* room? The strawberry flavor, like the many other flavors, has little resemblance to strawberries. We like Jello because it *is* light and buoyant, slithering easily down our gullet. Jello by itself is rather junky tasting—sticky kid's stuff—but when you add Cool Whip (also from General Foods) it becomes divine. The best flavors for eating plain are Mixed Fruit, Strawberry-Banana and Rapsberry.

PRODUCT	**JELLO PUDDINGS AND PIE FILLINGS**
MANUFACTURER	**General Foods**
INGREDIENTS	**Sugar, dextrose, cornstarch, cocoa processed with alkali, modified cornstarch, salt, calcium carrageenan, polysorbate 60, and artificial flavor.**
SUGAR QUOTIENT	**High**
DENTAL CHECKUP	**Average**
OIL QUOTIENT	**High**
NUTRIENT LEVEL	**Empty calories**
CALORIE COUNT	**90 per cup** **170 with milk**

The ingredients listed above are for the Chocolate Fudge flavor and a very chocolatey flavor it is. Before adding milk, there are 90 calories for each 8 ounces, all derived from the vast quantities of sugar in the mix. After preparing the pudding with milk there are almost double the calories (170) per cup. Is it worth it? If you enjoy pudding that is rich-tasting and velvety smooth it certainly is. General Foods dominates the national market with its Jello brand in numerous flavors. Because most of us do not have anything homemade to compare it to, we take it on its own merits, judged mainly by taste—and it tastes great. In the northeast, My-T-Fine, however, is a better brand (especially their Chocolate Nut flavor).

PRODUCT	**KELLOGG'S POP TARTS**
MANUFACTURER	**Kellogg**
INGREDIENTS	**Enriched wheat flour, vegetable shortening and oils, strawberry preserves, dextrose, sugar, corn syrup, whey, cracker-meal, apple preserves, corn cereal, gelatinized wheat starch, salt, tricalcium phosphate, baking powder, citric acid, baking soda, gelatin, natural flavoring, artificial coloring, vitamin A palmitate, iron, niacinamide, pyridoxine hydrochloride (B6), riboflavin (B2), thiamin hydrochloride (B1), and folic acid, with BHA and BHT.**
SUGAR QUOTIENT	**High**
DENTAL CHECKUP	**Tooth rotter**
OIL QUOTIENT	**High**
NUTRIENT LEVEL	**Minimum—some fortification present**
CALORIE COUNT	**210/each**

Each rather slender pop tart is topped with a dab of white sugar icing and decorated with Christmasy sprinkles. The tart is filled with "real preserves." More dessert than breakfast, heat these to get the intended flavor at its best (sweet but bland). Three foil packages to a box, two tarts to a pack, 210 calories (gasp!) per tart. Fortification equals 10 percent of daily recommended needs except for protein (4 percent) and vitamin C (none).

PRODUCT	**MORTON PASTRY SHOP MINI-PIES**
MANUFACTURER	**Morton Frozen Foods (ITT Continental Baking)**
INGREDIENTS	**Peach: peaches, corn syrup, water, food starch—modified, dextrose, salt, citric acid, and artificial color; Apple: apples, water, corn syrup, dextrose, food starch—modified, and seasoning (cinnamon, rye flour, gum arabic, malic acid, and natural and artificial flavors); Cherry: cherries, water, sugar, corn syrup, food starch—modified, citric acid, salt, dextrose, and artificial color. Crust: enriched flour, shortening, water, salt, and dextrose.**
SUGAR QUOTIENT	**High**
DENTAL CHECKUP	**Tooth rotter**
OIL QUOTIENT	**Moderate**
NUTRIENT LEVEL	**Empty calories**
CALORIE COUNT	**240 each average**

Each pie is loaded with large pieces of fruit. Forty-five minutes of baking yields a tart-sized pie with a barely acceptable pastry crust in an aluminum shell. Morton's Cherry (usually the sweetest and cheapest-tasting) is excellent, but their Apple (usually the best) is poorly flavored, with a faint scent of perfume. Morton's peach has the least seasoning; mercifully, they allow the peaches to provide the flavor.

PRODUCT	**MRS. SMITH'S APPLE PIE**
MANUFACTURER	**Mrs. Smith's Pie Co.**
INGREDIENTS	**Apples, water, flour, shortening, sugar, corn sugar, corn starch, salt, spice, and baking soda.**
SUGAR QUOTIENT	**High**
DENTAL CHECKUP	**Tooth rotter**
OIL QUOTIENT	**High**
NUTRIENT LEVEL	**Empty calories**
CALORIE COUNT	**295 per ⅙ pie portion, 340 (natural juice per ⅙ pie portion**

Mrs. Smith's probably makes the best prefrozen unbaked pies in America. All the pies are deep dish, and according to the company, "the flaky light crust contains 12 ounces of pure shortening for every 16 ounces of flour." The fillings are made with choice fruit and basic ingredients—there are no additives. What you get is wholesome, good ol' American pie. The apple variety is particularly well made and tastes as if it had just been made from scratch. The fruit is plentiful and subtly spiced. At prices just over a dollar mark for a 26-ounce pie, they are excellent value. Unless you *know* you can make it better, it doesn't seem worth the trouble to homebake a pie when Mrs. Smith will do all the dirty work. Beware, though: reheated leftovers are gummy.

PRODUCT	**PEPPERIDGE FARM (READY TO SERVE) LAYER CAKES**
MANUFACTURER	**Pepperidge Farm**
INGREDIENTS	Chocolate Fudge: Sugar, vegetable shortening, enriched flour, water, whole eggs, sugar syrups, cocoa, chocolate, non-fat dry milk, dextrose, salt, baking powder, emulsifiers, vanilla, modified food starch, gelatin, baking soda, modified milk protein.
SUGAR QUOTIENT	High
DENTAL CHECKUP	Tooth rotter
OIL QUOTIENT	High
NUTRIENT LEVEL	Empty calories
CALORIE COUNT	Not available

Available in about half a dozen flavors (Boston Cream, Lemon Coconut, Chocolate, etc.), I randomly tested their chocolate fudge cake. Chocolate iced chocolate cake can be exceedingly overbearing but P.F. has found a way to make its cake moist and light, while acceptably sweet for both adult and child. The icing is wet and smooth and wonderfully messy. The cake is chocolatey—more cocoa than fudge. All P.F. cakes are available by half-pound loaf size or by the pound square-shaped size. These cost less than if made from scratch or a mix.

PRODUCT	**SNOBALL CAKES**
MANUFACTURER	**Hostess (ITT-Continental Baking)**
INGREDIENTS	**Sugar, water, corn sweetener, enriched flour, coconut, shortening, cocoa, gelatin, leavening, mono- and diglycerides, polysorbate 6o, whey, salt, skim milk, modified foodstarch, artificial flavors and color, and sorbic acid.**
SUGAR QUOTIENT	**High**
DENTAL CHECKUP	**Tooth rotter**
OIL QUOTIENT	**High**
NUTRIENT LEVEL	**Empty calories**
CALORIE COUNT	**135 each**

Rubber doormats painted a pale mucilaginous pink, encapsulating a dark clump of chocolate-flavored cake pregnant with a dab of cotton-colored sugar creme. That's Snoball. It's supposed to be coconut on marshmallow frosting over a chocolate cupcake filled with sugar creme but it doesn't turn out quite that way. The cake is dry and the frosting is elastic. This is junk in the true sense of the word. It is an achievement of technological design that belongs in a science museum, certainly not in a stomach. Pass the Bromo.

PRODUCT	**STOUFFER'S LEMON POUND CAKE**
MANUFACTURER	**Stouffer Foods**
INGREDIENTS	**Flour, sugar, butter, egg white, egg yolks, water, margarine, corn syrup, emulsifier, sour-cream solids, baking powder, salt, vanilla powder, artificial lemon flavor, U.S. certified food coloring, lemon oil.**
SUGAR QUOTIENT	**High**
DENTAL CHECKUP	**Average**
OIL QUOTIENT	**High**
NUTRIENT LEVEL	**Empty calories**
CALORIE COUNT	**Not available**

Ostensibly Stouffer's wants to compete with Sara Lee. Realistically, it will never be equal, nor comparable. Stouffer's pinches pennies, while Sara Lee goes all out to insure that only the best ingredients are used in its products. For example, Stouffer's Lemon Pound Cake tastes oversweet and relies on artificial flavors and margarine instead of Sara Lee's all butter, all natural pound cake. Stouffer's cake has the consistency of a wet sponge. Sara Lee's is moist. Stouffer's still has a lot to learn. Its consumers don't, though. One lesson—one taste—is enough.

PRODUCT	**SUSIE Q'S CAKE**
MANUFACTURER	**Hostess (ITT Continental Baking)**
INGREDIENTS	**Sugar, water, enriched flour, shortening, corn sweetener, cocoa, modified food starch, leavening, whey, salt, skim milk, eggs, mono- and diglycerides, polysorbate 60, artificial flavor, and sorbic acid.**
SUGAR QUOTIENT	**High**
DENTAL CHECKUP	**Tooth rotter**
OIL QUOTIENT	**High**
NUTRIENT LEVEL	**Empty calories**
CALORIE COUNT	**230 each**

Another favorite from everybody's favorite corner conglomerate industrial baking factory, or, as ITT calls it, "the Hostess Bake Shoppe." A chocolate-flavored cake sandwich (two to a pack) with creme filling (whipped and apparently aerated), Susie Q's are not that different from the other chocolate-and-creme cakes Hostess grinds out. Water is the second largest ingredient (after sugar, of course) which may explain why the cake seems so wet. In this case, however, the wetness works well, enhancing the chocolatey flavor so that it *seems* rich and smooth. This is the same chocolate cake you find in other Hostess items, yet it seems to work better with the creme filling. Quiz Time: What does the Q stand for?

PRODUCT	**TASTYKAKE'S KRIMPETS**
MANUFACTURER	**TastyKake Inc.**
INGREDIENTS	**Sugar, enriched flour, skim milk, eggs, water, glucose, vegetable shortening, starches, butter, non-fat dry milk, leavening, salt, natural and artificial flavors, pectin, and spice.**
SUGAR QUOTIENT	**High**
DENTAL CHECKUP	**Tooth rotter**
OIL QUOTIENT	**High**
NUTRIENT LEVEL	**Empty calories**
CALORIE COUNT	**Not available**

Butterscotch flavor—and butter itself—pervades this TastyKake. However, just like the song "Smoke Gets in Your Eyes," here "Sugar Gets in Your Teeth," reducing the cake to an oversweet piece of kiddie litter. If you have sensitive teeth, beware! I don't know why this snack cake seems to have no more sugar than the others, seems sweeter, but it does. TastyKakes are found only in the Northeast but similar cakes are baked by other regional bakeries.

PRODUCT	**TWINKIES**
MANUFACTURER	Hostess (ITT-Continental Baking)
INGREDIENTS	Sugar, enriched flour, corn sweetener, water, shortening, eggs, leavening, whey, modified food starch, salt, skim milk, artificial color and flavor, and sorbic acid.
SUGAR QUOTIENT	High
DENTAL CHECKUP	Tooth rotter
OIL QUOTIENT	High
NUTRIENT LEVEL	Empty calories
CALORIE COUNT	**145** each

Prepare yourself for sacrilege! I expect to be pelted with stale Munchkins when I say that Twinkies are *terrible*: an overmoist spongecake, more sponge than cake. Into this yellow batter is injected a sugar creme that is white as a sheet. This is what Hostess calls "wholesome." Junk food doesn't have to be wholesome for me to eat it, but when it's advertised as wholesome I expect it to be so. There are legions of Twinkie freaks out there, proving once more that there is just no accounting for taste. The sweetness of Twinkies may affect people with sensitive teeth. Two to a pack.

PRODUCT	**WELCH'S DONUTS**
MANUFACTURER	Welch's Foods
INGREDIENTS	Glazed: enriched wheat flour, glaze, water, shortening, sugar, yeast, dextrose, non-fat dry milk, salt, lecithin, mono- and diglycerides, leavening, dough conditioners, sodium stearyl-2-lactylate, vegetable gum and cellulose gum, artificial colors, BHA, and BHT.
SUGAR QUOTIENT	High
DENTAL CHECKUP	Tooth rotter
OIL QUOTIENT	High
NUTRIENT LEVEL	Empty calories
CALORIE COUNT	Not available

You can't freeze donuts. They become sticky and gooey and taste nowhere near as good as those baked fresh. Welch's Jelly Donuts have Welch's Grape Jelly (big deal!) and are cakier than the airy Glazed raised ones. Neither are very good. No matter how much sodium stearyl-2-lactylate they put in these donuts as an emulsifier, they won't get any better. This is the same for Morton's Bake Shop Donuts, as well.

PRODUCT	**BREYER'S ICE CREAM**
MANUFACTURER	**KraftCo**
INGREDIENTS	**Law requires no listing of ingredients.**
	Available in Eastern half of U.S. Only
SUGAR QUOTIENT	**High**
DENTAL CHECKUP	**Average**
OIL QUOTIENT	**High**
NUTRIENT LEVEL	**Minimal, some fortification**
CALORIE COUNT	**130/½ cup (approximate)**

Breyer's is one of the many ice creams prepared by Kraft Foods, the world's largest food company. They call Breyer's the "all natural ice cream." Natural what? The vanilla, like the other flavors, is indeed creamy and smooth, with real vanilla bean specks sprinkled throughout. But the vanilla taste of this milk-white ice cream is overwhelmed by sugar. Mabe this is the way ice cream is supposed to taste; after eating so much processed stuff, ostensibly natural products taste peculiar. Breyer's is probably the best commercially packed bulk ice cream. But be warned: it tastes real.

PRODUCT	**SEALTEST ICE CREAM**
MANUFACTURER	**KraftCo**
INGREDIENTS	**Law requires no listing of ingredients.**
	Available in Eastern half of U.S. Only
SUGAR QUOTIENT	**High**
DENTAL CHECKUP	**Average**
OIL QUOTIENT	**High**
NUTRIENT LEVEL	**Minimal, some fortification**
CALORIE COUNT	**130/½ cup (approximate)**

Another Kraft Foods ice cream advertised as the one with the "ice-cream parlor taste." This is a parlor I never want to visit again. The flavors seem artificially derived and although they possess a smooth, quasi-creamy texture, they taste aerated and stretched. Sealtest has, however, chosen the flavors well. These don't really compare to ice-cream parlor taste, but are an acceptable quality, low cost, supermarket blend. The heavenly hash variety, a blend of chocolate, nuts and marshmallow, is aptly named. Their vanilla can be justifiably avoided.

PRODUCT	**DREYER'S ICE CREAM**
MANUFACTURER	Dreyer's Grand Ice Cream Co.
INGREDIENTS	Law requires no listing of ingredients.
SUGAR QUOTIENT	High
DENTAL CHECKUP	Average
OIL QUOTIENT	High
NUTRIENT LEVEL	Acceptable
CALORIE COUNT	130/½ cup (approximate)

Dreyer's is to the West coast what Breyer's Ice Cream is to the East. The difference is Dreyer's is a family run independent operation while Breyer's is owned and operated by Kraftco. Dreyer's is a rich, creamy ice cream and, for the most part, uses real (natural) ingredients. Dreyer's tastes less sweet than Breyer's—which means you can eat a generous portion of it without cloying your tastebuds. In addition to the standard flavors, this supermarket, bulk-packed ice cream comes in unusual flavors like cheesecake, and a mighty delectable bittersweet chocolate.

PRODUCT	**ESKIMO PIE**
MANUFACTURER	Eskimo Pie Corp.
INGREDIENTS	Vanilla ice cream flavored with real vanilla; chocolate flavored coating: vegetable oil, sugar, cocoa processed with alkali, non-fat dry milk, soya lecithin, and vanilla.
SUGAR QUOTIENT	High
DENTAL CHECKUP	Tooth rotter
OIL QUOTIENT	High
NUTRIENT LEVEL	Minimal
CALORIE COUNT	Not available

Eskimo Pies come with sticks and without. They are vanilla ice cream covered with a chocolate flavored coating. Many companies make similar pops but Eskimo Pies were one of the first. The ice cream is on the bland side with a consistency not far from cold cream. The chocolate coating is tissue-paper thin and adds little measurable flavor—of chocolate or anything else. Here you are buying a famous brand name more than anything else, since virtually every ice cream company has a chocolate-covered ice cream pop of their own, scads of which are 75% better.

PRODUCT	**IT'S IT**
MANUFACTURER	**It's It Ice Cream Co.**
INGREDIENTS	**Vanilla flavored ice cream, enriched flour, oatmeal, sugar, shortening, raisins, cocoa, dry sweet buttermilk, salt, vegetable oil, leavening, cinnamon, lecithin, emulsifier, vanilla, artificial flavor, artificial color.**
SUGAR QUOTIENT	**High**
DENTAL CHECKUP	**Tooth rotter**
OIL QUOTIENT	**High**
NUTRIENT LEVEL	**Minimal**
CALORIE COUNT	**Not available**

It says it all right on the package. It's It is a handmade ice cream treat that has been a San Francisco tradition since 1928. This is an ice cream sandwich with a difference. Instead of the ordinary chocolate wafers, a scoop of vanilla ice cream is sandwiched between two oatmeal raisin cookies. Then the whole she-bang is dipped into a dark (compound) chocolate. For about 35 cents you get your money's worth. I never can finish one without going into sugar shock. It's It is rich and easy to O.D. on. The yummy confection is now being copied elsewhere around the country under different names and slightly different formulas. This is still the best though. When you taste it, you'll know it's it.

Other Ice Creams

BORDEN OLD-FASHIONED ALL NATURAL with 150 calories per average half-cup serving is creamy and bland. The Dutch Chocolate and French Vanilla are particularly good. **HOWARD JOHNSON'S CHOCO-LATE** ice cream with 215 calories in half a cup stands out as one of the company's best flavors. High fat content puts it in the premium class. Supermarket brands that stand out include Safeway's **SNOWSTAR** (less than a dollar per gallon!) with just 135 calories per half cup; A & P's **CRESTMONT** runs about 150 per half cup average in calories and has a solid flavor for supermarket low-fat bulk blends. If the brand doesn't label its ice cream as all natural, any amount of chemical boosters and flavorings might be included in the blend. Beware.

THE BEST:

HAÄGEN DAZ, the continental European ice cream now sold around the U.S., had made its fine reputation from its superior ingredients and luxurious creamy blends. Its *Chocolate with Chocolate Chips* is obscenely delicious and incredibly rich. Don't keep this one in the "fridge"—put it in the safe-deposit box at your local bank.

A MEMBER OF THE JUNK FOOD BOOK HALL OF FAME.

COOKIES CRACKERS, AND CHIPS

PEPPERIDGE FARM is America's best cookie manufacturer. What Sara Lee is to cakes, Pepperidge Farm is to cookies. Almost the complete line up of PF cookies is listed here. Packaged in unique foil-and-paper bags in three lines, "Distinctive" (premium priced), "Old Fashioned" (moderately priced; less elaborate), and the newer "Kitchen Hearth" (moderately priced; natural, whole-earth, whole-grain assortment). All PF cookies are made from unbleached enriched white flour (noted in the lists of ingredients simply as "flour"). When butter is used it is U.S. Grade AA pure creamery butter. All other ingredients are 100 percent natural. No chemical additives or artificial flavors or colors are used. Most PF cookies are available nationwide. PF is so pro-consumer it even puts a freshness date on the side panel of the package, as well as the number of cookies inside. The company is now owned by Campbell Soup Company.

═══════════

PRODUCT	**BORDEAUX**
MANUFACTURER	**Pepperidge Farm**
INGREDIENTS	**Flour, sugar, vegetable shortening, sugar syrup, butter, non-fat dry milk, corn starch, salt, and leavening.**
SUGAR QUOTIENT	**High**
DENTAL CHECKUP	**Average**
OIL QUOTIENT	**High**
NUTRIENT LEVEL	**Empty calories**
CALORIE COUNT	**37 each**

Just 37 calories each, these "Distinctive Line" cookies are perhaps the plainest PF makes. The flavor is a bit syrupy-sweet. Each flat rectangular wafer is crispy and rather genteel in character. For junk food addicts, they're not quite junky enough; for those on the periphery, they're just right.

═══════════

PRODUCT	**BROWN SUGAR**
MANUFACTURER	**Pepperidge Farm**
INGREDIENTS	**Stone ground 100% whole wheat flour, sugar, vegetable shortening, brown sugar, whole eggs, baking soda, cinnamon, and vanilla.**
SUGAR QUOTIENT	**High**
DENTAL CHECKUP	**Tooth rotter**
OIL QUOTIENT	**High**
NUTRIENT LEVEL	**Empty calories**
CALORIE COUNT	**50 calories each**

This is a strange product, with a straw-like dryness, and a strong chemical flavor—yet there are no chemical additives in the batter. There is enough sugar on top and inside, thank you, to make you think you are eating straight sugar cane. PF is commended for its efforts in pioneering the use of 100% stone ground whole wheat in cookies. Let's just leave it at that.

========================

PRODUCT	**BROWNIE**
MANUFACTURER	Pepperidge Farm
INGREDIENTS	Flour, sugar, vegetable shortening, walnuts, sweet chocolate, cocoa, whole eggs, non-fat dry milk, leavening, salt and vanilla.
SUGAR QUOTIENT	High
DENTAL CHECKUP	Tooth rotter
OIL QUOTIENT	High
NUTRIENT LEVEL	Empty calories
CALORIE COUNT	55 calories each

The closest a cookie comes to tasting like a brownie. These have an intrinsic dryness which suggests stale cake but the genuine chocolate flavor and walnuts save the day. P.F.'s Fudge Chip Cookies are better. These are a more sedate chocolate cookie, designed for the timid. Fifty-five calories each.

========================

PRODUCT	**CAPRI**
MANUFACTURER	Pepperidge Farm
INGREDIENTS	Flour, vegetable shortening, cocoa, walnuts, chocolate liquor, whole eggs, butter, non-fat dry milk, leavening, salt, and vanilla.
SUGAR QUOTIENT	High
DENTAL CHECKUP	Tooth rotter
OIL QUOTIENT	High
NUTRIENT LEVEL	Empty calories
CALORIE COUNT	83 each

Take two brownie-nut cookie wafers and spread a heavenly layer of sugar creme filling in between. At a dozen or so cookies for just under a buck, eat these when you want to treat yourself royally. But beware, each cookie has a whopping 83 calories. Move over, Oreos.

A MEMBER OF THE JUNK FOOD BOOK HALL OF FAME.

PRODUCT	**CHOCOLATE CHIP**
MANUFACTURER	**Pepperidge Farm**
INGREDIENTS	**Flour, sugar, chocolate, vegetable shortening, eggs, butter, egg white solids, non-fat dry milk, salt, vanilla, and leavening.**
SUGAR QUOTIENT	**High**
DENTAL CHECKUP	**Tooth rotter**
OIL QUOTIENT	**High**
NUTRIENT LEVEL	**Empty calories**
CALORIE COUNT	**53 each**

Somewhat dryish, these don't measure up to PF's best. Lots of chocolate chips are put into a bland batter nowhere near as good as Toll House's. Still they are much better than most other chocolate chip brands. Each one has 53 calories.

PRODUCT	**CINNAMON SUGAR**
MANUFACTURER	**Pepperidge Farm**
INGREDIENTS	**Flour, sugar, vegetable shortening, whole eggs, butter, salt, cinnamon, non-fat dry milk, and leavening.**
SUGAR QUOTIENT	**High**
DENTAL CHECKUP	**Tooth rotter**
OIL QUOTIENT	**High**
NUTRIENT LEVEL	**Empty calories**
CALORIE COUNT	**53 each**

Labeled "old fashioned," these cookies really do taste like the ones my grandmother used to make. Lots of sugar, butter, and eggs in a well-balanced ratio produces a plain yet remarkably pleasing biscuit, containing 53 calories apiece. Perfect for eating in rocking chairs. PF also makes a plain Sugar cookie identical to this but without the cinnamon.

PRODUCT	**FUDGE CHIP**
MANUFACTURER	**Pepperidge Farm**
INGREDIENTS	**Flour, sugar, vegetable shortening, whole eggs, butter, cocoa, sweet chocolate, baking soda, non-fat dry milk, salt, and vanilla.**
SUGAR QUOTIENT	**High**
DENTAL CHECKUP	**Tooth rotter**
OIL QUOTIENT	**High**
NUTRIENT LEVEL	**Empty calories**
CALORIE COUNT	**53 each**

A strong chocolate flavor dominates these chocolate fudge cookies. The quality is apparent. The eggs and butter add an uncommon richness to the taste and texture of what would have been total trash in the hands of another manufacturer. Fifty-three calories each.

PRODUCT	**GINGERMAN**
MANUFACTURER	**Pepperidge Farm**
INGREDIENTS	**Flour, sugar, brown sugar, vegetable shortening, whole eggs, molasses, salt, ginger, cinnamon, and baking soda.**
SUGAR QUOTIENT	**High**
DENTAL CHECKUP	**Tooth rotter**
OIL QUOTIENT	**High**
NUTRIENT LEVEL	**Empty calories**
CALORIE COUNT	**33 each**

The shape of these 33-calorie molasses and ginger cookies is, as the name implies, that of a gingerman. Sprinkles of coarse refined sugar add unwanted sweetness to an already diabolically oversweet flavor. Heavy on the molasses, this creation is obviously aimed at the kiddie litter set—surprising for PF.

PRODUCT	**GOLDFISH**
MANUFACTURER	**Pepperidge Farm**
INGREDIENTS	**See text below**
SUGAR QUOTIENT	**Low to none**
DENTAL CHECKUP	**Low**
OIL QUOTIENT	**High**
NUTRIENT LEVEL	**Low**
CALORIE COUNT	**3 per fish**

There are six varieties of Goldfish crackers, all packaged in 6-ounce bags. They are based on a European recipe and are made with Pepperidge Farm's exceptionally high standards for ingredients and production.

The most popular flavor is **Cheddar Cheese** (flour, cheddar cheese, vegetable shortening, salt, yeast, leavening, butter, sugar, spices, and onion powder). Light, golden-colored goldfish-shaped crackers with a mild cheddar flavor, these are delicious and remarkably low in calories (three calories per fish). While the cheddar stands out, the spices added also help to make this a zesty nibble.

Equally infectious is **Sesame Garlic** (flour, vegetable shortening, sesame seed, salt, yeast, leavening agents, sugar, and garlic powder). The pungent garlicky flavor blends smoothly with the sesames to create an aristocratic taste.

Pretzel (flour, vegetable shortening, salt, malt, yeast, soda) has hollow air holes caused by the soda used in their preparation; nevertheless it is enjoyable and not overly salty (as many actual pretzels tend to be).

Parmesan (flour, vegetable shortening, parmesan cheese, salt, yeast, dried pasteurized process cheddar cheese, leavening agents, onion powder, and sugar) is a very mild snack cracker and works well for the adult who likes his pop food mellow.

Pizza is the knockout flavor (flour, vegetable shortening, tomato paste, cheddar cheese, salt, yeast, leavening agents, butter, herbs, spices, onion powder, and protease). Even though this doesn't really resemble a pizza taste, PF has the right idea. They have taken quality ingredients and masterchefed a robustly seasoned cracker with a taste that lasts through fish after fish. If real fish tasted like this, more people would turn to seafood for their sustenance.

The **Lightly Salted** variety (flour, vegetable shortening, non-fat dry milk, salt, yeast, leavening, butter, sugar, spices, and onion powder) has a bland flavor and none of the pizazz the other Goldfish have.

PRODUCT	**IRISH OATMEAL**
MANUFACTURER	**Pepperidge Farm**
INGREDIENTS	**Flour, sugar, vegetable shortening, oatmeal, whole eggs, sugar syrup, salt, baking soda, spices, and vanilla.**
SUGAR QUOTIENT	**High**
DENTAL CHECKUP	**Average**
OIL QUOTIENT	**High**
NUTRIENT LEVEL	**Empty calories**
CALORIE COUNT	**50 each**

Crisp, brittle, round cookies with a puny oatmeal flavor. Heavy doses of nutmeg and cinnamon dominate the taste. Less sweet than PF's Oatmeal Raisin but the sugar is persistently cloying.

PRODUCT	**LEMON NUT CRUNCH**
MANUFACTURER	**Pepperidge Farm**
INGREDIENTS	**Flour, sugar, vegetable shortening, walnuts, whole eggs, non-fat dry milk, lemon oil, baking soda, salt, citric acid, and lecithin.**
SUGAR QUOTIENT	**High**
DENTAL CHECKUP	**Average**
OIL QUOTIENT	**High**
NUTRIENT LEVEL	**Empty calories**
CALORIE COUNT	**58 each**

Very lemony, very nutty, very crunchy, very good.

PRODUCT	**MILANO**
MANUFACTURER	**Pepperidge Farm**
INGREDIENTS	**Sweet chocolate, flour, vegetable shortening, sugar, whole eggs, cornstarch, non-fat dry milk, egg-white solids, salt, vanilla, baking soda, and vegetable gum.**
SUGAR QUOTIENT	**High**
DENTAL CHECKUP	**Tooth rotter**
OIL QUOTIENT	**High**
NUTRIENT LEVEL	**Empty calories**
CALORIE COUNT	**63 each**

Probably the most popular cookie PF makes—or at least the most habit-forming. Milanos are ladyfinger-shaped sandwiches made of light golden batter wafers on either side of pure sweet chocolate. This cookie, despite its 63 calories, makes wading through all the other junk worthwhile. Based on a European recipe, the cookie is light and properly sweet, with a melts-in-your-mouth consistency.

A MEMBER OF THE JUNK FOOD BOOK HALL OF FAME.

PRODUCT	**MOLASSES CRISP**
MANUFACTURER	**Pepperidge Farm**
INGREDIENTS	**Flour, molasses, vegetable shortening, brown sugar, sugar, non-fat dry milk, leavening, salt, and cinnamon.**
SUGAR QUOTIENT	**High**
DENTAL CHECKUP	**Tooth rotter**
OIL QUOTIENT	**High**
NUTRIENT LEVEL	**Empty calories**
CALORIE COUNT	**30 each**

Crisp, thin wafers baked a golden brown. The ample molasses supplied makes them more spicy than sweet. By themselves or with vanilla ice cream, these are delicious, well-made cookies. Try spreading peanut butter between two of them for an out-of-this-world sandwich.

PRODUCT	**NASSAU**
MANUFACTURER	**Pepperidge Farm**
INGREDIENTS	**Flour, sugar, sweet chocolate, vegetable shortening, peanut butter, butter, whole eggs, non-fat dry milk, leavening, salt, and vanilla.**
SUGAR QUOTIENT	**High**
DENTAL CHECKUP	**Tooth rotter**
OIL QUOTIENT	**High**
NUTRIENT LEVEL	**Empty calories**
CALORIE COUNT	**83 each**

Here is a peanut butter cookie made the way it should be. The peanut butter doesn't overwhelm you; it blends perfectly with sweet, pure chocolate sandwiched between cookies shaped like hunchbacked clams. As 83 calories each and a price tag of just under a dollar a dozen, Nassau can get to be an expensive habit. But it's better than gambling.

PRODUCT	**OATMEAL RAISIN**
MANUFACTURER	**Pepperidge Farm**
INGREDIENTS	**Flour, vegetable shortening, raisin, oatmeal, sugar, whole eggs, molasses, sugar syrup, baking soda, salt, and vanilla.**
SUGAR QUOTIENT	**High**
DENTAL CHECKUP	**Average**
OIL QUOTIENT	**High**
NUTRIENT LEVEL	**Empty calories**
CALORIE COUNT	**55 each**

Chewy oatmeal cookies with 55 calories each that don't taste factory made. Perhaps a slight bit sweeter than necessary, they overflow with oatmeal flavor and raisins. If you like your oatmeal cookies soft and chewy with that just-baked flavor these are for you.

PRODUCT	**ORLEANS**
MANUFACTURER	**Pepperidge Farm**
INGREDIENTS	**Chocolate, flour, sugar, vegetable shortening, non-fat dry milk, egg-white solids, vanilla, salt, and lecithin.**
SUGAR QUOTIENT	**High**
DENTAL CHECKUP	**Tooth rotter**
OIL QUOTIENT	**High**
NUTRIENT LEVEL	**Empty calories**
CALORIE COUNT	**30 each**

REAL CHOCOLATE! Better than any candybar, these cookies are so well made and so delicious I'd like to cement them to my tongue. A super thin round wafer, similar to, but thinner than, the Milano, is drenched with the smoothest, best-tasting, dark sweet chocolate this side of heaven. And at 30 calories each, you can eat more than one and not feel guilty. But they are incredibly contagious: one leads to another and another. Let yourself go. Be a disconcerning nibbler.

A MEMBER OF THE JUNK FOOD BOOK HALL OF FAME.

PRODUCT	**PEANUT**
MANUFACTURER	**Pepperidge farm**
INGREDIENTS	**Flour, sugar, peanut butter, vegetable shortening, peanuts, whole eggs, non-fat dry milk, salt, leavening, and lecithin.**
SUGAR QUOTIENT	**High**
DENTAL CHECKUP	**Average**
OIL QUOTIENT	**High**
NUTRIENT LEVEL	**Empty calories**
CALORIE COUNT	**55 each**

Double peanut power: PF gives us both chopped peanuts and peanut butter in crisp, pleasantly sweet, wafer-shaped cookies. If you like peanut butter cookies without the Nassau's chocolate, PF has them for you at 55 calories each.

PRODUCT	**SHORTBREAD**
MANUFACTURER	**Pepperidge Farm**
INGREDIENTS	**Flour, vegetable shortening, sugar, butter, sugar syrup, cornstarch, non-fat dry milk, egg-white solids, salt, vanilla, and baking soda.**
SUGAR QUOTIENT	**High**
DENTAL CHECKUP	**Tooth rotter**
OIL QUOTIENT	**High**
NUTRIENT LEVEL	**Empty calories**
CALORIE COUNT	**73 each**

American shortbread can never duplicate the authentic Scottish, but PF comes the closest. By its very nature, Shortbread is a plain cookie, heavy on the shortening and butter found in comparable amounts here. The sweetness could be a bit more subdued though. Still this is a rich-tasting, filling cookie—no doubt as it should be with all that fat content. It is similar to a poundcake cookie—and light years ahead of a Lorna Doone. PF's Chessman is similar but more expensive.

PRODUCT	**TAHITI**
MANUFACTURER	**Pepperidge Farm**
INGREDIENTS	**Flour, sweet chocolate, coconut, sugar, vegetable shortening, cornstarch, whole eggs, sugar syrup, non-fat dry milk, leavening, and salt.**
SUGAR QUOTIENT	**High**
DENTAL CHECKUP	**Tooth rotter**
OIL QUOTIENT	**High**
NUTRIENT LEVEL	**Empty calories**
CALORIE COUNT	**80 each**

This light, crumbly cookie, loaded with coconut power, sandwiches a layer of rich, real chocolate. The coconut flavor endures from first sniff to last bite—and then some. I would readily call this creation ambrosia.

PRODUCT	**BARNUM'S ANIMALS**
MANUFACTURER	**Nabisco**
INGREDIENTS	**Enriched wheat flour, rye flour, sugar, shortening, corn sweetener, corn flour, whey solids, salt, leavening, and artificial flavor.**
SUGAR QUOTIENT	**Moderate**
DENTAL CHECKUP	**Average**
OIL QUOTIENT	**Moderate**
NUTRIENT LEVEL	**Empty calories**
CALORIE COUNT	**65/oz.**

The original cookie for young children is very much the same as it was in the early 1900s, except for the addition of obligatory artificial flavors. Barnum's Animals still arrive in a small box with a carrier string with modest animal crackers inside. While these animal crackers are more floury than sweet, they provide pleasing textures and familiar shapes to which a child can relate. They are conveniently placed on low shelves in supermarkets in line with small children's field of vision. Sunshine's version, Toy Crackers, are very much the same but because they do not have artificial flavors they are a wiser choice.

PRODUCT	**BISCOS SUGAR WAFERS**
MANUFACTURER	Nabisco
INGREDIENTS	Sugar, enriched wheat flour, rye flour, shortening, whey solids, salt, leavening, lecithin, and artificial flavor.
SUGAR QUOTIENT	High
DENTAL CHECKUP	Tooth rotter
OIL QUOTIENT	Moderate
NUTRIENT LEVEL	Empty calories
CALORIE COUNT	150/oz.

One of Nabisco's original mainstays, these finger-length crispy wafers have layers of white sugar and shortening in between. Biscos seem airy, almost puffy, in texture, and are habit-forming. Each package contains long sheets of them which break apart at perforations.

A MEMBER OF THE JUNK FOOD BOOK HALL OF FAME.

PRODUCT	**BROWN EDGE WAFERS**
MANUFACTURER	Nabisco
INGREDIENTS	Enriched wheat flour, rye flour, sugar, shortening, whey solids, butter, salt, leavening, and artificial flavors.
SUGAR QUOTIENT	High
DENTAL CHECKUP	Average
OIL QUOTIENT	High
NUTRIENT LEVEL	Empty calories
CALORIE COUNT	Four = 115

These round, paper-thin wafers are timidly sweet with a varely identifiable artificial flavor. Genteel in appearance and texture, they are "tres-elegant," perfect for milady's afternoon teas, but hardly fit for a red-blooded junk food junkie. As usual, Nabisco adds artificial flavor, but in this case, why they do is a mystery since you can hardly taste anything anyway.

PRODUCT	**BUGLES**
MANUFACTURER	**General Mills**
INGREDIENTS	**Degermed yellow corn grits, coconut oil (with BHA and BHT), sugar, salt, soda, niacin, iron, thiamin, and riboflavin.**
SUGAR QUOTIENT	**Moderate**
DENTAL CHECKUP	**Average**
OIL QUOTIENT	**High**
NUTRIENT LEVEL	**Empty calories**
CALORIE COUNT	**105/oz.**

Bugles are nothing to toot about. Prepared with degermed yellow corn grits, they taste more gritty than corny. While their cornucopia horn shape is fun, and handy for picking up dip, their oily, oversalted taste makes them less than appetizing. All the ingredients for a perfect junk food are here, but somehow Bugles come out tasting more like salted cereal than a habit-forming snack. Although four vitamins have been added to the ingredients, you will still receive less than 6 percent of the U.S. recommended daily allowance of each per ounce. They come in a 7-ounce box, and have 150 calories per 1-ounce serving. Stick to Fritos: they may have no nutrients and just as many calories, but they taste a lot better.

PRODUCT	**BURRY'S BEST CHOCOLATE CHIP COOKIES**
MANUFACTURER	**Burry (Quaker Oats)**
INGREDIENTS	**Enriched flour, chocolate, vegetable shortening (with BHA, propyl gallate and citric acid), sugar, brown sugar, corn flour, dried whey, salt, leavening, natural and artificial flavors, and lecithin.**
SUGAR QUOTIENT	**High**
DENTAL CHECKUP	**Tooth rotter**
OIL QUOTIENT	**High**
NUTRIENT LEVEL	**Empty calories**
CALORIE COUNT	**150/oz. (2 cookies)**

Burry's Best is the company's premium line, and their chocolate chip variety is well worth the extra cost. Baked in the Toll House tradition with plenty of mammoth chocolate chips, these are among the best cookies on the market. Keep them in the refrigerator to restore the original fresh, crisp flavor. If you don't, they tend to get soft and bready. The random shape of each cookie indicates a refreshing lack of factory uniformity. They are not available in western states.

===

PRODUCT **BURRY'S BEST OATMEAL COOKIES**

MANUFACTURER **Burry (Quaker Oats)**

INGREDIENTS **Enriched flour, vegetable shortening (with BHA, propyl gallate, citric acid), sugar, cereal oats, raisins, brown sugar, corn flour, dried whey, salt, leavening, spice, lecithin, and artificial and natural flavors.**

SUGAR QUOTIENT **High**

DENTAL CHECKUP **Average**

OIL QUOTIENT **High**

NUTRIENT LEVEL **Empty calories**

CALORIE COUNT **6o each**

Somewhat disappointing, the occasional raisin isn't enough to make up for the ersatz spice flavor in these crumbly, not-very-oatmealy cookies. Burry's is a division of Quaker Oats—the manufacturer of America's leading oatmeal. What a surprise! Not available in western states.

===

PRODUCT **C.C. BIGGS CHOCOLATE CHIP COOKIES**

MANUFACTURER **Keebler**

INGREDIENTS **Enriched wheat flour, shortening, sugar, sweet chocolate, molasses, corn syrup, diary whey solids, leavening, salt, malt, whole egg solids, and artificial flavor.**

SUGAR QUOTIENT **High**

DENTAL CHECKUP **Tooth rotter**

OIL QUOTIENT **High**

NUTRIENT LEVEL **Empty calories**

CALORIE COUNT **Not available**

These factory prepared chocolate chip cookies are surprisingly satisfying. In general, Keebler does high quality cookies, but they package them in fold-top paper bags, and as a result, many of the cookies arrive broken into pieces. This company offers a number of different chocolate chip cookies; C.C. Biggs are the most chocolatey, with lots of "bigg" chips in each cookie. Not available in some western states.

PRODUCT	**CHEE-TOS**
MANUFACTURER	**Frito-Lay**
INGREDIENTS	**Enriched corn meal, vegetable oil with BHA and BHT, salt, cheese, whey solids, sour cream, artificial color, and lactic acid.**
SUGAR QUOTIENT	**Minimal**
DENTAL CHECKUP	**Average**
OIL QUOTIENT	**High**
NUTRIENT LEVEL	**Empty calories**
CALORIE COUNT	**160/oz.**

I am not sure what type of cheese is used in these quick-fried "puffs," but the "Chee" in Chee-tos and the coloring suggests American or mild cheddar. The taste doesn't. Still these are habit forming, airy and crunchy, orange colored curly sticks. Rather messy to eat because the coloring comes off on your fingers. Chee-tos are available in either quick-fried or baked varieties. The baked version is lighter, less oily and not as tasty. Chee-tos is the only brand of cheese puffs distributed nationally.

PRODUCT	**CHIPS AHOY/CHOCOLATE CHOCOLATE-CHIP COOKIES**
MANUFACTURER	**Nabisco**
INGREDIENTS	**Chocolate Chocolate-Chip: enriched wheat flour, rye flour, sugar, chocolate, shortening, whey solids, corn sweetener, malted barley flour, salt, leavening, lecithin, and artificial flavors. (Chips Ahoy have the same ingredients, only with less chocolate.)**

SUGAR QUOTIENT	**High**
DENTAL CHECKUP	**Tooth rotter**
OIL QUOTIENT	**High**
NUTRIENT LEVEL	**Empty calories**
CALORIE COUNT	**53 each**

America's favorite cookies, chocolate chip, will *sell* no matter how they taste. Nabisco's contribution has a mass-manufactured taste, look, and texture. Of all the chocolate chip cookies I have ever eaten, these rank the lowest. An odd aftertaste remains from the Chips Ahoy, less so from the chocolate chocolate chip. Chips Ahoy are made with a tasteless batter, and, at about $1 for nine ounces, they are a rip-off besides.

PRODUCT	**CHIP-A-ROOS**
MANUFACTURER	**Sunshine**
INGREDIENTS	**Enriched flour, shortening, chocolate, sugar, brown sugar, high fructose corn syrup, leavening, corn flour, salt, whey, eggs, natural and artificial flavors, and lecithin.**
SUGAR QUOTIENT	**High**
DENTAL CHECKUP	**Tooth rotter**
OIL QUOTIENT	**High**
NUTRIENT LEVEL	**Empty calories**
CALORIE COUNT	**63 each**

Similar in design and taste to Nabisco's Chips Ahoy, these cheap cookies have teeny chipettes but little chocolate flavor. While the quantity has been adjusted upward, Sunshine's usual high quality seems to have been adjusted downward. Well, everybody makes mistakes.

PRODUCT	**CHOCOLATE NUGGETS**
MANUFACTURER	Sunshine
INGREDIENTS	Enriched flour, sugar, sweet chocolate, shortening, rye flour, cashews, whole egg solids, leavening, non-fat dry milk, salt, modified corn starch, whey solids, lecithin, artificial flavor, vanilla, and spice.
SUGAR QUOTIENT	High
DENTAL CHECKUP	Tooth rotter
OIL QUOTIENT	High
NUTRIENT LEVEL	Empty calories
CALORIE COUNT	30 each

A mini-chocolate chip cookie made from a marbleized batter and hordes of chocolate chips. The 14-ounce box seems to overflow with these choice little morsels. Their bite size and comfortable crunchiness make them endlessly munchable. The well-balanced flavor is due in part to the cashews blended in. Most appealing.

PRODUCT	**CHOCOLATE PINWHEELS**
MANUFACTURER	Nabisco
INGREDIENTS	Sweet chocolate, corn sweeteners, enriched wheat flour, rye flour, sugar, shortening, cocoa, malted barley flour, caramel color, gelatin, salt, leavening, lecithin and artificial flavors.
SUGAR QUOTIENT	High
DENTAL CHECKUP	Tooth rotter
OIL QUOTIENT	High
NUTRIENT LEVEL	Empty calories
CALORIE COUNT	53 each

More candy than cookie, sweet chocolate covers a donut-shaped chocolate cake cookie foundation with marshmallow on top. The taste is sweeter than a

Milky Way but milder than Devil's food. Actually this is a Mallomar in disguise. Mallomars are sold only in the East—mainly in New York. They are marshmallow puffs placed on top of a graham-colored cookie base, then drenched in chocolate. Pinwheels look as if they were baked in a Bundt pan. If you like your cookies sweet and chocolatey, this is for you. But at more than $1.30 a pound, the price is kinda steep.

PRODUCT	**CORNNUTS**
MANUFACTURER	**Cornnuts Inc.**
INGREDIENTS	**Corn, vegetable oil, and salt.**
SUGAR QUOTIENT	**None**
DENTAL CHECKUP	**Average**
OIL QUOTIENT	**High**
NUTRIENT LEVEL	**Empty calories**
CALORIE COUNT	**50/ounce**

These are great snacks to feed your pet gopher. Human consumption should probably be limited to those with granite teeth. Cornnuts are oversized kernels of corn that have not been popped but roasted and salted. The consistency of this dried corn seems harder than Gibraltar. But, still, if you can get past the hardness obstacle, Cornnuts are rather tasty, even habit-forming little rascals. And after a while, when the pain has numbed your mouth, they are fun to gnaw on. Popular in the western states, these are gradually moving eastward.

PRODUCT	**CREME WAFER STICKS**
MANUFACTURER	**Nabisco**
INGREDIENTS	**Sugar, shortening, enriched wheat flour, rye flour, whey solids, cocoa processed with alkali, sorbitan monostearate, lecithin and polysorbate 60, salt, leavening, and artificial flavor.**

SUGAR QUOTIENT	High
DENTAL CHECKUP	Tooth rotter
OIL QUOTIENT	High
NUTRIENT LEVEL	Empty calories
CALORIE COUNT	50 each

These sugar wafers have a compound chocolate coating and are proportionately sweet. They are oblong sticks with about three layers of wafer and sugar. Light and delicate, they practically melt in your mouth. Yummy.

PRODUCT	**DADDY CRISP FRENCH FRIED POTATO CHIPS**
MANUFACTURER	Daddy Crisp (Intext)
INGREDIENTS	Potatoes, pure vegetable oil, salt
SUGAR QUOTIENT	None
DENTAL CHECKUP	Average
OIL QUOTIENT	High
NUTRIENT LEVEL	Empty calories
CALORIE COUNT	Not available

Flattened potato sticks packed in a tennis-ball canister, these are rather tasty morsels, but the content of the packages I purchased had broken into confetti-sized chips. The price is about 60 cents for 4 ounces, or about the price of regular potato chips. Daddy Crisp comes in three varieties: Regular, Barbeque,

and Sour Cream and Onion Dip. All have an authentic taste. The built-in dip flavor in particular almost exactly duplicates the flavor of potato chips dunked in dip. The regular flavor has a greasy feel, but that didn't interfere with the taste. Regionally distributed in states east of the Mississippi River.

PRODUCT	**DEVILS CAKE**
MANUFACTURER	**Sunshine**
INGREDIENTS	**Sugar, enriched flour, invert sugar, corn syrup, cocoa, shortening, gelatin, leavening, non-fat dry milk, corn starch, salt, pure chocolate, lecithin, artificial color, imitation flavors, and sorbic acid.**
SUGAR QUOTIENT	**High**
DENTAL CHECKUP	**Tooth rotter**
OIL QUOTIENT	**High**
NUTRIENT LEVEL	**Empty calories**
CALORIE COUNT	**48 each**

This is the black sheep of Sunshine Biscuits. Almost all of their products exude quality and care but this nauseating abomination, consummate junk that it is, is barely edible. Each very brown square is coated in a plaster-of-Paris-type chocolate. Inside is a devil's food cake with the consistency of asbestos and a taste not unlike a dry Handi-Wipe. I wonder if kids hold their breath when they eat these things. I know I did.

PRODUCT	**DOO DADS**
MANUFACTURER	**Nabisco**
INGREDIENTS	**Enriched wheat flour, rye flour, whole wheat, rice, shortening, peanuts, salt, aged whole milk cheddar cheese, malted barley flour, sugar, leavening, spices and extractives of spices, vegetable protein derivative, monosodium glutamate, whey, soda, niacin, iron, thiamine, artificial flavors and artificial color, BHA, propyl gallate, and citric acid.**

SUGAR QUOTIENT	Low
DENTAL CHECKUP	Average
OIL QUOTIENT	Moderate
NUTRIENT LEVEL	Empty calories
CALORIE COUNT	**200 pieces** = **480** approximate

Based on a European snack recipe, Doo Dads are a mix of wheat and rice cereals (similar in appearance to Wheat and Rice Chex), cheese crackers, (Cheese Nibs), pretzel sticks, and salted peanuts. This is a winning combination, either individually or freely mixed, a tasty adult snack that works especially well with cocktails or beer. The small 7-ounce package may look rather diminutive but this snack is concentrated—a little goes a long way. Some may object to the saltiness of the mix, which does seem quite strong if you aren't drinking.

PRODUCT	**DORITOS NACHO™ CHEESE TORTILLA CHIPS**
MANUFACTURER	**Frito-Lay**
INGREDIENTS	Corn, vegetable oil, salt. Cheese flavor: salt, Romano cheese made from cow's milk, dried whey, flour, cheddar cheese, tomato powder, monosodium glutamate, buttermilk powder, onion, parmesan cheese, garlic, artificial color, dextrose, citric acid, sugar, spice, disodium inosinate, disodium guanylate, lactic acid, BHA, and BHT.
SUGAR QUOTIENT	Low
DENTAL CHECKUP	Average
OIL QUOTIENT	High
NUTRIENT LEVEL	Empty calories
CALORIE COUNT	All flavors = **140**/oz

Also available in Regular (unflavored) and Taco, Doritos Tortilla Chips are crisp and crunchy with a heavy flavor. Nacho Cheese is a trademarked word for a mishmash of ingredients which gives the basic triangular corn chip a faintly sweet, richly spiced taste. In fact the spice is so strong it completely overwhelms the corn ship it covers. You have to acquire a taste for Nacho chips, but the Regular corn chips are immediately delicious with no training necessary.

<hr>

PRODUCT	**FIG BARS**
MANUFACTURER	Sunshine
INGREDIENTS	Sugar, enriched flour, corn syrup, figs, oats, shortening, corn starch, whey solids, salt, leavening, whole egg solids, citric acid, oil of lemon, artificial flavor, lecithin, and U.S. certified colors.
SUGAR QUOTIENT	High
DENTAL CHECKUP	Tooth rotter
OIL QUOTIENT	Moderate
NUTRIENT LEVEL	Empty calories
CALORIE COUNT	45 each

The difference between Sunshine Fig Bars and Nabisco's Fig Newtons is the figs. The figs are Sunshine's fourth largest ingredient; Nabisco has figs as the first ingredient. The difference in quality and taste is immediately apparent even in a blindfold test. Sunshine makes its fig bars thicker and more cakey, with neither the fig flavor nor the cookie texture we expect them to have. In a word, these are a disappointment.

<hr>

PRODUCT	**FIG NEWTONS**
MANUFACTURER	Nabisco
INGREDIENTS	Figs, sugar, enriched wheat flour, rye flour, corn sweeteners, shortening, whey solids, salt, leavening, confectioners flaked corn, and artificial flavors.
SUGAR QUOTIENT	High
DENTAL CHECKUP	Tooth rotter

OIL QUOTIENT	Moderate
NUTRIENT LEVEL	Minimal—some fortification present
CALORIE COUNT	**55** each

The "one and only" fig cookies, these are really mini-cakes. A thin layer of dough wraps around a fig filling that is divinely overloaded with figs and moderately sweetened. The result is the classic Fig Newton, the name derived from a town near Boston. You don't even have to like figs to enjoy Fig Newtons. The fruit has been turned into a jelly-type filling which can be seen at the open ends of the cake. This is one of the original cookies Nabisco started with at the turn of the century.

PRODUCT	**FLINGS**
MANUFACTURER	Nabisco
INGREDIENTS	Corn meal, vegetable oil, dehydrated aged cheddar cheese (with added sodium phosphate and lactic acid), corn starch, whey solids, salt, artificial flavors, vegetable protein derivative, artificial color, BHA, propyl gallate, and citric acid.
SUGAR QUOTIENT	Minimal
DENTAL CHECKUP	Average
OIL QUOTIENT	High
NUTRIENT LEVEL	Empty calories
CALORIE COUNT	Ten = **107**

Packed in a foil-lined box, these messy little fritters are similar to Chee-tos, but Nabisco pours in many more extraneous ingredients to produce the same type of snack—an orange-colored puffy curl of extruded corn. There are so many preservatives to keep this snack on the grocer's shelf, that one wonders if they are preparing it for a time capsule. Flings aren't as crispy or crunchy as Chee-tos, nor do they have the same lipsmacking flavor. They do have the same messy, finger licking appearance. Overall, Flings are nothing special—just another junk food.

<hr>

PRODUCT	**FRITOS**
MANUFACTURER	Frito-Lay
INGREDIENTS	Corn, vegetable oil with BHA and BHT, salt.
SUGAR QUOTIENT	Minimal—almost none
DENTAL CHECKUP	Average
OIL QUOTIENT	High
NUTRIENT LEVEL	Empty calories
CALORIE COUNT	**160/oz**

Ole! Fritos were one of the first corn chips to be sold in the United States and have remained popular since their local Texas days in the 1930s. Today they are the only nationally distributed corn chip. Fortunately, they are also the best. Available in regular or wide dip shape, they are crunchy flat chips with a heavy corn and salt taste. The oil in Fritos plays an important part in the feel and taste of the chip. Call it the Frito mystique, but the slightly oily texture of each chip makes them intoxicating, satiating our craving for fat and crunchiness at the same time. Sublime junk food!

A MEMBER OF THE JUNK FOOD BOOK HALL OF FAME.

<hr>

PRODUCT	**GINGERY GINGER SNAPS**
MANUFACTURER	Sunshine
INGREDIENTS	Enriched flour, sugar, molasses, shortening, rye flour, leavening, ginger, whey solids, salt, and oil of lemon.
SUGAR QUOTIENT	High
DENTAL CHECKUP	Tooth rotter
OIL QUOTIENT	High
NUTRIENT LEVEL	Empty calories
CALORIE COUNT	**24 each**

These gingery bite sized cookies have quite a snap, but the texture somewhat reduces their inherent pleasure. In some cases, the center of the cookies were not as light as the edges, and the texture was mealy, almost as if they has been improperly baked. But the spicy flavor does linger in your mouth long after the cookies are eaten. Cookies this tangy are rare, indeed.

PRODUCT	**GINGER SNAPS, Old Fashioned**
MANUFACTURER	Nabisco
INGREDIENTS	Enriched wheat flour, rye flour, molasses, sugar, shortening, corn syrup, ginger, salt, leavening, and artificial flavor.
SUGAR QUOTIENT	Moderate
DENTAL CHECKUP	Average
OIL QUOTIENT	Moderate
NUTRIENT LEVEL	Minimal—some fortification present
CALORIE COUNT	**30 each**

Accurately named, Ginger Snaps have both the snap of ginger and molasses, and the snapability of a hard, crunchy cracker. Just sweet enough, each cookie has only 30 calories. Proper adult junk and one of Nabisco's best products, it has been in the company's line for nearly the entire century. Their Zuzu Cracker, not rated here, is almost identical, but smaller in size.

PRODUCT	**GIRL SCOUT COOKIES: THIN MINTS**
MANUFACTURER	Burry (Quaker Oats) for GSUSA
INGREDIENTS	Sugar, enriched flour, vegetable shortening (with BHA, propyl gallate and citric acid), cocoa (partially processed with alkali) corn flour, bleached rye flour, invert syrup, salt, leavening, lecithin, artificial flavors, oil of peppermint, baked with vegetable shortening.

SUGAR QUOTIENT	High
DENTAL CHECKUP	Tooth rotter
OIL QUOTIENT	High
NUTRIENT LEVEL	Empty calories
CALORIE COUNT	Not available

Why, oh why, did the Girl Scouts change the manufacturer of their cookies? Once a delightful quality product, they are now just a shadow of their former stature. The most popular cookie was the very chocolatey, very minty, Thin Mint. Now it really *is* thin on mint and the chocolate is just a compound cocoa blend that imparts more aftertaste than anything else. Burry's makes a number of top quality cookies under its own name so it is surprising that these are so inferior. Perhaps the Girl Scouts asked Burry's to cut corners to raise the profit margin on these $1.25 boxes. (The various Girl Scout Councils around the U.S. use different suppliers, each uses the same recipes—it is what they do with them that is questioned here.)

PRODUCT	**GOLDEN FRUIT RAISIN BISCUITS**
MANUFACTURER	**Sunshine**
INGREDIENTS	Raisins, enriched flour, vegetable shortening, corn syrup, sugar, rye flour, corn flour, non-fat dry milk, whey solids, salt, leavening, and oil of lemon.
SUGAR QUOTIENT	Moderate
DENTAL CHECKUP	Average
OIL QUOTIENT	High
NUTRIENT LEVEL	Minimal—some fortification present
CALORIE COUNT	61 each

Here are mountains of raisins pressed flat as pancakes between two equally thin layers of chewy cookie dough. If this doesn't quite seem like junk food it's because of all those healthy raisins. It's hard to feel guilty about eating this. I finished an entire package in one day (about fifteen biscuits). I won't tell you what happened the next day.

PRODUCT	**GRANNY GOOSE OLD FASHIONED STONE GROUND TORTILLOS**
MANUFACTURER	Granny Goose Foods (Del Monte)
INGREDIENTS	Corn, vegetable oil, salt, dextrose, onion powder, garlic powder, and natural flavorings.
SUGAR QUOTIENT	Moderate to low
DENTAL CHECKUP	Average
OIL QUOTIENT	High
NUTRIENT LEVEL	Empty calories
CALORIE COUNT	175/oz

The package screams that they're "100% natural" and they well may be—but that's not the point. These are delicious, among the best tortillos chips available in the United States, prepared extra thin, they are "crisp as the dickens" and "tasty as can be." Granny Goose Tortillos come in Regular and Cheese flavors. The regular holds up better and the taste lasts longer. The habit-forming 7-ounce bag empties very quickly. This is not a nationally distributed brand, but are so exceptional that they must be mentioned.

PRODUCT	**GRANNY GOOSE THICK POTATO CHIPS**
MANUFACTURER	Granny Goose Foods (Del Monte)
INGREDIENTS	Selected unpeeled potatoes, vegetable oil, salt.
SUGAR QUOTIENT	None
DENTAL CHECKUP	Average
OIL QUOTIENT	High
NUTRIENT LEVEL	Empty calories
CALORIE COUNT	175/oz

In my years and years of junk fooding I have never tasted as delicious a potato chip as the ones Granny Goose has fried up. I have found Nirvana. The potatoes are unpeeled and sliced extra thick. They are still crispy, but with more body and potato flavor. You can practically make sandwiches from these chips, as many of them are sliced from exceedingly large potatoes. The thicker the chip, the less oil is absorbed, which must have a lot to do with the extraordinary taste imparted. You still get some greasy oil taste—there's no escaping that—but it is more subtle, allowing the potato to shine through. Packed in a heavy foil pouch and distributed only in the far western states and Hawaii.

A MEMBER OF THE JUNK FOOD BOOK HALL OF FAME.

PRODUCT	**HOME STYLE OATMEAL COOKIES WITH GROUND RAISINS**
MANUFACTURER	Sunshine
INGREDIENTS	Enriched flour, sugar, oats, shortening, raisins, leavening, salt, artificial flavor, and spice.
SUGAR QUOTIENT	High
DENTAL CHECKUP	Tooth rotter
OIL QUOTIENT	High
NUTRIENT LEVEL	Empty calories
CALORIE COUNT	58 each

Thirty-three cookies to a package are a solid value. Add a firm, crunchy texture and a genuine oat flavor, and you have a "best bet" in oatmeal cookies. These are honest to goodness "home-style" oatmeal cookies. The raisins are ground exceedingly fine and their pungent flavor enhances the basic oatmeal and flour base. One of the better oatmeal cookies available from a commercial baking factory.

PRODUCT	**HYDROX**
MANUFACTURER	Sunshine
INGREDIENTS	Sugar, enriched flour, vegetable shortening, cocoa, corn flour, salt, leavening, chocolate, whey solids, lecithin, and natural and artificial flavors.

SUGAR QUOTIENT	High
DENTAL CHECKUP	Tooth rotter
OIL QUOTIENT	High
NUTRIENT LEVEL	Empty calories
CALORIE COUNT	48 each

Hydrox is, of course, an obvious copy of Nabisco's classic Oreos. But Hydrox is notably sweeter—the sugar-and-shortening creme filling emphasizes sugar over shortening—just the reverse of Oreo's recipe. A bit more chocolatey and less cocoa-dry than Oreos, these are easier to consume in quantity. The name Hydrox comes from combining the words "hydrogen" and "oxygen." What that has to do with the cookie is anybody's guess.

PRODUCT	**IDEAL CHOCOLATE PEANUT BARS**
MANUFACTURER	**Nabisco**
INGREDIENTS	Sweet chocolate, enriched wheat flour, rye flour, crushed roasted peanuts, coconut, sugar, shortening, corn sweeteners, molasses, whey solids, hydrogenated peanut oil, salt, leavening, and lecithin.
SUGAR QUOTIENT	High
DENTAL CHECKUP	Tooth rotter
OIL QUOTIENT	High
NUTRIENT LEVEL	Empty calories
CALORIE COUNT	90 each

How do I love thee: let me count the *way!* Solid chocolate and peanut butter flavors are folded into a light, graham-crackery log. Scrumptious. There's just one problem—a faintly nauseating aftertaste. Could these be just a pinch too sweet? Or is it a Motown problem—something in the basic design? Enjoyable, but go slow.

PRODUCT	**LAY'S POTATO CHIPS/RUFFLES**
MANUFACTURER	**Frito-Lay**
INGREDIENTS	**Potatoes, vegetable oil with BHA, and salt.**
SUGAR QUOTIENT	**None**
DENTAL CHECKUP	**Average**
OIL QUOTIENT	**High**
NUTRIENT LEVEL	**Empty calories**
CALORIE COUNT	**160/oz.—Ruffles: 150/oz.**

The only nationally distributed potato chip is, alas, far from the best. Lay's and its ridge-cut brand, Ruffles, are somewhat dry. Whether this is because the oil is absorbed into the chip or because the chips aren't fried as long as other brands are, the result is a parched potato chip. Ruffles are slightly better than Lay's because the ridges have a more satisfying texture for the snacker. Lay's chips have a manufactured appearance, with a suspicious uniformity about each chip. Although they taste okay, this is by no means inspired junk food. Stick to the company's topnotch corn chips and find your potato chips elsewhere.

PRODUCT	**LEMON COOLERS**
MANUFACTURER	**Sunshine**
INGREDIENTS	**Enriched flour, sugar, vegetable shortening, dextrose, starch, egg, leavening, salt, natural flavors, artificial color, oil of lemon, and lecithin.**
SUGAR QUOTIENT	**High**
DENTAL CHECKUP	**Average**
OIL QUOTIENT	**High**
NUTRIENT LEVEL	**Empty calories**
CALORIE COUNT	**29 each**

Small, round clumps dusted with powdered sugar and loaded with a very real lemon flavor. If you hold the cookie in your mouth, you will wince and blink from the tart lemon oil on the top. The cracker itself is hard and crunchy. Despite the powdered sugar on top, these have only a slight sweetness, and leave no aftertaste, as many fruit-flavored cookies do. There is only one other lemon cookie—made by Pepperidge Farm—that can compare with the zesty lemon flavor found here.

PRODUCT	**LORNA DOONE SHORTBREAD**
MANUFACTURER	Nabisco
INGREDIENTS	Enriched wheat flour, rye flour, shortening, sugar, corn flour, eggs, whey solids, salt, leavening, and artificial flavor.
SUGAR QUOTIENT	Moderate
DENTAL CHECKUP	Tooth rotter
OIL QUOTIENT	High
NUTRIENT LEVEL	Minimal—some fortification present
CALORIE COUNT	37 each

Shortening and artificial flavor have been substituted for the butter that should predominate in these Scottish shortbread cookies. Still, for mass-made cookies they're quite tasty. Lorna Doone is one of the cookies that launched Nabisco's success. Each square has a rich butter taste even if the cheapskates haven't put any in. Be warned: these are plain janes but habit-forming nonetheless.

PRODUCT	**MELT-AWAY-SHORTCAKE**
MANUFACTURER	Nabisco
INGREDIENTS	Enriched flour, vegetable shortening, sugar, non-fat milk solids, whole eggs, baking powder, salt, and artificial flavor.
SUGAR QUOTIENT	High
DENTAL CHECKUP	Tooth rotter
OIL QUOTIENT	High
NUTRIENT LEVEL	Minimal—some fortification present
CALORIE COUNT	Not available

Dreamy, airy shortbread with sugar swirled throughout. Like all shortbread, these cookies are loaded with shortening. No butter, just eggs. Made in Holland expressly for Nabisco, they cost an expensive $2.00 a pound.

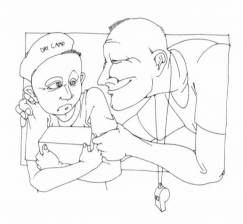

PRODUCT	**MISTER SALTY PRETZELS**
MANUFACTURER	**Nabisco**
INGREDIENTS	**Enriched wheat flour, rye flour, salt, shortening, malted barley flour, leavening, and sodium carbonate.**
SUGAR QUOTIENT	**None**
DENTAL CHECKUP	**Average**
OIL QUOTIENT	**Moderate**
NUTRIENT LEVEL	**Minimal—some fortification present**
CALORIE COUNT	**20 each**

One of the few nationally distributed pretzels, Mister Salty's are good tasting. Although there are many superior local brands, particularly in the Northeast, Mister Salty's are thin, salted proportionately, and baked to a pleasing, buttery flavored crunchiness. They are packaged in a cardboard box, supposedly to reduce breakage. It doesn't. Very few whole pretzels were found in the boxes sampled around the country. But this is an aesthetic quibble and shouldn't concern you if your main use for pretzels is as snacks or aids to beer consumption.

PRODUCT	**MYSTIC MINT SANDWICH COOKIES**
MANUFACTURER	Nabisco
INGREDIENTS	Sugar, shortening, enriched wheat flour, rye flour, cocoa (processed with alkali), whey solids, corn sweetener, corn flour, sorbitan monostearate, lecithin and polysorbate 60 emulsifier, chocolate, salt, leavening, oil of peppermint, and artificial flavor.
SUGAR QUOTIENT	High
DENTAL CHECKUP	Tooth rotter
OIL QUOTIENT	High
NUTRIENT LEVEL	Empty calories
CALORIE COUNT	65 each

These are sinfully delicious cookie sandwiches made up of two mint-flavored Oreo wafers (with chocolate coating hiding the Oreo insignia), and everybody's favorite sugar-and-shortening creme center. These glorified Oreos are reminiscent of the wonderful way Girl Scout Mint Cookies used to taste. These cookies are somewhat expensive and quite rich—it doesn't take too many to O.D.

===

PRODUCT	**NILLA WAFERS**
MANUFACTURER	Nabisco
INGREDIENTS	Enriched wheat flour, rye flour, sugar, shortening, corn sweetener, whey solids, eggs, butter emulsifier, salt, leavening, vanillin, and other artificial flavor.
SUGAR QUOTIENT	High
DENTAL CHECKUP	Average
OIL QUOTIENT	Moderate
NUTRIENT LEVEL	Empty calories
CALORIE COUNT	19 each

Just as Lorna Doone Shortbread has no butter, Nilla Wafers have no vanilla. For this ersatz delicacy we are asked to pay about $1.10 a pound. Sunshine's *Vanilla Wafers* cost about 20 cents less than Nabisco's and they have not only real vanilla but other real ingredients as well. Vanilla wafers by their nature are bland and moderately sweet. Nabisco's Nilla Wafers are sweeter than Sunshine's *Vanilla Wafers* and are slightly larger in size. The choice is yours: phony or genuine, more money or less?

===

PRODUCT	**NUTTER BUTTER**
MANUFACTURER	Nabisco
INGREDIENTS	Enriched wheat flour, rye flour, sugar, shortening, oatmeal, roasted peanuts, eggs, whey solids, corn sweetener, salt, leavening, lecithin, hydrogenated peanut oil, and artificial flavor.
SUGAR QUOTIENT	High
DENTAL CHECKUP	Average
OIL QUOTIENT	High
NUTRIENT LEVEL	Empty calories
CALORIE COUNT	70 each

These are finger-shaped sandwich cookies with a sugar and peanut butter filling. The cookie is oatmealy, gritty and untantalizing. The filling is more sugary than peanut buttery. There are many better peanut butter cookies around.

PRODUCT	**OATMEAL PEANUT SANDWICH**
MANUFACTURER	**Sunshine**
INGREDIENTS	**Enriched flour, oat flakes, sugar, shortening, corn syrup, peanut butter, molasses, leavening, corn flour, salt, artificial flavor, and spice.**
SUGAR QUOTIENT	**High**
DENTAL CHECKUP	**Average**
OIL QUOTIENT	**High**
NUTRIENT LEVEL	**Minimal—some fortification present.**
CALORIE COUNT	**79 each**

Oatmeal cookies are an American favorite. Peanut butter is national passion. You'd think the two together would be a perfect match. Wrong. The oatmeal here tastes mealy and oversweet; the peanut butter center is like a stiff pasty glue. Too many tastes converge in this cookie, each trying to overpower the other.

PRODUCT	**OREO CHOCOLATE SANDWICH COOKIES/ DOUBLE STUF**
MANUFACTURER	**Nabisco**
INGREDIENTS	**Sugar, enriched wheat flour, rye flour, shortening, cocoa (processed with alkali), whey solids, corn sweetener, corn flour, chocolate, salt, leavening, lecithin, and artificial flavor.**
SUGAR QUOTIENT	**High**
DENTAL CHECKUP	**Tooth rotter**

OIL QUOTIENT	High
NUTRIENT LEVEL	Empty calories
CALORIE COUNT	50 each; Double Stuf: 60

One of the most enduring cookie recipes in America is two chocolate wafers with a sugar-and-shortening creme filling slapped between. Everybody loves to first separate the wafers and sensuously lick away the center, ignoring the chocolate cookie part. Nabisco caught on and kept adding more and more filling. Now they have Double Stuf—Oreos with double the amount of filling—which proves that too much of a good thing is not as good as just enough. The cookie wafers are on the dry, chalky side (from the cocoa no doubt), and are not as sweet as they could or should be. (Sunshine *Hydrox* fixed this problem with their formula.) I know these cookies are legendary, the stuff dreams are made of, but they taste as if they are missing something—T L C maybe?

═══════════════

PRODUCT	**PEANUT CREME PATTIES**
MANUFACTURER	Nabisco
INGREDIENTS	Roasted peanuts, sugar, enriched white flour, rye flour, shortening, whey solids, hydrogenated peanut oil, salt, leavening, and lecithin.
SUGAR QUOTIENT	High
DENTAL CHECKUP	Average
OIL QUOTIENT	High
NUTRIENT LEVEL	Empty calories
CALORIE COUNT	35 each

A dried-out sugar wafer filled with a smidgeon of peanut creme (*not* peanut butter!) baked in a long continuous sheet. If there is anything exceptional about these cookies it's their drab tastelessness. The flavor is hardly detectable. "Stale"mate!

PRODUCT	**PECAN SANDIES**
MANUFACTURER	Keebler
INGREDIENTS	Enriched wheat flour, shortening, sugar, pecans, corn syrup, salt, leavening, artificial flavor, and lecithin.
SUGAR QUOTIENT	High
DENTAL CHECKUP	Average
OIL QUOTIENT	High
NUTRIENT LEVEL	Empty calories
CALORIE COUNT	Not available

Big, thick cookies with piles of pecans blended throughout and a wonderfully "sandy" crumbly texture. These classic cookies have been an American favorite for decades. Although Pecan Sandies are a shortbread cookie, rich and heavy, the flavor of the pecans places them in a class by themselves. Like all Keebler cookies, these may not be available in the western United States.

PRODUCT	**PINATA REAL TORTILLA CHIPS**
MANUFACTURER	**Pinata Foods (S & W Fine Foods)**
INGREDIENTS	Stone ground corn, hydrogenated vegetable oil, salt, and lime.
SUGAR QUOTIENT	None
DENTAL CHECKUP	Average
OIL QUOTIENT	High
NUTRIENT LEVEL	Empty calories
CALORIE COUNT	**20 each**

Don't let the Pringles-type canister fool you. Inside are the best commercially prepared tortilla chips for snacking and dipping in the United States. Available in Regular, Taco, or Nacho Flavor, the circular chips are flat and come stacked in the can. Brittle and crunchy, the Regular ones need no artificial flavorings to create authentic South-of-the-Border flavor. These corn chips come as close to the Mexican specialty as you will find in a supermarket. Hopefully their ready acceptance in the Pacific Coast States will inspire S & W Fine Foods to deliver them to the entire nation. They're that good!

PRODUCT	**PITTER PATTER**
MANUFACTURER	**Keebler**
INGREDIENTS	**Sugar, peanut butter, graham flour, oats, shortening, enriched flour, corn syrup, peanuts, diary whey solids, corn starch, leavening, salt, glycerine, and emulsifier.**
SUGAR QUOTIENT	**High**
DENTAL CHECKUP	**Tooth rotter**
OIL QUOTIENT	**High**
NUTRIENT LEVEL	**Minimal**
CALORIE COUNT	**Not available**

If these weren't so obnoxiously sweet, they might well be the best peanut butter sandwich cookies in the United States. The graham flour and oats mix was a stroke of genius and the texture is not mealy like most of its competitors. But sugar, sugar, and more sugar prevents Pitter Patter from hopping to the head of the class.

PRODUCT	**POPCORNS—*VARIOUS BRANDS***
MANUFACTURER	**Jolly Time, Jiffy Pop, TV Time, Orville Redenbacher's Gourmet**
INGREDIENTS	**Popcorn (Jiffy and TV Time include oil and salt).**

Popcorn is popcorn, right? According to the manufacturers the answer seems to be an emphatic *no. Jolly Time,* for example, "is the only popcorn which is 'Volumized' by our patented process. This insures the exact percentage of moisture for perfect popping and tenderness—everytime." *Orville Redenbacher's Gourmet Popping Corn* is alleged to be high grade corn, guaranteed to pop 90 plus percent of the time and to taste better than the others. *Jiffy Pop* comes in its own aluminum pan ready for popping. It costs more and produces less but is super convenient to prepare. *TV Time* has packets of premeasured oil and corn so you will make perfect corn. In a taste test at a party, I set out four bowls of the different popcorns and asked people to choose the corn they preferred. The results: *Orville Redenbacher's* was preferred by all judges, followed by *Jolly Time, TV Time* and *Jiffy Pop. Jolly Time* is the least expensive and the taste difference between it and Orville's seems slim. For 65¢, Jolly Time gives you 20 ounces. Orville provides just 15 ounces for nearly a buck.

PRODUCT	**PRINGLES NEW FANGLED POTATO CHIPS**
MANUFACTURER	**Proctor & Gamble**
INGREDIENTS	**Dehydrated potatoes, vegetable shortening, mono- and diglycerides, salt, ascorbic acid, and BHA.**
SUGAR QUOTIENT	**None**
DENTAL CHECKUP	**Average**
OIL QUOTIENT	**High**
NUTRIENT LEVEL	**Empty calories**
CALORIE COUNT	**7.5 each chip**

Corrugated cardboard, emery boards, flavored paper—anything but potato chips. This seems the best way to describe Pringles. Proctor & Gamble should stick to what it knows best: detergents, soaps, and tooth paste. But P&G wants it all and some hefty advertising (approximately $10 million) has helped them corner 15% of the potato chip market. Shaped in concave ovals, one stacked upon the next, each thin chip has a dry, ungreasy quality and looks as manufactured as it tastes. You can't fool the tastebuds all that easily; Pringles taste reconstituted. The ads say "There's nothing else like a Pringles." Thank God.

PRODUCT	**RAISIN FRUIT BISCUITS**
MANUFACTURER	Nabisco
INGREDIENTS	Raisins, enriched flour, rye flour, sugar, corn sweeteners, shortening, whey, leavening, and salt.
SUGAR QUOTIENT	High
DENTAL CHECKUP	Average
OIL QUOTIENT	Moderate
NUTRIENT LEVEL	Acceptable
CALORIE COUNT	54 each

It's a raisin riot! These crepe-flat cookies in three long sheets have perforations dividing each sheet into five cookies. The cookie dough is rather dry and chalky, which tends to interfere with the taste of the raisins which are pressed flat between the two layers of dough. There isn't enough shortening, but these are still better than most. Sunshine's version, Golden Fruit, has a raisin sweet, chewier consistency—they are probably the best raisin cookies available in groceries.

PRODUCT	**RICH 'N CHIPS**
MANUFACTURER	Keebler
INGREDIENTS	Enriched wheat flour, shortening, sugar, sweet chocolate, dairy whey solids, peanut butter, corn syrup, cocoa powder, salt, lecithin, sorbitan monostearate, polysorbate 60, molasses, leavening, and artificial coloring.
SUGAR QUOTIENT	High
DENTAL CHECKUP	Tooth rotter
OIL QUOTIENT	High
NUTRIENT LEVEL	Empty calories
CALORIE COUNT	Not available

These cookies are rich in chips but not all of them are chocolate. Some are caramel (or is it butterscotch?) but all are consistently crunchy, firm, and scattered profusely throughout. The basic cookie is peanut-butter-accented with a touch of molasses to give it a lively taste. A hearty cookie! Not available in some western states.

PRODUCT	**SANDWICH MINT COOKIES**
MANUFACTURER	**FFV (Famous Foods of Virginia)**
INGREDIENTS	Sugar, enriched flour, vegetable shortening, cocoa powder, dextrose, corn syrup, non-fat dry milk, salt, chocolate, leavening, artificial flavors, lecithin, oil of peppermint, mono- and diglycerides, artificial color, and sorbic acid.
SUGAR QUOTIENT	High
DENTAL CHECKUP	Tooth rotter
OIL QUOTIENT	High
NUTRIENT LEVEL	Empty calories
CALORIE COUNT	Not available

A sugar-shortening creme filling between two mint wafers drenched in chocolate. It is hard to determine from the label whether the chocolate is real or a cocoa-compound, but I think it is the compound type. The wafer sections were used in the Girl Scout Cookies of old, and the taste is still pepperminty and chocolatey. It's a shame FFV feels compelled to add the gooky creme filling. Nevertheless, these are as close as you'll get to the mint cookies that sold in the halcyon days of the 1950s for 40 cents a box. Now you get half as much for twice the price.

PRODUCT	**SOCIAL TEA BISCUITS**
MANUFACTURER	**Nabisco**
INGREDIENTS	Enriched wheat flour, rye flour, sugar, shortening, butter, eggs, corn sweetener, whey solids, salt, leavening, and artificial flavor.

SUGAR QUOTIENT	Moderate
DENTAL CHECKUP	Average
OIL QUOTIENT	Moderate
NUTRIENT LEVEL	Empty calories
CALORIE COUNT	**20 each**

At $1.15 a pound, Social Tea Biscuits—bland wafer rectangles in the shortbread family—might not seem the ideal junk food. But for the better part of this century Social Teas have been a staple junk food for people who like to think they aren't eating junk food.

PRODUCT	**TOLL GATE INN CHOCOLATE CHIP COOKIES**
MANUFACTURER	**Kungsholm Baking Co.**
INGREDIENTS	**Unbleached flour, vegetable shortening, pure chocolate drops, sugar, brown sugar, fresh eggs, salt, natural and artificial flavors and colors, and leavening.**
SUGAR QUOTIENT	**High**
DENTAL CHECKUP	**Tooth rotter**
OIL QUOTIENT	**High**
NUTRIENT LEVEL	**Empty calories**
CALORIE COUNT	**Not available**

Available in limited areas, these just may be the best *commercially available* chocolate chip cookies. Big chocolate drops are blended into a rich toll-house batter (hence: Toll Gate) to produce a cookie that tastes almost homemade.

The only chocolate chip cookies that come anywhere near these in quality and taste are Burry's Best (reviewed separately, see page 234). If you are a chocolate chip cookie freak, seek these out. If not available in your area protest loudly to the company, whose address is listed above.

PRODUCT	**VIENNA FINGERS**
MANUFACTURER	Sunshine
INGREDIENTS	Enriched flour, sugar, vegetable shortening, corn flour, leavening, whey solids, salt, artificial flavor, vanilla, and lecithin.
SUGAR QUOTIENT	High
DENTAL CHECKUP	Tooth rotter
OIL QUOTIENT	High
NUTRIENT LEVEL	Empty calories
CALORIE COUNT	71 each

These finger-shaped sandwich cookies are the vanilla equivalent of Hydrox. There are many take-offs and duplicates made by other companies so insist on the original—and still the best—vanilla sandwich: Vienna Fingers.

A MEMBER OF THE JUNK FOOD BOOK HALL OF FAME.

PRODUCT	**WISE POTATO CHIPS**
MANUFACTURER	Wise (Borden Foods)
INGREDIENTS	Potatoes, vegetable oil, and salt.
SUGAR QUOTIENT	None
DENTAL CHECKUP	Average
OIL QUOTIENT	High
NUTRIENT LEVEL	Empty calories
CALORIE COUNT	150/oz.

The Wise Potato Chip business started when a Pennsylvania grocer found an ingenious use for his overstock of potatoes. The demand for the chips he created in his garage grew so overwhelming that the grocer, Earl V. Wise, Sr. opened an entire plant devoted solely to their manufacture. Located in Berwick, Pa., the company has expanded to operate the largest single potato chip factory in the world, though it still confines distribution to the Eastern states. (In 1964 Borden Foods added Wise to its conglomerate of twenty-two other food companies.) Slightly oily, the chips come both in the regular style and with ridges and are rich in potato flavor. While they feel greasy, the oil doesn't interfere with the crispness or taste.

PRODUCT	**YUM YUMS**
MANUFACTURER	**Sunshine**
INGREDIENTS	**Sugar, corn syrup, coconut, shortening, enriched flour, condensed skim milk, whey, milk solids not fat, cocoa, salt, leavening, lecithin, and artificial flavor and color.**
SUGAR QUOTIENT	**High**
DENTAL CHECKUP	**Tooth rotter**
OIL QUOTIENT	**High**
NUTRIENT LEVEL	**Empty calories**
CALORIE COUNT	**83 each**

A two-inch long coconut caramel cookie-log with a compound-chocolate topping. In these extremely sweet candied cakes the coconut is in ample supply and provides a nifty crunch for a cookie that is otherwise soft and chewy. One Yum Yum a day and you'll feel as if you've had enough sugar for a week. The fake chocolate is superfluous and actually interferes with the coconut and caramel, reducing Yum Yums to Ho-Hums.

CHEWING GUM AND MINTS

NOTES ABOUT CHEWING GUM AND MINTS

Gum is low in calories, usually less than twelve per stick. Since mints are small, their calorie counts are low also. Ratings of gum and mints do not include sugar, oil quotients, or nutrient levels. You can assume gum and mints are proportionately high in sugar but have no oil. Nutrients are nonexistent. Mints are tooth rotters if you hold them in your mouth, and moderate if you don't. Gum is a definite tooth rotter.

PRODUCT	**BAZOOKA**
MANUFACTURER	**Topps Chewing Gum**
INGREDIENTS	**Dextrose, corn syrup, gum base, softeners, natural and artificial flavors, artificial colors, and BHT.**

Bazooka is made with dextrose rather than refined sugar, so it is not as syrupy sweet as other bubble gums. Once the hardish pink cube of gum is properly mashed, Bazooka is ready for bubble action. Like most gums the pleasing flavor lasts about five minutes. The price is 100 percent higher now than in 1973. Whether it is worth 2 cents to you depends on how much you enjoy blowing bubbles. The BHT added to preserve freshness seems to be a waste: the pieces I chewed were as tough as uncooked spaghetti.

PRODUCT	**BEECHIES CANDY COATED GUM**
MANUFACTURER	**Life Savers Inc.**
INGREDIENTS	**Sugar, gum base, corn syrup, dextrose, modified food starch, natural flavor, gum arabic, artificial colors, and BHT.**

Two pieces of any pellet-type gum are always needed for a substantial chew. The flavor of the Peppermint pellets is strong and would clean up a dragon's breath. Spearmint is too sweet. So are all the other flavors. Compared to the other major pellet gum, *Chiclets*, Beechies have a heavier candy taste. Back in the early 70s when gum was still a nickel, all pellet gum was white. Then the prices rose 200 percent. To make us think we were getting more for our money, the manufacturers reshaped the pellets, colored them ugly, and christened them with so-called "super flavors." The only thing that's really different is the higher price.

PRODUCT	**BEECH NUT GUM**
MANUFACTURER	**Life Savers Inc.**
INGREDIENTS	**Peppermint: sugar, gum base, corn syrup, dextrose, natural flavors, artificial colors, and BHT. (Spearmint also contains artificial flavors.)**

This gum was stale, even with preservatives. Funny about that—Wrigley's stays fresh *without* BHA or BHT. The consistency is cardboardy. Artificial colors are added but I wonder why, since the result is an unappetizing greyish brown. As with Beechies, peppermint stands out as the best flavor.

PRODUCT	**BEEMAN'S CHEWING GUM**
MANUFACTURER	**Warner Lambert**
INGREDIENTS	**Sugar, gum base, corn syrup, and artificial and natural flavor.**

Gums were first made as a medicinal remedy, but soon they were manufactured purely as confectionery products. Beeman's has a long history, and by now it should have followed this trend. But the pepsin flavor of these white-brown sticks still has a strong medicine taste, albeit combined with a saccharin sweetness. I suspect this gum is popular with old timers and those who secretly prefer to gnaw on paraffin.

PRODUCT	**BIG RED**
MANUFACTURER	**Wm. Wrigley Jr. Co.**
INGREDIENTS	**Sugar, gum base, corn syrup, softeners, artificial and natural flavors, and artificial colors.**

One of the newest additions to the Wrigley family, Big Red is a poor man's version of Dentyne. The normally grey color is dyed pink to suggest cinnamon flavor, but this tastes like a chemical surrogate. The flavor does, however, last slightly longer than other Wrigley gums.

PRODUCT **BUBBLE YUM**
MANUFACTURER **Life Savers**
INGREDIENTS **Sugar, corn syrup, gum base, corn starch, softeners, artificial flavors and colors, and BHT.**

The label says it all: "Soft 'n juicy." Bubble Yum *is* the softest bubble gum around. Any juiciness it has proceeds from the combination of the chewer's saliva with BY's extra cornsyrup and starch. You can actually feel the bits of sugar granules as you chew, leaving you to wonder whether you are tasting sugar, foreign elements, or, dare I mention loosened fillings. A most disconcerting drawback. The gum tastes all right; the flavor lasts for from 5 to 7 minutes.

PRODUCT **CARE*FREE SUGARLESS GUM**
MANUFACTURER **Life Savers**
INGREDIENTS **Sorbitol, gum base, mannitol, artificial flavors, sodium saccharin, artificial colors, and BHT.**

Although all sugarless gum tends to have a cardboard texture, Care*Free's is more readily apparent. Of its different varieties, the outstanding one is Bubblegum. Its flavor tastes the most authentic and lasts longer. The others lose their hokey artificial flavors quickly (thank goodness).

PRODUCT **CHICLETS**
MANUFACTURER **Warner Lambert**
INGREDIENTS **Peppermint: sugar, gum base, corn syrup, starch, and natural flavor. Other flavors use artificial flavors and colors.**

Peppermint Chiclets are the only ones with nothing artificial. The garish red cinnamon lacks any resemblance to real cinnamon; the fruit flavors all taste ersatz. Lemon is so sour you want to spit it out immediately. The orange flavor tastes like Aspergum. Spearmint is green and minty-looking, but candy sweet. You'll need at least two "tablets" per chew. The different flavors come in a vivid palette of colors.

=========

PRODUCT	**CLARK'S CINNAMINT/TEABERRY**
MANUFACTURER	**Clark-Reed**
INGREDIENTS	Gum base, sugar, corn syrup, softeners, food color, and imitation flavors.

Cinnamint: This used to be one of the best chewing gums in America. Then the Clark Company was shuffled around like a football from conglomerate to conglomerate, and since that time the gum seems bland and phony. Cinnamint once gave Dentyne a run for its money but now Dentyne is way out front.

Teaberry: This "one and only" has a taste reminiscent of bubblegum but is nevertheless unique. Clark seems to have maintained this gum's formula over the decades. The flavor is rapidly lost, but while it lasts, it is mild and properly sweetened.

=========

PRODUCT	**DENTYNE**
MANUFACTURER	**Werner Lambert**
INGREDIENTS	Sugar, gum base, dextrose, softeners, artificial and natural flavoring, and artificial colors.

Short cinnamon-flavored sticks (without cinnamon, of course) that are probably the most satisfactory cinnamon gum. Dentyne tastes almost real and lasts the longest. It is probably dyed pink because we associate that color with cinnamon. Dentyne was advertised for years as a gum that "helps keep teeth white— breath fresh"—even the name "Dentyne" has a hygenic ring to it. People *know* gum is bad for teeth and Dentyne uses reverse psychology. It's just as deleterious to your teeth as the next brand. But it does taste better.

PRODUCT   **DOUBLEMINT**
MANUFACTURER   **Wm. Wrigley Jr. Co.**
INGREDIENTS   Sugar, gum base, corn syrup, dextrose, softeners, natural flavor.

Five solid minutes of robust mint flavor. Then it goes flat, as all gums seem to. The sweet peppermint makes this the most popular gum in the United States.

PRODUCT   **DUBBLE BUBBLE**
MANUFACTURER   **Fleer Corp.**
INGREDIENTS   Gum base, dextrose, sugar, corn syrup, and artificial flavor and color.

One of the original bubble gums, Dubble Bubble is still one of the best (the top rival is Bazooka). For 2 cents a hit, you get a solid chunk of "bubble gum" flavor and good blowing consistency. The comics and premium offers on the wrapper are often more fun than the bubbles. Rather than inane four part cartoons they now feature vicious one-liner put-downs. No wonder kids are getting more sarcastic! An example:

First boy to second boy: Let's play *horse!* I'll be the *head* and you be *yourself!* Is Norman Lear writing for bubble gum wrappers, too?

PRODUCT   **FREEDENT** (Spearmint/Peppermint)
MANUFACTURER   **Wrigley**
INGREDIENTS   Sugar, gum base, corn syrup, softeners, natural flavors, artificial flavors, and BHA.

Why didn't they think of this years ago: a gum that doesn't pull out your fillings or dentures. The flavor seems much like other Wrigley gums; the chewing is a little stiffer. You trade the "improvement" in texture, for two less sticks per pack.

PRODUCT **FRESHEN-UP**
MANUFACTURER **Warner Lambert**
INGREDIENTS **Sugar, gum base, corn syrup, softeners, natural flavoring, artificial colors, magnesium stearate.**

The gum that comes. Each chlorophyl-green pellet has a liquid filling which spurts into your mouth when you bite into it. It tastes like most other spearmint gums, but a trifle too sweet. The selling point is the liquid center. It's a great gimmick for only a nickel more, but like any gimmick it loses its novelty after a pack or so. Soon to be available in peppermint and cinnamon.

PRODUCT **JUICY FRUIT**
MANUFACTURER **Wm. Wrigley Jr. Co.**
INGREDIENTS **Sugar, gum base, corn syrup, dextrose, softeners, and natural and artificial flavors.**

So this is a fruit taste? Whatever it's supposed to be, it is savory and unique. This five-minute sweetness blitz can become habit-forming, leading you to chew a whole pack quickly. Kids seem to like this Wrigley flavor the best—it's great for shutting them up on long trips. For a while anyway.

PRODUCT	**LIFE SAVERS MINTS (Peppermint, Spearmint, Winter-green, Cinnamon, Cryst-O-Mint, Stik-O-Pep)**
MANUFACTURER	**Life Savers Inc.**
INGREDIENTS	**Sugar, corn syrup, natural flavor, and stearic acid.**
CALORIE COUNT	**7 each**

The first Life Saver flavor was Peppermint. A roll sold for five cents "For That Stormy Breath." Clarence Crane, a Cleveland chocolate manufacturer, created these white circular mints with a pill machine borrowed from a pharmaceutical company. When an advertising salesman suggested he could "pyramid them into a fortune," Crane sold all rights for a mere $2,900. The patent for Life Savers describes them as "nothing enclosed by a hole," but they are a lot more. Flavorful, zesty mints, which use natural flavors, the Wintergreen is by far the best. Peppermint still kills even the strongest garlicky stink in your mouth. Cryst-O-Mint is a clear peppermint candy. Eleven "doughnut"-shaped mints to a roll.

PRODUCT	**LIFE SAVERS GUM** (Five Flavors/Mint Flavors)
MANUFACTURER	**Life Savers Inc.**
INGREDIENTS	**Sugar, gum base, corn syrup, dextrose, artificial flavors and color, and BHT. Peppermint uses natural instead of artificial flavor.**

Five Flavors: Surely the kids who eat this dreck could get their sugar fix from better fruit-flavored products. Does anyone at Life Savers bother to taste this stuff before they sic it on vulnerable small fry? Each stick is dutifully dyed the color of the fruit it's alleged to taste like, but the comparison ends there. The five different flavors are supposedly cherry, orange, fruit, lemon, lime. But they all taste the same: fake, phony, ersatz, unreal, horrible.

Peppermint: Turning a mint into a chewing gum seems miraculous, but the Fairy Godmothers at LS have done just that. If you want a peppermint mint to chew, this is it.

PRODUCT	**MIGHTY MINTS**
MANUFACTURER	**Life Savers**
INGREDIENTS	**Sugar, dextrin, magnesium hydroxide, gum arabic, calcium stearate, natural and artificial flavors, artificial colors, gelatin, menthol, beeswax, carnauba wax.**

It's difficult to figure out how they stuffed so much into these tiny mints. The ingredients read like a textbook for Chemistry 101, but the mints are compact, concentrated powerhouses of flavor. Forty mints in sundry flavors are packed in a 25-cent plastic dispenser. The first of this type of mint was Tic Tac; this brand and others like it are copies. *Dentyne's Dynamints*, not reviewed here, can be considered to have much the same story.

PRODUCT	**ORBIT SUGARFREE GUM** (Peppermint/Spearmint)
MANUFACTURER	**Wm. Wrigley Jr. Co.**
INGREDIENTS	Sorbitol, gum base, mannitol, xylitol, softeners, and natural flavor.
SUGAR QUOTIENT	None
DENTAL CHECKUP	Good
CALORIE COUNT	**7.7** calories

This revolutionary gum is the first to use Xylitol, a natural sweetener substitute clinically proven to *reduce and prevent* tooth decay. It may even make the gum taste better. Available in Peppermint, Spearmint, and Cinnamon, these are the most delicious sugar-free gums I've ever tasted. While cinnamon is artificially flavored and colored and preserved with BHR, the spearmint and peppermint are not. All have extraordinary flavor, even better than some of the gums that use sugar. You can hardly go wrong if Xylitol reduces the risk of cavities. [One note: mannitol, sorbitol and xylitol do eventually metabolize in the body as sugar but at a much slower rate.]

PRODUCT	**TIC TACS**
MANUFACTURER	**Progresso Foods Corp.**
INGREDIENTS	Sugar, dextrin, rice starch, sorbitol, magnesium stearate, natural flavors, artificial colors, and candellilla wax.

These forty concentrated mints, imported from Italy, clean the breath almost instantly, while they release a powerful amount of flavor. First produced in peppermint, other artificially flavored mint and fruit flavors are now available. Cinnamon holds up well but, considering the liberal use of chemicals, I wonder which one is used to get the red. The plastic packing is a plus, it prevents pocket lint from getting on the mints, and the packages are useful as substitute maracas.

PRODUCT **TRIDENT SUGARLESS GUM**
MANUFACTURER **Warner Lambert**
INGREDIENTS **Sorbitol, gum base, mannitol, acacia (a natural gum base), artificial and natural flavoring, sodium saccharin, artificial color, and magnesium stearate.**

This original sugarless gum is still the best. The cinnamon has the least cardboardy texture, and is also the most popular flavor. Trident Bubble Gum tastes fake, and has poor texture, and is not as good as *Care*Free*.

PRODUCT **WRIGLEY'S SPEARMINT**
MANUFACTURER **Wm. Wrigley Jr. Co.**
INGREDIENTS **Sugar, gum base, corn syrup, dextrose, softeners, and natural flavor.**

This real spearmint flavor comes on loud and strong and stays with you for one whole twelfth of an hour. After that, you'll probably start a new piece. For my money, it's the best spearmint gum sold.

SODA POP AND SOFT DRINKS

NOTES ABOUT SODA POP AND SOFT DRINKS

With more than 180 different brand names, and even more flavors to choose from, I have listed only those beverages which are franchised nationally or are widely available.

The soft drinks were judged by junk food fans for their real or phony taste (real: 10; phony: 0); degree of sweetness (cloying and oversweet: 0; proportioned correctly: 10); and overall quality: whether natural flavorings are used, whether chemical additives are used, whether the carbonation is effective, etc. Because the main ingredient, water, varies from city to city, bottlers are supposed to correct and purify it. A Pepsi in Philadelphia should taste exactly like one in Miami. It doesn't.

Individual bottlers rely on different methods of purification, depending on the type of water from the tap. Accordingly, local variations in taste do exist. When this has been noted by the tester, it is signified by an asterisk.

RATINGS LISTED BY COMPANY

brand or flavor	quality of flavor (phony: 0 real: 10)	sweetness (0 = sweetest)	overall quality: carbonation + ingredients (10 = best)
AMERICAN BEVERAGE CORP. Hoffman Flavors	8	4	7
Dr. Brown's			
Cel-Ray	8	8	8
Cream (vanilla)	5	3	5
Others (composite)	7	4–5	6
I-C INDUSTRIES Bubble Up	5	5	5
Dad's Root Beer	7	4	6–7
CANADA DRY CORP. Ginger Ale*	9	2	9
Wink	7	4	7
Barrelhead Root Beer	6	4	4
COCA-COLA Coca-Cola	7	4	7
Fresca	0	5	0
Sprite	5	4	7
Tab	3	3	6–7
Mr. PiBB	5	4	6
Fanta Flavors			
Orange	4	2	2
Grape	4	2	2
Root Beer	4	1	2
COTT CORP. Flavor Beverages (composite)	7	3–4	7
CRUSH INTERNATIONAL Orange Crush	5–6	2	4
Hires Root Beer (Real Draft)	8	3–4	8

brand or flavor	quality of flavor (phony: 0 real: 10)	sweetness (0 = sweetest)	overall quality: carbonation + ingredients (10 = best)
DR. PEPPER CO. Dr. Pepper	8	2	7
NO-CAL CORP. No-Cal/Lo-Cal Flavors (composite)	5	5	5
PEPSI-COLA CO. Pepsi-Cola*	8	3	7–8
Pepsi Light	8	8	7
Teem	7	4	6
Mountain Dew	5	2	5
Patio Flavors Orange Grape	4 4	2–3 2–3	3 3
ROYAL CROWN COLA CO. Royal Crown Cola	8	4–5	8
Diet Rite Cola	8	5	7
SCHWEPPES USA LTD. Ginger Ale*	3	3	3
Bitter Lemon	8	10	8
SEVEN UP CO. Seven Up	9	4–5	9–10
THE SQUIRT CO. Squirt	7	6	7–8
WHITE ROCK PRODUCTS Orange (Jaffa Joy) Black Cherry	6 7	3–4 3	6 6
YOO-HOO BEVERAGE CO. Yoo-Hoo Chocolate	5	3	7
Nedick's Orange	5	4	5

================

PRODUCT	**FRESCA**
MANUFACTURER	Coca-Cola
INGREDIENTS	Carbonated water, citric acid, gum arabic, sodium saccharin, sodium citrate, 1/40th of 1% sodium benzoate (preservative), natural and artificial flavors, salt, glycerol of wood rosin, brominated vegetable oil, and artificial color.
SUGAR QUOTIENT	None
DENTAL CHECKUP	Average to low
OIL QUOTIENT	Low
NUTRIENT LEVEL	Empty calories
CALORIE COUNT	**2/8 ounces**

The only reason Fresca sells at all is so people on diets can advertise their martyrdom. Anyone who drinks this diet soda *has* to be a Joan of Arc. Regular soda needs sugar to be palatable; otherwise it tends to taste medicinal. Fresca is no exception; it has faint grapefruit flavor but only until the saccharin taste takes over. Among Fresca's laboratory-size collection of chemicals is brominated vegetable oil, an oil mixed with bromine which helps the flavoring to stay mixed in the water without rising to the top. It also makes liquid look cloudy, for an illusory appearance of "body."

Canadian studies showed this additive to be harmful, causing damage to animals by accumulating in vital organs. The FDA removed it from the GRAS list of safe food additives but allowed manufacturers to go on using it until the FDA could conduct its own biological studies—a 2- to 3-year process. Fresca is not the only product to use BVO. Look for it in other fruit-flavored soft drinks.

================

PRODUCT	**HAWAIIAN PUNCH (FRUIT JUICY RED)**
MANUFACTURER	**RJR Foods (R. J. Reynolds Tobacco)**
INGREDIENTS	Water, sugar and corn syrups, fruit juices and purees (concentrated pineapple, orange, and grapefruit juices, passion-

fruit juice, apricot, papaya, and guava purees), citric acid, natural fruit flavors. Vitamin C, dextrin, artificial color, and ethyl maltol.

SUGAR QUOTIENT	High
DENTAL CHECKUP	Tooth rotter
OIL QUOTIENT	Low
NUTRIENT LEVEL	Empty calories (50% of daily vitamin C recommendations added)
CALORIE COUNT	90/6 ounces

This blood-red drink is 11 percent fruit juice and 89 percent water, sugar, and chemicals to make the juices taste better. No amount of ethyl maltel (a flavor enhancer) could help this taste. It doesn't even quench your thirst. Food processors call drinks "punch" when they have no definable flavor. If you drink this garbage, someone should "punch" some sense into you.

PRODUCT	**HI-C FLORIDA PUNCH**
MANUFACTURER	Coca-Cola
INGREDIENTS	Water, sugar and corn sweeteners, concentrated orange juice, concentrated grapefruit juice, natural flavors, fumaric and citric acid, concentrated grape juice, concentrated pineapple juice, guava juice, passionfruit juice, vitamin C, and artificial colors.
SUGAR QUOTIENT	High
DENTAL CHECKUP	Tooth rotter
OIL QUOTIENT	Low
NUTRIENT LEVEL	Empty calories (100% of daily vitamin C recommendations added)
CALORIE COUNT	100/6 ounces

Force-feeding prisoners of war this gory red liquid could have been an ideal torture during World War II. I would confess to *anything* if forced to drink more than two glassfuls of this concoction. Hi-C's other "flavors" (orange, grape, cherry, etc.) supposedly contain 10 percent real fruit juice. Six juices are included in each flavor, so that it contains less than 2 percent of each juice. The rest is sugar, water, and additives. The best time to drink this junk is when you're unconscious.

PRODUCT	**KOOL AID** (Sweetened)
MANUFACTURER	**General Foods**
INGREDIENTS	Sugar, citric acid, monocalcium phosphate, dried lemon juice with corn syrup solids, natural lemon flavor, modified corn starch, modified tapioca starch, vitamin C, partially hydrogenated coconut oil, vitamin A, tricalcium phosphate, artificial color, and BHA.
SUGAR QUOTIENT	High
DENTAL CHECKUP	Tooth rotter
OIL QUOTIENT	Low
NUTRIENT LEVEL	Empty calories (Contains **15**% of daily vitamin C recommendations, plus some vitamin A)
CALORIE COUNT	**90**/8 ounces (**720** per package)

Unsweetened, a Kool Aid package weighs in at .022 ounces. Sweetened—with only refined sugar added—the package weighs 6.71 ounces. This means sugar is 97% of the contents. In some flavors (orange, for example) sugar is added even to the unsweetened varieties! The flavors are rather washed out. The Lemonade comes close to duplicating chemically the taste of frozen concentrate but lacks the pulpy pizazz or tart tingle provided by the latter. Ultimately, Kool Aid is a rip-off because all you are buying is sugar with a teensy bit of test tube flavoring. The sugar masks the taste of the chemicals needed to give it flavor and color.

PRODUCT	**KOOL AID** (Unsweetened)
MANUFACTURER	**General Foods**
INGREDIENTS	Citric acid, monocalcium phosphate, natural lemon flavor, modified corn starch, modified tapioca starch, vitamin C, partially hydrogenated coconut oil, lemon juice dried with corn syrup solids, vitamin A palmitate, tricalcium phosphate, artificial color, and BHA.
SUGAR QUOTIENT	Before preparation: none; after preparation: high
DENTAL CHECKUP	Tooth rotter
OIL QUOTIENT	Low
NUTRIENT LEVEL	Empty calories (Contains 15% of daily vitamin C recommendations, plus some vitamin A)
CALORIE COUNT	See text below

Try this taste test. Wet your finger and dip it into this pale powder. Lick it. This is what Kool Aid is like without sugar. Horrible, isn't it? Sugar is what gives Kool Aid its life. Without sugar there are only sixteen (16) calories per package. With sugar, there are 100 calories per cup. One cup of sugar is added for every 2 quarts (the yield of one .022-ounce package). Kool Aid is lousy even as junk food since the taste is "watered down" and never quenches your thirst. General Foods points out though that Kool Aid is cheap. It certainly is.

PRODUCT	**ORANGE CRUSH**
MANUFACTURER	**Crush International**
INGREDIENTS	Carbonated water, sugar, concentrated orange juice, orange oil, other natural citrus oils, gum acacia, glycerol ester of wood rosin, brominated vegetable oil, citric acid, salt, artificial color, and 1/20 of 1% sodium benzoate.
SUGAR QUOTIENT	High
DENTAL CHECKUP	Tooth rotter
OIL QUOTIENT	Low to average
NUTRIENT LEVEL	Empty calories
CALORIE COUNT	Not available

Orange soda can taste either like paint or carbonated instant orange juice. Crush is a hybrid of the two. Its two main flavorings are orange juice and orange oil—a great start. Yet, the carbonation is not as strong as it should be (ordinarily, orange soda has the highest CO_2 concentration of any soda). The result is rather flat, and that's where the paint taste comes in. And what the hell is "glycerol ester of wood rosin" doing in the drink—sounds like some sort of shellac! The presence of brominated vegetable oil, a questionable additive, casts doubt over the worth of this beverage, even as junk food.

PRODUCT	**PEPSI LIGHT**
MANUFACTURER	PepsiCo
INGREDIENTS	Carbonated water, sugar, caramel color, phosphoric acid, citric acid, sodium saccharin, caffeine, natural and artificial flavor, 1/15 of 1% sodium saccharin.
SUGAR QUOTIENT	Low
DENTAL CHECKUP	Average
OIL QUOTIENT	Low
NUTRIENT LEVEL	Empty calories
CALORIE COUNT	See text below

The light lemony flavor reduces medicinal, saccharin taste, and adds needed zest to the cola. Not as sweet as regular Pepsi, with supposedly half the sugar. It has an "adult" flavor even kids can enjoy, yet this is still a cola drink with the usual caffeine and phosphoric acid. Each ounce contains 1.5 grams of sugar and 5.9 calories, or 94.4 calories per 16 ounces.

If you drink regular diet colas (Tab, Diet-Rite, and others), take a tip from Pepsi and add lemon juice to the soda for an improved flavor.

Phosphoric acid is found in all cola drinks. It acts as a sequestrant: a chemical that traps trace amounts of metal atoms that would otherwise discolor the food or make it go bad. Larger amounts of this acid are used to eat rust off metal.

PRODUCT	**SEVEN UP**
MANUFACTURER	**Seven Up Co.**
INGREDIENTS	**Carbonated water, sugar, citric acid, sodium citrate, and flavor derived from lemon and lime oils.**
SUGAR QUOTIENT	**High**
DENTAL CHECKUP	**Average to low**
OIL QUOTIENT	**Low**
NUTRIENT LEVEL	**Empty calories**
CALORIE COUNT	**97/8 ounces**

Not too sweet. Not too sour. Just right. Seven Up has a light, citrusy flavor. It's as colorless as water, with water's fresh, clean taste. Foibles of local bottlers sometimes make this one expensive. I purchased a 24-ounce bottle on the West coast for the same price as a quart bottle (32 ounces) in Florida. Still the most "natural" soda and one of the best on the market today. Junk food at its most endearing. A good way to UnCola™ your life.

PRODUCT	**WYLER'S LEMONADE MIX (Imitation flavor)**
MANUFACTURER	**Wyler's (Borden Foods)**
INGREDIENTS	**Sugar, citric acid, dehydrated lemon juice and corn syrup, corn starch, salt, ascorbic acid, malto dextrin, lemon oil, carrageenan, and U.S. certified artificial color.**
SUGAR QUOTIENT	**High**
DENTAL CHECKUP	**Tooth rotter**
OIL QUOTIENT	**None**
NUTRIENT LEVEL	**Empty calories (Contains 10% of daily vitamin C recommendations)**
CALORIE COUNT	**90/8 ounces**

Wyler's offers the most authentic-tasting lemonade from an imitation powdered mix, but it still lacks the snap you get from frozen concentrate. Nevertheless, it should yield sales at any kid's sidewalk stand. One 3-ounce package produces one quart—all you do is add water. An 8-ounce serving has 90 calories, all from sugar. The shelf life of powder is considerably longer than frozen lemonade, and much easier to use, but you sacrifice taste for convenience. Virtually all powdered brands of lemonade taste identical but Wyler's has a tart edge. Most sell for under 35 cents in packets; 50 cents and up for canisters.